Philosophy and Ps[illegible]
in the Abhidharma

PHILOSOPHY AND PSYCHOLOGY IN THE ABHIDHARMA

Herbert V. Guenther

SHAMBHALA
Berkeley & London
1976

Shambhala Publications, Inc.
2045 Francisco Street
Berkeley, California 94709
and
68 Carter Lane
London EC4V 5EL

ISBN 0-87773-081-4
LCC 75-40259

Distributed in the United States by Random House
and in Canada by Random House of Canada, Ltd.

Distributed in the Commonwealth by
Routledge & Kegan Paul Ltd.
London and Henley-on-Thames

Printed in the United States of America
from the Indian edition published 1974.

PREFACE

The title "Philosophy and Psychology in the Abhidharma" outlines the scope of this book. It attempts to deal with philosophy as the perennial quest for meaning and with psychology as the abstract understanding by which man is engaged in comprehending himself, as presented in the vast literature of the Abhidharma. It does not claim to deal with the whole of Abhidharma literature. Such an attempt would go far beyond the capacity of a single individual. Therefore only those topics which seem to have special significance have been selected. In restricting myself to a presentation of philosophical and psychological problems in the Abhidharma, I have chosen three authors of outstanding merit, each of them belonging to a different school of Buddhism. They are : the author of the Aṭṭhasālinī, who goes by the name of Buddhaghosa and who represents the Theravāda view; Vasubandhu, author of the Abhidharma-kośa, examining and reviewing the Sarvāstivāda-Vaibhāsika view from the Sautrāntika standpoint; and Asaṅga, author of the Abhidharmasamuccaya, propounding the Vijñānavāda (Yogācāra) view. In connexion with them I have mentioned such details from other authors as have value on account of some illustrative quality. Even in imposing such a restriction upon myself I had to compromise at every turn. I am fully aware of the fact that much would have deserved a more detailed treatment and that much more might have been included. Nevertheless I believe and hope that nothing of importance has been left out.

Since my primary interest has been philosophy and psychology, in dealing with the Abhidharma literature I have constantly tried to find out from the original texts what the authors themselves had to say and I have intentionally refrained from discussing opinions about the Abhidharma; these may be quite interesting (and sometimes highly amusing) as far as they reflect the attitudes of those learned men who have held them, but they are not the philosophy of the Abhidharma. I have always attempted to put what seems to me to be the fundamental meaning in modern terms and as plausible as possible. Any critique of the views of the various authors either follows the arguments of the criticizing rival school of Buddhism or is made from the forum of the Mādhyamika philosophy which up to the present day has kept philosophy as a quest for meaning alive and has prevented this gigantic task from degenerating into spiritless formalism.

I have to thank my friend Joseph E. Cann, whose name appears on the dedication page, for his appreciative criticism of and constant interest in my work which owes its origin to his suggestion to write on Buddhist philosophy from a Buddhist point of view. Unfailing help and inspiration has been given me by my wife whom in particular I have to thank for the preparation of the index. My thanks are also due to Rev. G. Prajnananda, Resident Bhikshu of the Buddha Vihara, Lucknow, for his constant encouragement. Last not least, I am greatly indebted to Mrs. Irene B. Hudson, M.D., for her generosity which has made it possible that a book on philosophy as a guide to a way of life sees the light of the world which on the whole is prejudiced against philosophy because of some contemporary misconceptions about the nature and function of philosophy.

Lucknow University Dr. H.V.G.
1957

PREFACE TO THE THIRD EDITION

The study of the Abhidharma is now seen to be an essential phase in the understanding of Buddhist thought in its development over the centuries. There is no philosophical school in the whole of Buddhism that does not accept this first systematization of suggestive ideas, however divergent the subsequent interpretation has turned out within the framework of specific emphasis on one topic or another. It was this importance of the Abhidharma that led, some twenty years ago, to the attempt to bring out some of the salient features which, in the context of Western thinking, cover the fields of both philosophy and psychology.

The present edition is basically the same as the second revised edition. The patchwork correction of minor detail is unnecessary and impossible to particularize and has been done without violence to the original.

I am grateful to Mr. Samuel Bercholz of Shambhala Publications Inc., to include this third edition in his publications.

1976 H.V.G.

To
Joseph E. Cann

CONTENTS

INTRODUCTION

ABHIDHARMA : ITS MEANING AND SCOPE

Throughout the varying phases of its historical development, Buddhist philosophy has unmistakably preserved certain traits which at the outset formed the very life force of Buddhist thought and which still vitally concern us as a truly spiritual force. These are the emphasis on immediate experience and the rejection of everything that might make us lose what is essential in our dealings with the problems of life. For by such a loss we are at once entangled in all sorts of speculations and arguments about something which has no longer any practical meaning for human life. The very fact that no amount of discursive reasoning will ever convey that which must be experienced within ourselves and which therefore is also known quite independently of logical method, may be gathered from the legendary history of the origin of the Abhidharma which the Buddha is said to have first revealed while residing in the heaven of the Tāvatiṁsa gods.[1] 'The world of gods' and what is commonly called the 'divine' is essentially a symbolic expression of the fact that interest and attention have been drawn away from the surface of sensuous objects and have been directed toward the within, the background and source of all things. The 'transcendency' of the world of gods is due to the fact that our senses deliver only specific, limited and determinate data within something indeterminate and unlimited, which precisely because of its indeterminateness and of its going beyond the narrow scope of mere intellectual judgments is so emotionally moving, so spiritually quickening, that a deep sense of reverence for the sanctity of all that exists is instilled in us. It is—as far as our mechanistic language devices allow to depict it—a heightened sense of reality. And that which leads to this heightened sense of reality, because the facts that are right here have been pointed out to us together with the possibilities and potentialities they

1. Aṭṭhasālinī I 76. See also I 1, 2 sqq. and I 36 where the Buddha is said to have revealed the Abhidharma for the benefit of his mother.

offer in practical living and in the formation of character, is laid down in the Abhidharma. For this reason the author of the Aṭṭhasālinī, who goes by the name of Buddhaghosa, informs us that "it is called Abhidhamma, because it excels in and is distinguished by several qualities".[1] These excellent qualities which make the Abhidharma rank foremost in Buddhist literature, are, according to Asaṅga, four: being face to face with the highest goal and the nature of Reality (*abhimukha*); the teaching of the necessary steps to be taken for the attainment of the goal and presenting them from various viewpoints (*abhīkṣṇa*); its standing above the petty controversies about the nature of Reality and its capacity to come to a definite answer (*abhibhava*); and penetration into the deeper import of the Buddha's teachings (*abhigati*).[2]

Indeed, it is through our contemplation and our taking in with one single glance the whole of the nature of things, that together with this heightened sense of reality a more intense emotional satisfaction and stability is achieved. As the author of the Aṭṭhasālinī informs us: "Those who study the Abhidhamma literature experience unending joy and serenity of mind"[3]. But while most men are content with merely looking at the surface of things and, instead of searching for the essence of things and thereby widening their horizon, confine themselves to the narrowest plane of meanness and prejudiced-

1. Aṭṭhasālinī I 2; *evam eva ayam pi dhammo dhammātireka-ahammavisesaṭṭhena abhidhammo ti vuccati.* In III 488 the Abhidhamma is said to be "the instruction in the ultimate nature of things"—*abhidhammo nāma paramatthadesanā* The ultimate way of explanation (*nippariyayadesana*) is also mentioned as the outstanding quality of the Abhidhamma in I 3; III 304; 484; 486; 488. It is because of the idea that the Abhidhamma is of highest importance that the author in this passage tries to harmonize the meanings of the prepositions *abhi-* and *ati-*. In I 49, however, he makes use of the preposition *abhi-* only, and the four qualities he mentions look like a dim recollection of Asaṅga's four qualities in Mahāyāna-Sūtrālaṅkāra XI 3. The relation of the Abhidharma to ultimate reality (*paramārtha*) is also expressed in Abhidharmakośavyākhyā I p. 10.

2. Mahāyāna-Sūtrālaṅkāra XI 3: *abhimukhato 'thābhīkṣṇyād abhibhavagatito 'bhidharmaś ca.* Each point has found its detailed explanation in the commentary, the gist of which has been incorporated in the quotation above.

3. Aṭṭhasālinī I 27 ; *Abhidhammatantipaccavekkhantānam anantam pītisomanassam uppajjati.*

ness, it is for those who want to rise above the level of the common place and above the limitations set up by mere reason and its standardized conventions, to look into the very essence of existence and of Reality. As a matter of fact, it was by thoroughly knowing the nature of things, not merely from the blinding glitter of the outer surface but from their illuminating glow from within, that the prince of the Sakya clan became The Buddha, The Enlightened One—"The Supremely Enlightened One was the first to know the Abhidhamma. While sitting under the Bodhi-tree He penetrated the Abhidhamma. He became The Buddha.."[1]. Furthermore, "The Abhidhamma is the sphere of the omniscient Buddhas, but not the sphere of others".[2] In other words, first we have to apprehend with immediacy and find the answer to the problems of life for ourselves, afterwards we may speak about that which we have seen and which we have found, if it should still be necessary to speak. Thus the Abhidharma, however dry its presentation in a highly technical language may appear to us at first sight, aims at nothing less than to open man's eyes to that which is not speculatively arrived at by the logical method of hypothesis and deductive verification, but which can be immediately apprehended and is applicable to ourselves.

1. Aṭṭhasālinī I 44 : *Sammāsambuddho va pathamataram Abhidhammiko. So hi nam mahābodhipallaṅke nisīditvā paṭivijjhi; buddho hutvā....*

2. Aṭṭhasālinī I 73: *Abhidhammo nāma esa sabbaññubuddhānam yeva visayo na aññesam visayo.* See also VI 2.

MIND AND ITS STATES

(*citta-caitta*)

THE IMPORTANCE OF A HEALTHY ATTITUDE

This insistence on immediate experience and on immediately grasping the facts that are right here in front of us, necessarily stresses and evaluates the present moment, though not as valuable for its own sake, but insofar as it functions as a conduit to that which in all its inexhaustible and overwhelming richness will only be attained, most intimately felt and known, in Enlightenment. It certainly will not do to cast one's eyes into the heavens for it and idly scan the endlessness of a dubious future, nor will it do to brood self-accusingly over the beginningless past. The one is as useless and we may say, as morbid as the other. We have to deal with the problems of the present as they arise, and in order to do so we must be alert and efficient. It is, therefore, not to be wondered at that the first book of the Pali Abhidhamma, the Dhammasaṅganī, begins with the significant and meaningful words, "When a healthy conscious attitude, belonging to the world of sensuous relatedness, accompanied by and permeated with serenity, and associated and linked up with knowledge, has arisen...."[1]

In this statement a certain conscious attitude has been specified with respect to a certain occasion and the occasion, in its turn, has been specified by a certain conscious attitude, for an attitude is the end product of all factors which can have an influence on, and in this way, can produce certain psychic operations ("effects"), while at the same time the attitude, thus group-patterned will either determine an action in this or that definite direction, or will comprehend a stimulus in this or that definite way. According to the author of the Aṭṭhasālinī the little word "when" (*yasmiṁ samaye*) is full of meaning.

1. Dhammasaṅganī, ed. P.V. Bapat and R.D. Vadekar, p. 21 : *yasmiṁ samaye kāmāvacaraṁ kusalaṁ cittam uppannaṁ hoti somanassasahagatam ñāṇasampayuttam.*

First of all it points to the totality of circumstances and conditions favouring and producing a definite operation ("effect") (*samavāya*), then it denotes the unique opportunity (of grasping the secret of all existence) (*khaṇa*),[1] furthermore it designates the momentariness of any given moment or situation (*kāla*), then it hints at the simultaneous co-operation of many other psychic functions (*samūha*), and finally it shows the interdependence and interrelatedness of everything involved (*hetu*).[2] All these factors which are thus present and effective are called *dharma*. The meaning of *dharma* is as follows: "They bear their intrinsic nature, or they are supported by conditions, or they are supported according to their intrinsic nature".[3] However, all these factors or *dharmas* are so entirely dependent upon the innumerable conditions that in no way can they or will they retain their individuality above all conditions, hence they are called "having no individuality of their own" (*nissattanijjīvatā*).[4]

The sensuousness of the immediate situation with its display of all the enticements of the world and the incessant dissipation of mind in the prodigal variety of the world, is clearly pointed out in the above definition of an attitude by the attribute 'belonging to the world of sensuous relatedness' (*kāmāvacara*). By this term is encompassed the whole range between the lowest hell, called Avīci, and the highest heaven, the heaven

1. The unique opportunity (*kṣaṇa*), which is essentially the human status, has been much insisted upon in Mahāyāna writings. See for instance Bodhicaryāvatāra I 4 and the commentary.

2. Aṭṭhasālinī III 14 sqq.

3. Aṭṭhasālinī II 10; *attano pana sabhāvam dhārentī ti dhammā, dhāriyanti vā paccayehi, dhāriyanti vā yathāsabhāvato ti dhammā.*

The first part of this definition is also met with in the Prasannapadā, p. 304 : *Svalakṣaṇadhāraṇārthena*. Abhidharmakośa I 4 : In Visuddhimagga VIII 2 46 Buddhaghosa treats *dharma* and *svabhāva* as synonymous : *dhammā ti sabhāvā.*

4. Aṭṭhasālinī II 9. The translation of these terms by 'without a soul', found in most European translations, is silly. Whether a thing has a soul or not may have been a problem for Christian Fathers and apologetians. It certainly has never been a Buddhist problem, since Buddhism did not share a dualistic view. What is colloquially termed 'body' and 'soul' is on the same level of transitoriness. Only the ultimate is permanent and even beyond permanence.

of the Paranirmitavaśavartin gods. It may sound strange to our modern "enlightened" ears that the world of sensuousness not only comprises the world of men, plants, and animals, but also the world of ghosts and gods. However, it should not be forgotten that an abstract idea, such as god or demon,—at least we nowadays try to conceive them as an abstract idea—is not arbitrarily hypostatized and transplanted into a world of the beyond, but that which is called heaven or hell is essentially the term for the psychic reverberation of strongly emotionally toned experiences which, when they appear reproduced, are so sensuous that we actually see or feel them. There is absolutely no reason to deride the fact that we may at any time experience for ourselves the tormenting pains of hell and the all-surpassing bliss of heaven. We would only commit a grave fault if we ignored the symbolic character of such terms as heaven and hell and transferred a mere linguistic device to the realm of metaphysics. However, this sensuous realism contains a grave danger, for it implies the identity of the object with the emotion of the moment which, of course, destroys or at least greatly curtails the possibility of cognition. This the author of the Aṭṭhasālinī has clearly brought out in explaining the term 'world of sensuous relatedness'. He states that "sensuous relatedness (*kāma*) is twofold: object and emotion. Emotion means passionate desire, and object means the triple realm of existence (i.e., the hells, the human world, and the heavens). Emotion is spoken of here, because it passionately desires, and object is spoken of here, because it is passionately desired".[1] The identity of the emotion with the object, as pointed out by the comprehensive term 'sensuous relatedness' (*kāma*), implies that any object whatsoever can have an effect on the individual to any degree and that any sort of emotion on the part of the individual immediately violates the object. Such a mentality which may be called autoerotic, because the individual loves himself in and through the object, is a serious handicap and certainly cannot be called a healthy and dexterous attitude,

1. Aṭṭhasālinī III 26 : *uddānato dve kāmā vatthukāmo ca kilesakāmo. tattha kilesakāmo atthato chandarāgo vā, vatthukāmo tebhūmakavaṭṭam: kilesakāmo c'ettha kāmetī ti kāmo, itaro kāmiyatī ti.*

This latter explanation of *kāma* is also found with Yaśomitra, commenting on Abhidharmakośa III 3 : *kāmaḥ, kāmyate 'neneti kāma iti kṛtvā.*

hence the insistence on the healthiness of attitude in the Abhidharma literature.

Although healthiness is the fundamental and most outstanding quality, yet the term 'healthy' (*kusala*) comprises still other connotations which evolve out of the basic 'healthiness' of an attitude. These qualities are 'faultlessness', 'efficiency', and 'production of happy results'.[1] The author of the Aṭṭhasālinī gives quite a long explanation of this term 'healthy' (*kusala*), which is not without interest. He says that those factors operating at a particular moment "are called *kusala,* because they make base factors tremble, shake, be upset, and finally be abolished. Or, the word *kusa* means those factors which lie in an individual in a base form and the term *kusala* has the meaning of chopping off, cutting off those base factors which are called 'unhealthy' (*akusala*). Or, *kusa* is another word for knowledge, because it curtails, reduces, and eradicates that which is base, and *kusala* is that which should be grasped and activated, since it is to be taken hold of by this knowledge. Or, just as the kusa grass cuts any part of the hand with both edges of its blade, so also it cuts the emotions both in their actual manifestation and in their latent potentiality; and therefore *kusala* is so called, because like the kusa grass it cuts off that which is base".[2]

1 Aṭṭhasālinī II 8 : *kusalasaddo tāva ārogyānāvajjacchekasukhavipākesu dissati.* Similarly in III 29, we are told that "kusala has the meaning of healthiness, faultlessness, and skilfulness"—*api ca ārogyaṭṭhena anāvajjaṭṭhena kosallasambhūtaṭṭhena ca kusalam.* This latter aspect has become most important in Mahāyāna philosophy.

2. Aṭṭhasālinī II 10: *vacanattho pan' etthe kucchite pāpake dhamme salayanti calayanti kıppenti viddhamsentī ti kusalam kucchitena vā ākārena sayanti ti kusā, te akusalasankhāte kuse luṇanti chindantī ti kusala. Kucchitānam vā sānato tanukaraṇato osānakaraṇato ñāṇam kusam nāma, tena kusena lātabbā ti kusala gahetabbā pavatteṭabbā ti atiṇn; yathā vā kusā ubhayabhāgagatam hatthappaoesam lunanti evam ime pi uppannānuppannabhāvena ubhayabhāgagatam sankilesapakkham lunanti, tasmā kusā viya lunantī ti kusalā.* See also III 29 where the first of these explanations has been repeated.

A similar and, in one aspect, identical explanation has been given by Yaśomitra in his Abhidharmakośavyākhyā and Abhidharmakośa I 30 : "The base factors have moved away, have gone, have gone away, therefore one speaks of *kuśala.* Or, kuśa is a term for knowledge, because, it is sharp like kuśa grass. It takes, acquires, therefore one speaks of *kuśala*"—*kutsitāś chalitā gatā apakrāntā iti kuśalāḥ. prajñā vā kuśa iva tīkṣṇeti kuśaḥ; tam lānti ādadata iti kuśalāḥ.*

By pointing to the emotions our author has made a very important observation. Both the actual emotional explosion and the latent potentiality of an emotion are no doubt a great hindrance to our dealings with the problems of life as they arise. Moreover, the fact should not be overlooked that an emotion complex always and entirely depends upon the fact that a real conscious adaptation to an immediate object situation has been impossible, and this failure of adaptation results in the explosion of an emotion. This liability to become at any time overpowered by an emotion makes man weak, and just as a man who is physically ailing is unable to attend to his work in a proper way, so much more so is a man who is mentally unbalanced unable to deal with any problem that may confront him. No doubt, mental instability is a very serious disease. So also, by way of a simile, we are told that "Just as a man is called healthy when he is neither ill nor sick nor unwell in body, so also one may speak of healthiness in mental-spiritual matters when there is absence of illness, sickness, and disease through (and in the form of) affects".[1]

One other point has to be noted in this connection. Even when the emotional outburst has worn off and man has regained his senses, he will, only too often, with the same lack of comprehension, pour forth self-accusations and feel utterly ill at ease because of the sickening and gloomy feeling of moral guilt. It is therefore not to be wondered, that 'faultlessness' or 'irreproachableness' has been described as absence of emotional outburst[2] and that the domestication of man's untamed and unbridled emotive nature plays such an important role in the whole of Buddhism. But this domestication, to be sure, is brought about only by a change of attitude, never by grand talk about 'moral', 'immoral', and other more or less selfish interests.

Emotional outbursts, i.e. feelings and emotions attached to ideas, are forces that will inevitably carry the individual away with them and color any and all sorts of human response. Very often they tend to become complexes, and as often as not complexes are a matter of the everyday experience of every body and not necessarily a matter of abnormal psychology. It

1. Aṭṭhasālinī III 29.

2. ibid. III 29 *kilesāvajjassa pana kilesadosassa kilesadarathassa ca abhāvā anāvajjaṭṭhena kusalam.*

is this tendency to react by emotions that is called 'the world', Saṁsāra, as opposed to the tranquil equanimity of Nirvāṇa which is attained by a radical change of attitude. Sthiramati has dealt with this problem of the power of emotions and the necessary change of attitude in connection with the idea of an existent substratum to the phenomena of Saṁsāra and Nirvāṇa (*ālayavijñāna*). His words are so significant that they are given here in extenso:[1]

"Karman and the emotions are the reason for the way of the world, and among them the emotions are the principal condition. By way of the dominating influence of the emotions, Karman is able to project a new existence (*punarbhavākṣepasamartha*); it cannot be otherwise. Karman which has been enabled to project a new existence will become this new existence under the conditions of the dominating influence of the emotions; it cannot be otherwise. Therefore, the emotions are, indeed, the root of the fact that the way of the world (*saṁsāra*) continues to exist, since it is well-known that the emotions are the principal condition. But when the power of the emotions has been exhausted then the world will cease to exist; it cannot be otherwise. The exhaustion of their power, however, is not possible unless a substratum (*ālayavijñāna*) is assumed. But why is it not possible without this substratum, it may be argued. The problem is whether it is sufficient that the emotion be exhausted in its actuality (*sammukhībhūta*) or in its state of potentiality (*bījāvasthā*).

"That the exhaustion of the emotion in its actuality is sufficient for the cessation of the way of the world, is impossible; being on the way of exhaustion the potentiality of the emotion has not yet become exhausted. At this moment, nothing else can be assumed but the substratum in which the latent potentialities of the emotions (*kleśabīja*) reside. Otherwise we would have to assume that the very remedy (*pratipakṣacitta*) is inherent in the latent potentiality of the emotions (*kleśabījānuṣakta*). But that which is inherent in the latent potentiality of an emotion can by no means be the remedy against its power. And as long as the latent potentialities of emotional outbursts have not been eliminated the cessation of the world will not come about. For

1. Triṁśikāvijñaptibhāṣya, p. 38.

this reason it is necessary to assume a substratum (*ālayavijñāna*) which is affected ("charged", *bhavyate*) by the various emotions (*kleśopakleśa*) which co-exist with sense perceptions which are different from the substratum, because this substratum is the nutritive soil for the maturation of the emotions lying in it in a potential state (*svabījapuṣṭyādhānataḥ*).

"The potential state of the various emotions which appear as actual emotional outbursts when the residua of former emotional experiences are suitably stimulated (*vāsanāvṛttilābhe sati*) in the particular course of a homogeneous series (representing our individual existence), becomes eliminated by the remedy against the emotional disturbances which is co-existent with the substratum. Therefore, when the potential state has been eliminated, Nirvāṇa during our lifetime (*sopādhiśeṣo nirvāṇadhātu*) has been attained, because by this spiritual adjustment (*āśraya-āśrayaparāvṛtti*)[1] emotional distractions can no longer come about. And when the existence projected by the former Karman has come to an end, ultimate Nirvāṇa (*nirupādhiśeṣo nirvāṇadhātu*) has been attained, because another existence is not produced. Though there be still psychic activity (*karman*) this psychic activity cannot produce a new existence, because the emotional outbursts, having become exhausted, are no longer able to co-operate in the production of a new exis-

1. That *āśraya* is used here in the sense of *āśrayaparāvṛtti* is born out by Triṁśikā, p. 15 and p. 44. The spiritual adjustment is a radical change of the former narrow and egocentric attitude, as is pointed out by Sthiramati:

"*āśraya* designates the *ālayavijñāna* endowed with all potentialities. Its radical change consists in the fact that there does not exist any longer the potential state which will manifest itself as the duality of incapacity (to act properly) and of affective experience (*dausṭhulyavipākadvayavāsanābhāvena*), but that there is efficiency, the Dharmakāya and non-dual wisdom (*karmaṇyatādharmakāyādvayajñānabhāvena*). By giving up which factors is this radical change obtained? The author (Vasubandhu) says: 'By giving up the twofold inefficiency.' Twofold means inefficiency consisting in the veiling power of emotional instability and inefficiency consisting in the veiling power of the beliefs concerning the knowable (*kleśāvaraṇa, jñeyāvaraṇa*). Inefficiency means that the psychic substratum cannot function properly......"

On p. 15 Sthiramati declares that "Emotional instability is a hindrance for the attainment of liberation. When it has lost its power, liberation is gained. Beliefs about the knowable are a hindrance for the functioning of true knowledge. When beliefs have been given up, true knowledge functions."

tence (*sahakārikaraṇābhāvāt*). In this way, the continuation as well as the cessation of Saṁsāra comes about, when there is a substratum; it cannot be otherwise."

Whether or not it is necessary to assume an entity as the substratum for Saṁsāra and Nirvāṇa can be left undecided. Important are the following points and their observation gives high credit to Sthiramati. In declaring that the exhaustion of the working power of an emotion is not sufficient for the cessation of further unpleasant and disagreeable experiences which make up the world we encounter—the pleasant experiences because of their transitory nature also being basically unpleasant, Sthiramati obviously has in mind the fact that very often impulses to actions which are in conflict with the ego-ideal are blocked and to a greater or lesser extent are repressed. But in spite of repression these impulses do not submit to defeat and die out; on the contrary, they continue to be active and contribute largely to the fact that the world gradually comes to be perceived in a distorted manner. Of course, many of those impulses will gradually subside and eventually disappear entirely, others, however, will linger with the individual in spite of all attempts to forget them, intentional forgetting being identical with repression. These impulses will only die out when the individual develops spiritually, and the spiritual development is essentially a restoration of the psychic equilibrium that has been disturbed by the emotional outbursts and remains disturbed due to possible emotional outbreaks. The disturbances by emotionality will be removed by changes in interpretation. With the passage of time the individual will see things in a different light. Old experiences that once disturbed the individual and which he tried to forget take on a new meaning and gradually recede before the new that appears out of the unknown. This restoration of the psychic equilibrium is meant by Sthiramati when he speaks of spiritual adjustment (*āśraya-parāvṛtti-nirvāṇa*) which is equal to seeing things in a different light. That which formerly was the cause of troubles, is now no longer repressed but has lost its power and is viewed from a different level, the attainment of which is effected by meditative processes. And it is this interconnection between emotionality and interpretation that gives rise to the Mahāyānic demand that emotionality as well as interpretation has to be changed into a feeling of bliss and comprehensive understanding.

The importance of attitude has so far escaped the notice of many scholars, and yet it alone provides a satisfactory explanation for such peculiar and complex psychological phenomena as those in which certain stimuli exercise a strong effect at one time, while their effect is rather weak or even absent at another. Having a certain attitude means to be ready for something, and this readiness for something is due to the presence of a certain subjective group-pattern, being a definite combination of many factors in the human psyche. This group-pattern may have been brought about by various events. Unconsciously it may have been brought about by the innate disposition; in a subtle, partly unconscious and partly conscious, way by the influence of our environment; and consciously by our experiences in life, to mention only some of the numerous and varied contributing events. Moreover, any strongly toned factor in consciousness may, either alone or in connection with others, form a certain constellation which favours a certain way of perception and apperception insofar as those qualities or motives are stressed which seem to belong to or fit into the subjective content, while at the same time everything that is dissimilar is inhibited. Thus an attitude is both the resultant of many factors and the determining element in our life, inasmuch as it moulds our actions and even our ideas down to the minutest details. It is, therefore, obvious that there is not only one attitude valid for all human beings but that there are a number of attitudes in accordance with the group-patterning factors or events. All these points just mentioned are referred to by the author of the Aṭṭhasālinī who, far from being a philosopher, gives a cross-section of the opinions held about what we call an attitude. He says:[1]

"Attitude is so called, because it is concerned with (*cinteti*) an objective; 'it discriminates' is the meaning (of *citta*—attitude). Or, since the term *citta* is the common denominator for all mental operations (i.e., the generic term 'attitude' admits of various qualifications and distinctions according to the constellating factors as well as to the resultants), that which is called

1. Aṭṭhasālinī III 33.

a worldly, healthy, unhealthy, and unprompted attitude and which builds up its own continuity by way of apperceptive processes, is termed *citta*[1]. As a resultant it is also called *citta* because it is built up (*cita*) by activity and affectivity[3]. Moreover, all *citta* may be understood in the sense that it varies according to circumstances (and constellating factors) and that it is capable of producing a variety of operations or resultants ("effects")".[3]

It is true that without an attitude apperception is impossible, for in the act of apperception a new content or a new combination of contents is articulated to similar contents which already exist, in such a way that not only are those qualities emphasized which appear to belong to the subjective content but the new content, too, is understood and is clear. But it is erroneous to assume that an attitude is just apperception. This mistake was committed by the Pāli philosophers and the usefulness of a healthy attitude came to a dead end.[4]

An attitude, to be sure, is not a phenomenon existing per se and detached from all psychic factors but is intimately connected with all of them and only precedes them (and also, of course, accompanies them). As we are told: "An attitude does not arise as something single. Therefore, just as in the saying,

1. This is the explanation also given in Yaśomitra's commentary on Abhidharmakośa II 34 : "It builds up, therefore it is called *citta*. The meaning is that citta builds up what is healthy or unhealthy"—*cinotīti cittam iti; kuśalam akuśalaṁ vā cinotīty arthaḥ.*

2. This is the view of the Sautrāntikas and Yogācāras as stated by Yaśomitra, loc. cit. "it is built up by bright and dark elements, therefore it is called citta"—*citaṁ śubhāśubhair dhātubhir iti cittam.*

Insofar as an attitude is largely preconsciously determined, the Yogācāras emphasizing this aspect define the *ālayavijñāna* as *citta* in the sense of being built up by the residua of former experiences: *tad vāsanācitātam upādāya.* Abhidharmasamuccaya, p. 12.

3. For this interpretation see also L. de la Vallée Poussin's translation of the Abhidharmakośa, chapter II, verse 34.

4. See for instance Abhidhammāvatāra, p. 1 sq. : *citta* is called so, because it is cognition of objects. The meaning of this is to be understood in the following way : *citta* is a generic term. It is called so because it reflects or because it builds up its own continuity."—*tattaḥ cittan ti visayavijñānam cittam tasmā pana ko vacanattho. vuccate. sabbasaṁgāhakavasena pana cintetī ti cittam, attano saṁtānam vā cinotīti pi cittam.*

'the king has arrived', it is understood that he has not arrived alone and without his retinue, but that he has come together with his attendants, so also it should be understood that an attitude has come with more than fifty healthy factors. Attitude as such has come as a forerunner".[1]

Without taking into account the importance of attitude in our lives it would be impossible to account for the differences in individuals. In obedience to His Majesty the King, i.e., the attitude, not only the relation between the various functions is modified but also the emotional value as regards likes and dislikes is regulated. For, it may be asked, when has there not been something which at one time has been passionately desired and at another time most violently been detested, and what has not attracted the queerest notions at one time or another ? And how else could it be explained, if not by the fundamental importance of attitude, that one man just lives blindly that which he experiences, while another man thinks about and tries to fathom the meaning of what he experiences ? The author of the Aṭṭhasālinī correctly observes that "An attitude in which passion is predominant is different from an attitude in which aversion prevails and different from an attitude in which bewilderment holds its sway. And an attitude concerned with the world of sensual objects (*kāmāvacara*) is different from an attitude concerned with the world of Gestalten (*rūpāvacara*).[1]

In our daily life and as long as we struggle to find that standpoint from which we will be able to look at the world of multiplicity without becoming the victim of emotional outbursts and from which we are able to deal with any problem whatsoever in a way which will not violate the object and which will not make us over-self-righteous, a healthy attitude is most important. But it has also to be borne in mind that especially in matters spiritual, an attitude alone will not do but that understanding must come as the ripe fruits as it were of a healthy attitude. Understanding has in Buddhist philosophy, as we shall see later, a specific meaning which, though of intellectual quality, is not theoretical in nature. Of this distinction bet-

1. Aṭṭhasālinī III 43.

2. Aṭṭhasālinī III 34. At the same place the variety of attitudes as regards the constellating contents has been fully discussed.

ween attitude for practical purposes and understanding as regards spiritual matters, the author of the Aṭṭhasālinī says that "In worldly matters an attitude is the chief, an attitude is the leader, an attitude is the forerunner; but in matters spiritual analytical appreciative understanding is the leader, analytical appreciative understanding is the forerunner".[1]

The importance of *citta*—attitude—whether it tends to become involved in Saṁsāra or whether it tends to find its fulfilment and expression in Nirvāṇa, is the key to Buddhist philosophy and psychology. Although the various schools of thought in Buddhism wrangled about the logical nature of the substantive *citta*, whether it is existent or subsistent, none of them ever challenged the primacy of *citta*.[2] This fact may be taken as an indication, that *citta* as something which can and must be experienced is of primary importance, and of secondary importance with respect to its formulation.

Perception and Apperception

Intimately connected with the importance of attitude is active perception and apperception. It is therefore necessary to give a detailed account of these processes as they occur according to the Buddhist conception, which did not fail to see that any total state of mind appears as a 'unity of centre'[3].

Perception is divided into sensuous and non-sensuous. Sensuous perception is based on the sensation of certain interrelated sensa, on a selection of sensa, and on using sensed and selected sensa for perceiving.[4] This is clearly stated in the oldest available texts from which the Abhidharma derives its material. The classical passage runs as follows: "These five senses,

1. Aṭṭhasālinī III 44. See also III 45 and 46 where this difference has been discussed in connection with modes of questioning a person about worldly or spiritual matters.

2. Passages to this effect are: Saṁyuttanikāya I 39; Abhidharmakośa II 105; Aṅguttaranikāya II 177: Śikṣāsamuccaya, p. 121; Daśabhūmikasūtra, p. 49; Laṅkāvatārasūtra X 134; Kāśyapaparivarta 98; Subhāṣitasaṁgraha, p. 19; Jñānasiddhi IX 7; 9; Pañcakrama IV 16; Tattvasaṁgrahapañjikā, p. 184; etc. etc.

3. I owe this term to C.D. Broad, The Mind and Its Place in Nature.

4. C. D. Broad, The Mind and Its Place in Nature, p. 420.

seeing, hearing, smelling, tasting, and touching, have each their own field of functioning and corresponding objects and none of them enjoys the field and the object of the others. These five senses, of which each has its own field and object and of which none enjoys the field and object of the others, take refuge in the *manas*; the *manas* enjoys their field and objects".[1] Similarly, but much more exhaustively and more precisely the Aṭṭhasālinī describes the nature of the *manas* which is next to *citta*, the most important term in Buddhist philosophy and psychology. In this work we read: "Because the psychic total situation (*phassa*, Gesamtsituation) and the other psychic factors connected with it have their origin here (in the *manas*), the term *āyatana* (in *mano āyatana*) has the meaning of birth-place; because the without assembles here in the form of visible, audible, olfactory, gustatory, and tactile objects, it also has the meaning of meeting-place; because it is the immediate and indispensable antecedent in the sense of simultaneity for the psychic total situation, and the other psychic factors connected with it and thus is the cause of them, it also has the meaning of cause".[2] In the first passage just mentioned 'refuge' can hardly mean anything else but that the single sense perceptions with their percepts have given up their isolation and independence, and the 'enjoying' of their fields and objects by the *manas*, would signify that the material presented by the senses to the perceiving subject is arranged, ordered, and interpreted in a certain way. For the world of things and persons in which commonsense believes, is a synthesis of the data brought to the knower by means of the senses and of the ordering and regulating concepts brought to the data by the knower. This synthesis is, as we shall see presently, brought about unconsciously, in other words, the idea of an external object is not derived from inference. In the second passage, 'birth-place', 'meeting-place', and 'cause' refer to the fact that the subjective factor is rather a complex phenomenon and not just an imaginary blank tablet called a mental substance. The *manas* according to these passages denotes what we might call the subjective disposition

1. Majjhimanikāya I 295; Saṁyuttanikāya V 218; Mahāyānasaṅgraha II 12.

2. Aṭṭhasālinī III 275.

that receives the sense stimuli and comprises them, giving them the peculiar subjective admixture that is never absent in either perception or cognition. As a comprehensive term it is mentioned last in enumerations—"because the field and object of the five senses is experienced by the *manas* it is mentioned last";[1] and as a power that cannot simply be ignored, it controls and subordinates the co-existent psychic material—"as a controlling power the *manas* puts the co-existent psychic factors under its dominance".[2]

While the *manas* may be spoken of as 'the subjective disposition' in general, it is possible to describe its function in very precise terms. It is well to bear in mind that Buddhism acknowledges only a fluxional nature of all entities, the fluxional nature being aptly compared with the flowing water of a river. Therefore also the *manas* or the 'subjective disposition' is not at all a permanent or unchanging entity, but in a state of continuous flux. This means that the fluxional character of the *manas* is nothing distinct from the *manas* itself and therefore cannot be regarded as an antecedent or subsequent event with respect to its own nature, though it may be conceived as either an antecedent or a subsequent event with respect to the immediately following or immediately preceding phase of the psychic process. In this way the *manas* is a characteristic relation backwards or forwards. This is obviously what Buddhaghosa, the author of the Visuddhimagga, means: "The *manas*, according to its origination, may be conceived as either antecedent or subsequent to sense perceptions such as visual perceptions and the like".[3]

Insofar as the manas precedes the sense perceptions, i.e., before the actual process of sense perception sets in, it performs the function of attention. As Buddhaghosa says "The *manas* which precedes the activity of visual perception and other sense perceptions and which discriminates the visual object from other objects, has the function of attention, its actual phase is the becoming confronted with visual and other objects, and the moment and basis from which its function starts and operates, is the interruption of the unconscious stream (by the object

1. Visuddhimagga XV 11.
2. Visuddhimagga XVI 10.
3. Visuddhimagga XV 42.

that has come into the range of psychic activity)".[1] When Buddhaghosa speaks here of the discriminating action of the *manas* he does not mean so much the actual conscious discrimination but the initial stage of the process of becoming conscious, which is marked by utilizing the sensum selected and discriminated.

Becoming attentive (*āvajjana*) is an absolutely automatic phenomenon and, therefore, it is technically termed *kiriyamanodhātu* to distinguish it from other non-automatic processes. Stated more precisely, the meaning is that the *manas* which becomes attentive to the stimulation of the sense apparatus does not produce any effect and hence passes off as a relatively subsidiary phenomenon within the whole of the psychic process. The merely functional character is stated in the Aṭṭhasālinī in the following way: "*kiriya* simply means activity. In all automatic psychic processes, that which has not attained the stage of apperception is like a flower in the wind, and that which comes up to the stage of apperception is fruitless (i.e., bearing no result or effect) like the flower of a tree that has been cut down at its root. Because such a process only performs its function, it is called mere activity, and as such is spoken of as an automatic phenomenon".[2]

Nevertheless, however unimportant in the whole of the psychic activity this process of becoming attentive may appear, it is the only phase which makes it possible for the senses to operate according to their nature and which, in addition, assists and helps the operation of the senses. In this way, it is, as has been pointed out by Buddhaghosa, both antecedent and subsequent (*purecarānucara*). In its aspect of antecedent it makes the internal psychic process possible, while in its aspect of subsequent, i.e., following immediately after the sense perception has set in, it marks the actual beginning of the internal psychic process, which, in course of time, leads to an actual awareness of an object. This initial stage is designated as the reception of the object (*sampaṭicchanakiccā manodhātu*).[3] Thus Buddhaghosa states that "Immediately after the activity of visual

1. Visuddhimagga XIV 107. See also XIV 115.
2. Aṭṭhasālinī III 659.
3. Visuddhimagga XIV 95; 101.

perception or other sense perceptions has ceased, the *manas* which discriminates the visual object from other objects begins to function; its function is receiving the visual percept or the other percepts; its actual manifestation is suchness; and the moment from whence it starts its action, is the moment or situation when the activity of visual perception or of the other sense perceptions has ceased".[1]

This receiving the sensum is the very activity of the *manas* though not the sense of a special faculty, since it comes into play in all basic forms of psychic activity. It is best understood as the intensity of the psychic process which becomes manifest, even if it should be only in a subliminal way, as a certain effect. For this reason, it is called *vipāka* 'developing toward a certain effect'.[2] Buddhaghosa remarks on the receptive process of the *manas*: "Immediately after visual perception or other perceptions there springs up the *manas* which receives their respective objects and which is developing toward and in a healthy operation or effect (*kusalavipāka*) after (psychic processes that are) developing toward and in a healthy atmosphere, and which is developing toward and in an unhealthy operation after processes that go on in and toward an unhealthy atmosphere".[3] The terms 'healthy' and 'unhealthy' refer to the general attitude under whose dominance the manas functions, as is evident from the opening statement of the Dhammasaṅgani.

That such a process comes about is solely due to Karman. This term has created great confusion due to its misuse by Western writers who did not understand the Eastern mind, as well as by Easterners who, in their desire to appear as modernists, simply copied the misconceptions. In Buddhist reasoning Karman is no outside force, but the inherent activity of every process. Since activity is limited by the amount of energy available—there is no single action which is not energy-determined—Karman represents both the potential and kinetic

1. Visuddhimagga XIV 97. See also Aṭṭhasālinī III 578.

2. *vipāka* denotes both the process and the final product. In the former case its etymology is *vipacyata iti vipākaḥ. karmakartari ghañ*; in the latter, it is *phalaṁ tu vipaktir eveti vipāka iti bhāve ghañ*. See Abhidharmakośavyākhyā and Abhidh.-kośa I 37.

3. Visuddhimagga XIV 118.

energy of a process. Moreover, since energy cannot be lost it is always present either as kinetic or potential energy. In its potential stage energy is 'heaped up' (*upacita*), while in its kinetic state it develops (*vipacyate*) toward a certain effect. Thus, the functioning of the manas is due to the 'heaped-up' potential energy invested in the psychic phenomenon called *manas*. The way in which the *manas* operates after the energy discharge has been effected, is due to the fact that the *manas* owes its origin and mode of functioning to innumerable, similar processes which have left their function traces (*vāsanā*), and therefore the *manas* represents a certain basic form of a certain ever-recurring psychic process. This double nature, as it were, of owing its nature to similar processes that have been going on since time immemorial and of being able to function in a proper way because of its heaped-up or potential energy, has already been indicated in the Dhammasaṅgani: "Because the process has gone on in a healthy manner (i.e., within a compass of a healthy attitude), belonging to our ordinary world of sensuous relatedness, and because energy has been heaped up, the *manas* which represents an energic process, has originated (i.e., has started performing its proper function)".[1] Also its determination as 'suchness'[2] points to the explanation given above.

In connection with the *manas* which, as the above analysis has shown, designates the subjective disposition and its incipient activity in a process of perception and apperception, we have to discuss another phenomenon which is technically termed *manoviññāṇadhātu* in the Pāli text. This term and the function it performs must be carefully distinguished from another *manoviññāṇa* (Skt. *manovijñāna*) which will be discussed later on.

The *manoviññāṇa* (*dhātu*) under consideration is a single 'entity' which represents a further stage in the process of becoming conscious. As the author of the Aṭṭhasālinī informs us, it is called by such a long name as it is made up of three elements (*manas, vijñāna, dhātu*), and because of its character of

1. Dhammasaṅgani 455 : *kāmāvacarassa kusalassa kammassa katatā, upacitattā vipākā manodhātu uppannā hoti.*

See also Visuddhimagga XVII 121: *vipākaṁ h'etaṁ, vipākañ ca na upacitakammābhāve uppajjati*, which may be rendered freely: "This is an energic process, but an energic process does not come about without Potential energy".

2. See for instance Visuddhimagga XIV 97; etc. etc.

'measuring' or 'taking stock' of the material presented to it by the sensory functions, because of its character of being a psychological process leading up to awareness of 'things' and 'ideas', and because of its intrinsic nature which is its fluxional nature and not an unchanging entity beyond origination and destruction.[1]

Buddhaghosa in his Visuddhimagga speaks of the autonomy of this factor in the following way : "The *manoviññāṇadhātu* should be considered as a monkey in a forest (jumping from one branch to another), because it does not stop with the objects (presented to it); as a restive horse, because it is controlled only with difficulty; as a stick thrown into the air, because it falls down wherever it likes (i.e., our mental life is absolutely autonomous and we are never quite sure of what we will experience next); and as a dancer, because it is dressed in the various garments of passionate actions and reactions such as greed and aversion".[2]

This last qualification gains importance when we consider the following passage : "*The manoviññāṇadhātu* is twofold: of a general kind and of a special kind. In its general aspect it is associated with an indeterminate feeling tone, it has no causal characteristic and is simply automatic; its function is the discrimination of the six kinds of objects (i.e., the five sense objects and the objects of introspection); its operation as expressed by its mode of action is the determination of the sensed data conveyed by the five senses and attentiveness to the continuously flowing stream of the subjective factor; its actual manifestation is suchness; and the moment and place from whence it starts its action, is the moment or the situation when either the energic process of the *manoviññāṇadhātu*, which has no causal characteristic and which is simply automatic, has ceased its activity, or when the stream of the unconscious has been interrupted (i.e., when attention has set in).—In its special aspect it is associated with cheerfulness, has no causal characteristic and is simply automatic; its function is the discrimination

1. Aṭṭhasālinī III 276: *imasmiṁ hi pade ekam eva cittaṁ minanaṭīṭhena mano, vijānanaṭṭhena viññāṇaṁ, sabhāvaṭṭhena nissattaṭṭhena vā dhātu ti thi nāmehi vuttaṁ.*

2. Visuddhimagga XV 43.

of the six kinds of objects; it operates in such a way that the Saints (*arhant*) are able to take the minor things of life in a gay and joyous mood; its actual manifestation is suchness; and it operates exclusively from the heart".[1]

Here two kinds of a *manoviññāṇadhātu* are distinguished : the one is operating in the case of ordinary human beings, while the other operates only in the case of the Arhants or Buddhist Saints who excel in a cheerful temperament. But certain basic functions such as cognition and interpretation of sensed data are common to both kinds. It is important to note that the same distinction is found in the works of the Yogācāras. That which operates in the case of ordinary beings is called the *kliṣṭa manas* which literally translated means 'tainted *manas*'—'tainted', because the ordinary human being is too much fettered by his egocentricity and hence is unable to see things (and above all himself) in a more detached way or to let the natural richness of his spiritual side burst forth. [His self-centredness actually makes it impossible for him to appreciate or to participate joyfully in any thing that is not immediatly related to for his whims.] The feeling of indifference aptly illustrates the narrowness of outlook and poverty of thinking and feeling in general. Therefore, to see things while in a joyous and gay mood is an art that will be mastered only by and after hard work—by overcoming the self-centredness which is so characteristic of the 'tainted' *manas*. It is precisely this taintedness that distinguishes an ordinary human being from the Arhant and from those who have realized the transcendental, for, [psychologically speaking, the transcendental is the going beyond the limits of egocentricity.] Vasubandhu therefore declares that the 'tainted' *manas* does not operate in the Arhants.[2]

We have seen above that the *manas* or the subjective disposition is divided into an automatic process (*kiriya*) which has no effect, and an energic process (*vipāka*) leading up to a certain effect, which, according to the general attitude of the individual, will be either healthy or unhealthy. This same

1. Visuddhimagga XIV 108.
2. Triṁśikāvijñapti, verse 7......*arhato na tat*. See also Sthiramati's commentary on this verse.

distinction is met with in the case of the *manoviññāṇa*. Anticipatingly it may be stated that both the *manas* and the *manoviññāṇa* (*dhātu*) (this differentiation is met with only in the works of the Pāli tradition, while the Yogācāras use only one term, viz., *manas*[1] to denote subliminal processes leading up to an actual awareness.

While the *manas* and its twofold operation as either automatic or energic denotes simply the initial stage of the individual's psychic activity in perception, the *manoviññāṇadhātu* denotes the subliminal process which later appears as a definite conscious content. Of the automatic process Buddhaghosa states, "Immediately after the unconscious stream has been disturbed, because one or the other of the six kinds of objects has come into the realm (of the senses and the subjective factor), as the *manas* there begins to operate the *manoviññāṇadhātu* which has no causal characteristic and is simply automatic, and which performs the function of attentiveness, as if interrupting the unconscious stream. It is associated with a feeling tone of indifference".[2] This attentiveness releases, as it were, the energic process that leads up to constellating a definite content in consciousness. This process itself is a most complicated one. It is a well known fact that two persons, for example, though they see the same object, never see it in such a way as to receive two identically similar impressions of it. Apart from the differences in organic acuteness there are in it also marked psychic variations which would be inexplicable if the subjective factor were not operative in an influential manner. The final result, i.e., the conscious content, is the most accurate synthesis and blending of all the inner and outer factors and processes. This synthesis and blending, or, as it has been termed in the Pāli texts, 'the bridging over (of the gulf between the subjective disposition and readiness to act and the outer object)' (*santīraṇa*) is an energetic process of which three aspects are distinguished according to the general attitude of the individual, and the feeling-emotional tone that accompanies every attitude.

1. The term *manovijñāna* is ambiguous, because it may be conceived as a tatpuruṣa-compound "the perception of the *manas*". Actually it is meant as a karmadhāraya compound "perception which is *manas*". See Vijñaptimātratāsiddhi. La Siddhi de Hiuan-tsang, p. 226.

2. Visuddhimagga XIV 116.

Buddhaghosa says about these three aspects: "The *manoviññāṇadhātu* which is an energetic process and is without causal characteristics (*vipākāhetukamanoviññāṇadhātu*), and which performs the function of bridging over the gulf between the subjective factor, (*manas, manodhātu*) and the object that has been received by the subjective factor operates (i) as developing into an unhealthy process immediately after the subjective factor which itself develops in and towards an unhealthy atmosphere, (has received the object), (ii) as accompanied by a joyous feeling with respect to a desirable object immediately after the subjective factor, which itself develops in and toward a healthy atmosphere, (has received the object), and (iii) as accompanied by an indifferent feeling tone with respect to an object of medium desirability".[1] This bridging over is only the initial stage, its final stage being the actual apperception of the object, viz., the relating of the new content to other contents already present in consciousness. In between these two stages, bridging over and apperception, there also operates the automatic *manoviññāṇadhātu*. Its operation consists of determining and fixing, as it were, (*voṭṭhapana*) the new content to be connected with the other contents in consciousness. And furthermore there is also the operation of several apperceptional phases (*javana*), all of which are wholly automatic (*kiriya*).[2]

It is rather surprising that the object should have feeling qualities of varying degrees, while at the same time also the subjective disposition has a certain feeling tone. The solution of this problem lies obviously in the fact that the division between subject and object in Buddhist philosophy is not so rigid as it is for a thorough dualist. Bearing in mind that cognition is essentially experiencing for the Buddhists, experiencing does not imply a subject-object relation as ultimate, nor does it necessarily imply a neutral stuff out of which later mind and matter are constructed. Attributing feeling qualities to objects is, perhaps, only an attempt to convey something of the intensity of an experience.

The intensity of the psychic process or the intensity of the experience in general accounts for the various functions

1. Visuddhimagga XIV 119.
2. Visuddhimagga XIV 120-121.

as described by Buddhaghosa who distinguishes two main qualitatively different *manoviññāṇas*. He says : "Its difference lies in the fact that it is accompanied either by a joyous feeling tone or by indifference and that accordingly it operates either at two or at five stages of the psychic process. The former of these two, because of its proceeding with respect to an exclusively desirable object, is accompanied by a joyous feeling tone, and operating as bridging over and apperception by the five senses and continuing the apperceptional process, it operates on two levels(i.e., bridging over and apperception). The latter, because of its proceeding with respect to objects of medium desirability, is accompanied by a feeling of indifference and operates on five levels as (i) bridging over, (ii) apperception, (iii) 'rebirth' or connecting psychic process, (iv) the unconscious continuum, and (v) death or ceasing psychic process".[1]

The author of the Aṭṭhasālinī is more exhaustive and definitely points out the intensity of the process. He says regarding the two aspects of the *manoviññāṇa* : "In the first instance the term 'joy' (*pīti*) is used additionally. The feeling tone is one of joyousness and serenity (*somanassa*). This joy and serenity is felt when the object is exclusively desirable.—In the second instance an object of medium desirability is involved, therefore the feeling tone is indifference....The mode of action of the *manoviññāṇadhātu* is twofold (and it has to be borne in mind) that it has no causal characteristic and is a merely energetic process (*ahetukavipāka*), that its characteristic is the discrimination of the six kinds of objects (the five sense objects and the objects of introspection), that its function is bridging over, that its ever-recurring manifestation is suchness, and that the basis from which it operates is the heart.—The first named process (accompanied by a joyous feeling tone) manifests itself on two levels. It develops (*vipaccati*) into the function of bridging over the five senses which act like doors, immediately after the *manodhātu* which itself is an energetic process (*vipākamanodhātu*) has received the sense object, as soon as the functions of visual perception and other sense perceptions, operating in a wholesome or healthy direction and atmosphere, have ceased to operate (i.e., have transmitted the sense stimulus to the perceiving subject). If the stimulus coming from the

1. Visuddhimagga XIV 98.

object is very intense in the senses, the process mentioned will develop into the function of taking a firm hold of the object perceived. How is this to be understood? Just as the wake follows a boat which has forced its way through a rapid current, thereby dividing the water of the stream for a while, (before the wake disappears in the current once more) so also the process of apperception has come about, when a desirable object appears at one of the six senses creating a very intense stimulus; but while generally after conscious perception the unconscious continuum will take its turn again (i.e., the conscious content will disappear into the unconscious continuum and be succeeded by a new content penetrating into consciousness), this last named function will not allow (the unconscious continuum to take its turn at once), but will take a firm hold of the image won by conscious perception for one or two moments, and only after that will it allow the unconscious continuum to take its turn. (Instead of using the simile of a boat) the back of a bull crossing a river might also be used for an example of how the process of apperception comes about. In this way, the image that has been grasped in conscious perception, because of it having been taken hold of firmly, becomes the apperceptive process (*tadārammaṇaṁ nāma hutvā vipaccati*).—The second aspect (accompanied by an indifferent feeling tone) appears on five levels. It develops (i) into that psychic event which forms the connection with the new existence (*paṭisandhi*), if the being should be reborn in human existence, being either blind or deaf or stupid or insane or a hermaphrodite or even sexless by nature, (ii) into the unconscious continuum (*bhavanga*), as soon as the moment of connection has passed, and this unconscious continuum will last as long as the lifetime of this sentient being, (iii) into the function of bridging over (*santīraṇa*) if the object is of medium desirability, (iv) into the function of taking a firm hold of the object (*tadārammaṇa*), if the stimulus to the six senses by the object is very intense, and (v) into that kind of psychic process which at the moment of death departs from the present existence (*cuti*). On these five levels the psychic process under consideration manifests itself".[1]

1. Aṭṭhasālinī III 581-583.

Apart from the connection of the *manoviññāṇadhātu* with rebirth, most interesting is the statement that apperception depends upon the intensity of the stimulus. Usually we go through life without ever being conscious in the true sense of the word. We mark things and forget them almost as soon as we mark them. It actually requires more, to be, or to become actually conscious of a thing or a situation than just noting the items of our everyday life.

Since the process of becoming conscious is not merely a reaction process to the object stimulus but also is a most active process, one in which the sensed material is used for perceiving, or what amounts to the same, where meaning accrues to forms, though this dual presentation of sensed forms and given meanings is due only to the limitation of language with its linear successive order of words, while actually seeing, hearing and so on are themselves processes of formulation, we are now able to appreciate the statement concerning the simultaneity of sensation and formulation: "Each object makes its way (into consciousness) by way of two doors. Thus, a visible object simultaneously with stimulating the sensitivity of the eye appears at the *manas* (*manodvāre*). The meaning is that the visible object is the irremissible condition for the activation of the unconscious (i.e., of the latent image or deposit of former similar experiences). The process in respect to an audible, olfactory, gustatory, and tactile object is exactly the same (as in respect to a visible object). (This process may be illustrated by a simile:) Just as a bird flying through the air and alighting on the top of a tree touches a branch of the tree and its shadow strikes the ground, the touching of the branch and the spreading of the shadow on the ground taking place simultaneously, so also the stimulation of the sensitivity of the eye by the visible object and its appearance at the subjective factor (*manas*) by virtue of its ability to activate the (latent image of the object in the) unconscious takes place simultaneously. After that, the image having been selected from the unconscious continuum immediately after the process just described, and having started with attention and ended with judgment as to the visible object, a conscious perception with respect to any aspect among the visible objects as its objective comes into existence."[1] Bearing in mind the function of the *manas* as 'measuring' or 'taking stock', it is obvious that the immediately sensed colours, sounds, fragrances, flavours, are not the mere effects of the action of material substances upon the otherwise absolutely blank mental substances which by means of some mysterious faculty then project out of themselves what we call our conscious world. Sense perception is essentially a process of symbolic formulation.[2]

Non-sensuous perception, as the name implies, comes about without the co-operation of the senses.[3] As the examples adduced in the Aṭṭhasālinī make clear, non-sensuous perception refers to perceptual memory situations. It will suffice to quote one example : "Someone has circumambulated a great shrine, which is well plastered, decorated with such colours as orpiment, realgar, and the like, which is bedecked with various kinds of flags and banners, interlaced with garlands and wreaths, encircled by rows of lamps, and is shining in gorgeous splendor, and adorned in every respect. On the sixteen platforms the visitor has paid homage in prostrating himself, and with folded hands he has stood looking at the statue of the Buddha, with a deep feeling of joy. Thus having seen the shrine and having derived a deep feeling of joy from looking at the statue of the Buddha, wherever he may subsequently go or seat himself; be it in a place reserved for the night or a place reserved for the day, the shrine adorned in every respect seems to appear before his eyes on reflection just as it was when he actually circumambulated the shrine and paid his homage. Thus by previous sight a visible object is non-sensuously perceived".[4] The gist of the matter is that according to this view the memory situation does contain as its objective constituent a visual, auditory, olfactory, gustatory, and tactile image, as the case may be, and that such an image is very much like a sensum perceived in sensuous perception.[5]

It is important to note that in non-sensuous perception

1. Aṭṭhasālinī III 55.
2. See Susanne K. Langer, Philosophy in a New Key (Mentor Book), p. 73.
3. Aṭṭhasālinī III 56. *suddhamanodvāre pasādaghaṭṭanakiccaṁ natthi*.
4. Aṭṭhasālinī III 56.
5. See C. D. Broad, The Mind and Its Place in Nature, p. 230.

the intensity of the sense impression is decisive for whether there will be a perceptual situation or not.[1] However, since the *manas* (*manovijñāna*) is always present in sense perception,[2] the very fact that sometimes an object is not registered with the *manas* because of its low intensity, might suggest that in this case we have simultaneous undiscriminating awareness, to use a term of C. D. Broad.[3] To give an example. If I look for a certain slip with notes on my writing table, but fail to find it, though it was staring me in the face all the time, I am aware of the papers scattered over my writing table which registered with my eyes and my *manas*, to use Buddhist terms, but I am unaware of the slip with notes which registered neither with my eyes nor with my *manas*.

I shall conclude this section by considering very briefly the *manovijñāna* mentioned on a par with *cakṣurvijñāna* and different from the *manas*, *manovijñāna* discussed so far, and the nature of the *manas*.

The term *vijñāna* means 'discrimination' in the sense of cutting up a whole into parts and selecting them.[4] This function is connected with the senses so that, strictly speaking, *vijñāna* corresponds to our 'sensing'. In this way we have five sense *vijñānas* (eye, ear, nose, tongue, skin), each *vijñāna* named after the basis on which it operates. Similarly a *manovijñāna* has been listed as having the *manas* for its basis.[5] However, since the *manas* (sometimes called *manovijñāna* as pointed out above) is sufficient for accounting for the formulated content in consciousness, the assumption of a special *manovijñāna* in the sense of another sensory *vijñāna* (*cakṣurvijñāna*, etc.) is redundant and only apt to create confusion.[6]

1. Abhidhammatthasaṅgaha IV 11.
2. Madhyamika-vṛtti, p. 72. Hiuan-tsang's Vijñaptimātratāsiddhi, pp. 244, 245, 412, 413. Mahāyāna-sūtrālaṅkāra XI 40.
3. loc. cit., p. 380.
4. Laṅkāvatārasūtra ... 461 : *vijñānaṁ cittaviṣayaṁ vijñānaiḥ saha chindati*.
5. Abhidharmakośa I 17 ed.
6. For this reason Śāntarakṣita thinks it discreet to slur over it, while Kamalaśīla declares it to be a well-known piece of the Buddhist doctrine.

See Satkari Mookerjee, The Buddhist Philosophy of Universal Flux, pp. 311 sq.

It is a fact that at any moment a man's total state of mind may be, and generally is, differentiated both qualitatively and objectively. At the same time a certain series of successive total mental states are said to belong to a single mind. And as is conclusively proved by language, the unity of a set of sensa which are apprehended by a person is the unity of centre.[1] This centre is, as the discussion about the *manas* as the meeting-place has indicated, the *manas*. It is the nature of this *manas* that has found various interpretations in Buddhist philosophy. According to the Yogācāras it is an existent, though not in the sense of a Pure Ego but in the sense of an event which is of the same nature as the events which it unifies. The authors of the Pāli Abhidhamma take more or less a purely physiological view, for them the centre is the heart. But here also two interpretations are found. For the author of the Visuddhimagga the heart is the physical organ, while for the author of the Aṭṭhasālinī heart means only 'inwardness',[2] so that he is more closely related to the Vaibhāṣikas for whom the centre is not an existent, but only a fact about the relation of terms in a particular way, hence its mode of being is subsistence and not existence.

Concomitant Function—Events in An Attitude I

While in life a healthy attitude is of utmost importance, it has to be borne in mind that an attitude is not a single entity that can be dealt with as such, but a definite organization of many factors, which by reason of the Buddhist conception of momentariness I shall term function-events. This is borne out by one of the earliest Abhidharma works, the Dhammasaṅgani. Yaśomitra, too, states concisely : "An attitude does not arise without psychic function-events, nor do these psychic function-events operate without an attitude. However, not every attitude comes into existence with all psychic function-events, nor do all psychic function-events necessarily come into existence with every attitude".[3] Vasubandhu and Sthira-

1. C. D. Broad, The Mind and Its Place in Nature, p. 212.
2. Aṭṭhasālinī III 274. But Visuddhimagga VIII 111. See also the discussion of the various views by Hiuan-tsang, Vijñaptimātratāsiddhi, p. 281.
3. Yaśomitra ad Abhidh.-kośa II 23 : *na cittaṁ caittair vinā utpadyate*

mati have fully elaborated the problem: which function-events are always present, and which may not or may be present.[1] With only a minor deviation the list of these authors is identical with the one given by the author of the Aṭṭhasālinī. As always being present in an attitude the following five function-events are mentioned:

sparśa (Pāli *phassa*), *vedanā*, *saṁjñā* (Pāli *saññā*), *cetanā*, and *citta*.[2]

nāpi caittā vinā cittenety avadhāryate. na tu sarvaṁ cittaṁ sarvacaittaniyatasahotpādam, nāpi sarvacaittāḥ sarvacittaniyatasahotpādā iti. The explanation of *caitta* which I have translated by 'psychic function-events' runs in Yaśomitra's Vyākhyā and Abhidh.-kośa I 2 as follows : "*cittasyeme citte vā bhavāś caittā iti*" state of or in mind.

1. Triṁśikā, verses 3 and 10, and commentary.

2. With the exception of the rather ambiguous term *citta*, which, for this reason, seems to have been replaced by the more exact term *manaskāra*, the four other function-events are acknowledged as belonging to an attitude in all schools of Buddhist thought. Thus Vasubandhu says in his Triṁśikā 3 cd:

sadā sparśamanaskāravitsaṁjñācetanānvitam

Always accompanied by *sparśa*, attention, feeling, sensation, and motivation. In his Pañcaskandhaka he calls these five function-events *sarvaga* 'ever-accompanying'.

The Vaibhāṣikas admit of ten function-events as belonging to every attitude, *mahābhūmika*, a view which is not shared by Vasubandhu, Śthiramati, and probably also not by the author of the Aṭṭhasālinī who, though there is a strong evidence that he inclines to the views of the Sautrāntikas-Yogācāras, does not make such subtle distinctions with respect to the psychic function-events as does Vasubandhu. Abhidharmakośa II 24 representing the view of the Vaibhāṣikas, runs as follows:

vedanā cetanā saṁjñā chandaḥ sparśo matiḥ smṛtih
manaskāro, dhimokṣaś ca samādhiḥ sarvacetasi

"Feeling, motivation, sensation, desire, *sparśa*, discrimination, memory, attention, intention, and concentration are found in every attitudinal operation."

The order of these function-events is not fixed. In the Dhātukāya the order is :

vedanā, saṁjñā, cetanā, sparśa, manaskāra, chandaḥ, adhimukti, smṛti, samādhi, and prajñā.

prajñā corresponds, according to Yaśomitra, with *mati* in the kārikā of the Abhidharmakośa, and both *mati* and *prajñā* as 'discernment' 'discrimination' are related to *citta* in its aspect of 'discrimination' in Aṭṭhasālinī.

That there is no fixed order is also asserted in Aṭṭhasālinī III 178. It is interesting to note that *chandaḥ, adhimokṣa, manaskāra* are mentioned in Aṭṭhasālinī III 252, 253, 254 as belonging to those called *yevāpanaka* "whatever

A. The first of these terms, *sparśa*, cannot be translated without giving rise to misunderstanding[1] and it can only be circumscribed as the totality of a given situation (*Gesamtsituation*) or the being in tune of various events and circumstances out of which there results and is maintained a certain relationship; this relationship, however, lasting only as long as the circumstances which have brought about the respective situation, are the same. This means that what we call a given situation is not just a disconnected set of isolated items, but all these together in a harmonious pattern or structure. The author of the Aṭṭhasālinī explains this general character of *sparśa* by the simile of the main pillar and the adjoining rafters of a palace structure, each one having its recognized differences and yet forming a harmoniously connected whole. His words are : "This *phassa* is like a pillar in a palace being the firm support to the rest of the structure; and just as beams, cross-beams, wing-supports, roof-rafters, cross-rafters, and neck-pieces are fastened to the pillar, are fixed on the pillar, so also is *phassa* a firm support to the simultaneous and associated events. It is like the pillar, the rest of the psychic events are like the other materials forming the structure.[2]

Although this description seems to advocate a static conception of *sparśa*, since we are apt to overlook the state of mutual tension between the various parts of the structure, it would be erroneous to assume that *sparśa* or the totality of a given situation is a static entity. It is actually an action which seizes and limits the object just as much as it is seized and limited by the object. Thus, its further definition runs as follows:

events there may be". Their definite presence in a healthy attitude is apparently taken over from the Vaibhāṣikas. The term *yevāpanaka* does not convey definite presence.

Anuruddha in his Abhidhammatthasaṅgaha II 2-3 declares that *manasikāra* is present in every attitude, but that *adhimokṣa* and *chandaḥ* are restricted to certain attitudes, among others a healthy attitude. This distinction introduces a new classification of the *mahābhūmikas* of the Vaibhāṣika, but does not have special merits.

1. *sparśa* is usually translated by 'contact'. However, in psychology 'contact' is a feeling of actual accord in spite of recognised differences between the representatives of the different psychological types. *sparśa* does not have this sense and therefore the translation by 'contact' had better be avoided.

2. Aṭṭhasālinī III 177.

"*sparśa* is called so, because it 'touches' (i.e., relates). Its nature is 'touching', its accomplishment is close contact; its actuality is the tuning-in (of the three events concerned in its formation); and the basis on which it rests is the object that has come into the focus of consciousness".[1] Our author is quite aware of the fact that this description is not at all adequate. The fact is that the very moment the character of thingness disappears, as is the case with such an abstraction as 'totality of a situation', with it goes the quality of representation. At this point the conflict about the 'nature' of *sparśa* (or whatever other abstraction there may be) appears : whether it is purely conceptual and abstract, a piece of our mental calculus, so to say, or whether it is something real and tangible. The reality of the purely conceptual which always creeps into our process of abstraction because of the perseverance of perception and because of the limitation of de-sensualization, is brought out in the statement that "though it is non-sensuous it functions with respect to an object in the manner of touching'.[2] Elsewhere the dynamic aspect of *sparśa* is described as "touching, establishing a close contact, and the resultant of the process of establishing a close contact".[3] This latter aspect is again pointed out by the statement that *sparśa* is not merely the coming together of the three factors: sense organ, sense object and sense perception, but that which results out of this coming together, in addition to the coming together.[4] The manner by

1. Aṭṭhasālinī III 179.

2. Aṭṭhasālinī III 179. This fact that it is 'like touching' is explicitly pointed out by Yaśomitra in his Vyākhyā ad Abhidh.-kośa II 24 : *spṛṣṭir iva spṛṣṭiḥ. yadyogād indriyaviṣayavijñānāny anyonyaṁ spṛśantīva sa sparśaḥ*—"*spṛṣṭi* because it is like touch. Because of it, it is as if the sense organ, the sense object, and the perception touch each other. Therefore one speaks of *sparśa*."

3. Aṭṭhasālinī III 266. It is here further stated that every factor in our mental and spiritual life is to be understood in this way, viz., general description (*vyañjana*), its intensity as pointed out by the addition of a preposition (*upasagga*), and its meaning (*attha*), being the product of some elementary factors. However, though it may appear as something derived and something secondary, it has an autonomous existence as a given possibility of thought-connections. As such it is a determining psychological factor.

4. Thus also Yaśomitra in his Vyākhyā ad Abhidh.-kośa II 24 states: "*sparśa* is the situation born out of the coming together of sense organ, sense object, and sensory perceptiod"—*sparśa indriyaviṣayavijñānasannipātajā spṛṣṭir iti. indriyaviṣayavijñānānāṁ sannipātāj jātā spṛṣṭiḥ.*

which the author of the Aṭṭhasālinī explains this characteristic of *sparśa* is highly suggestive and remarkable. He says that "Since it is known through its own cause which is the coming together of three factors, its actuality is the tuning-in of these three factors. This is pointed out at several places by the Sūtra phrase, '*sparśa* is the coming together of three'; the meaning of this Sūtra phrase is that it is *sparśa* because of the coming together (and subsequent tuning-in) of the three, but not that it is the mere coming together".[1] That *sparśa* is both cause and effect is also the view of the Yogācāras, and Sthiramati states that "The sense organ, the sense object, and the sense perception form a trinity. The state of this trinity as being both cause and effect is the coming together and tuning-in of the three factors of this trinity".[2]

There is a marked contrast between the solidness as it were, of sense perception and the subtleness of non-sensuous perception, for while with respect to sense perception there is both 'touching and close contact', in non-sensuous perception there is merely 'touching'.[3] Sense perception is so strong and solid and concrete in hue and texture that it is compared with two fighting rams or two hands being clapped together, the one ram or the one hand representing the sense organ, for instance, the eye, and the other ram or the other hand, the sense object, the colours and so on. It is in this connection that the author of the Aṭṭhasālinī makes some important remarks which clearly show the line of thought he follows and which are also most relevant for assigning to the Pāli Abhidhamma a definite place in the history and development of Buddhist thought, thus liberating it from the barren isolation into which scholars not knowing Sanskrit have exiled it. Our author says that though we are accustomed to say, 'what the eye sees', when we actually mean, it is the mind which sees,

1. Aṭṭhasālinī III 182.

2. Triṁśikā, p. 20.

3. Aṭṭhasālinī III 180 : "Close contact is established only by the five senses. With respect to perception by the five senses there is 'touching' and close contact; with respect to non-sensuous perception there is only touching' but not close contact"—*saṁghaṭṭanaraso pana pañcadvāriko hoti. pañcadvārikassa hi phusanalakkhaṇo ti pi saṁgaṭṭanaraso ti pi nāmam; manodvārikassa phusanalakkhaṇo tv eva nāmam, na saṁghaṭṭanaraso.*

by taking its stand on the eye as its basis, and utilizing it as its medium for seeing. In support of this explanation which attempts to convey the spirit of the living process instead of clinging to the dead letter of the text, he quotes the Ancients who stated that "The eye does not see, because it is not of the nature of mind, and mind does not see, because it is not of the nature of the eye. But by the close contact of the object with the 'door' (i.e., the sense organ) one sees by consciousness which takes the sensitivity of the sense organ as its basis." Such an explanation is, moreover, supported by such phrases as, 'one pierces with a bow' (though actually it is the arrow shot from the bow that pierces its target). Therefore the meaning of the phrase 'seeing colours by the eye' is 'seeing colours with visual consciousness'.[1] This instrumental theory of perception is precisely the view of the Yogācāras, as Yaśomitra informs us in his Abhidharmakośavyākhyā, commenting on a long controversy between the Yogācāra philosopher upholding the view that mind sees by means of the eye, and the Vaibhāṣika who clings to the theory that it is the eye that sees and not mind.[2] Moreover, the Yogācāras also acknowledged the sensitivity (*pasāda*) of the sense organs through which mind does the actual seeing, hearing etc. That it is not the physical eye that sees, but that seeing is due to the sensitivity of the eye is pointed out in a verse which is ascribed to Śāriputra and has often been repeated in the Abhidharma literature. This verse runs as follows:—

> The sensitivity of the eye by which one sees forms /
> Is small, fine, and like the head of a louse.[3]

1. Aṭṭhasālinī V 131. See also III 181.

2. Abhidharmakośa-vyākhyā ad Abhidh.-kośa I 42:
cakṣuḥ paśyati rūpāṇi sabhāgaṁ na tadāśritam
vijñānaṁ dṛśyate rūpaṁ na kilāntaritaṁ yataḥ
'The eye sees forms, when it is *sabhāga* (conform), but not mind that takes its stand on it. For an object is not seen when it is hidden. Such is the opinion of the Vaibhāṣikas.'

The Vaibhāṣika means that since mind is immaterial and can go everywhere there is no reason why it should not see what is hidden. He only overlooks the condition by which visual perception arises.

3. Aṭṭhasālinī IV 28; Paramatthavinicchaya 664: Nāmarūpapariccheda:
yena cakkhupasādena rūpāni-m-anupassati
parittaṁ sukhumam etam ūkāsirasamūpamam

But the most decisive fact is that the definition of 'sensitivity' given by the Author of the Aṭṭhasālinī tallies exactly with the one given by Asaṅga, who is the most prominent representative of the Yogācāra school of Buddhist thought. 'Sensitivity' is explained as the 'organised four elements'.[1] This proves beyond a shadow of doubt that the acknowledged interpreter and commentator of the Pali Abhidhamma texts is in line with the Yogācāra way of thought. The claim of the Pali school that they have preserved the 'original' Buddhism, on the evidence of the material available is unfounded and is nothing but sectarianism.

Insofar as the *sparśa* is a unique harmony of cause and effect it also provides the possibility for the functioning of other psychic function-events. One of the most important function-events is *vedanā*, feeling. Thus, *sparśa* is said "To produce feeling, to give rise to it",[2] though not in the sense of mechanistic cause and effect relation but insofar as within the totality of a certain situation as pointed out by *sparśa* the whole mental-spiritual potential is able to work. As a simile the following is adduced. "Just as heat in heated lac which has become manifest on account of the outer heat, produces softness in its material (i.e., the lac), but not in its condition, the outer burning coals, so also because there are such outer conditions as basis and object, *sparśa* produces feeling in the conscious attitude as its material, but not in the basis or in the object which are its condition".[3]

1. Aṭṭhasālinī IV 28; 29 : *catuṇṇam mahābhūtānam upādāya pasādo.*

Abhidharmasamuccaya, p. 3 : *catvāri mahābhūtāny upādāya cakṣur-vijñānāśrayo rūpaprasādaḥ.* "The organized four elements which form the basis for sensory consciousness are sensitivity.

2. Aṭṭhasālinī III 183.

3. Aṭṭhasālinī III 183. In the Abhidharmasamuccaya, p. 6 sparśa is said "to act as a basis for feeling"—*vedanāsanniśrayadānakarmaka*. The same term occurs in Sthiramati's commentary on Vasubandhu's Triṁśikā, p. 20. In the Madhyamakavṛtti, p. 118, feeling is said to be sparśasahaja 'co-existent with sparśa, denoting simultaneity (*sahotpannatva*) and the relation of cause and effect (*janyajanakabhāva*). The relation of 'feeling' to sparśa is expressed in this way that 'feeling' has its root in *sparśa* as its condition On p. 534 we read:

"Just as one speaks of feeling with respect to *sparśa* whose characteristic is the coming together and tuning-in of the three factors, object, consciousness,

B. Feeling (*vedanā*) is a basic psychological function which imparts to every conscious content, of whatever kind it may be, a definite value in the sense of acceptance ("like") or rejection ("dislike") or indifference, for even indifference is a certain valuation.[1] It enjoys the content either as a whole or only in its more desirable portion.[2] Thus, feeling is a kind of judging, although it does not establish an intellectual connection, but merely sets up a subjective criterion of acceptance, rejection, or indifference. Of course, the nature of feeling itself cannot be defined, because every definition has to be given in terms which belong to the realm of the intellect and the intellect is quite incommensurable with feeling. Moreover, no basic psychological function can be expressed by another. This autonomous character of feeling is, therefore, indicated by the simile of a king who by virtue of his lordship, expertness, and mastery, tastes and enjoys that which others have prepared, in a way nobody else can account for, since everybody else is only partly concerned with what is the issue.[3] This supremacy of feeling clearly shows that in our life the emotional value which we attach to any content is more important and decisive than the merely cognitive meaning, for how else could it be possible that the so-called civilized nations for such abstractions as God, mother-

and sense organ, so also feeling is to be spoken of as being conditioned and having its root in *sparśa* whose characteristic is the coming together of three factors, viz., sense organ, object, and sensory consciousness".

1. That "feeling' is an imparting of value is also brought out by the terminology itself, inasmuch as the past participle passive has been used, denoting the resultant out of the process itself. Aṭṭhasālinī III 184: *vedayita-lakkhaṇa*.

2. Aṭṭhasālinī III 184. This latter aspect has been explained in III 186 as : "In the second meaning it is here understood that feeling just enjoys the desired portion of an object and therefore its function has been called 'enjoying the desirable part".

The Abhidharmasamuccaya, p. 2 defines feeling simply by "enjoying" (*anubhava*) and adds that by it one tastes to the end the results of one's pure and impure actions.

The Madhyamakavṛtti gives both views,. i.e., total enjoyment and partial enjoyment, as is evident from p. 534: *iṣṭāniṣṭobhayaviparītaviṣayānubhūtir viṣayānubhavo vedanaṁ vittir vedanety ucyate*.

3. Aṭṭhasālinī III 186. In III 185 we are told that "*phassa* is only touching, *saññā* is only sensing, *cetanā* is only motivating, *viññāṇa* is only discriminating, but *vedanā* because of its lordship, expertness, and mastery relishes the taste of the object".

land, etc., unhesitatingly waged war against each other and thought it very meritorious to commit wholesale murder.

However, feeling can also appear quite apart from the momentary content in consciousness in the form of a 'mood', which has been referred to in the statement that "as regards its presence in the pure form of 'mental-spiritual relishing' (*cetasika-assādato*) it has been said that its actuality is 'mood' (*cetasika-assāda*).[1] Mood, too, signifies a valuation, though not of a definite content but of the whole conscious situation at the moment. The fact that feeling in the form of 'mood' may appear quite independently of the momentary sensations, although by some exiguous reasoning it may be causally related to some previous conscious content, is brought out in the Buddhist texts by terming this kind of feeling *cetasikā vedanā* which may be translated as 'abstract feeling', inasmuch as it is raised above the different individual feeling values of concrete feeling. It is clearly distinguished from *kāyika vedanā* or 'concrete feeling' which denotes that kind of feeling which is mixed up with and joins in with sensation; being only concerned with transmitting to the perceiving subject the data of the senses, such as colours, sounds, fragrances, and flavours, but not giving them an emotional meaning and arranging them according to their feeling value. The independence of mood from the momentary contents of consciousness and from the momentary sensations, is furthermore stressed by the statement that it functions or operates in a situation, or out of the conjunction (*samphassaja*) with that function of the psyche which orders, regulates, and gives meaning (*manoviññāṇadhātu*) to the contents of consciousness which due to the decisive function of an attitude have been selected in such a way as to be acceptable to the group-patterning function-events of the attitude and may be interpreted and evaluated accordingly (*tajja*).[2] In other words, an attitude

1. Aṭṭhasālinī III 187.

2. Dhammasaṅgaṇi 6. In his Aṭṭhasālinī the author gives the following explanation; "Created by such objects as colours which serve as a condition for the respective pleasurable feeling" (*iehi va rūpādīhi ārammaṇehi imassa ca sukhassa paccayehi jātā ti pi tajja*). samphassaja—born out of a certain situation or born within a certain situation (*samphassato jātam, samphasse vā jātaṁ samphassajam*). *cetasika* he defines by *cittanissitattā* "because of its

which is characterized by the feeling of serenity of mind will naturally take a bright view of life and interpret and value whatever comes up in a joyful way and in this manner the individual is able to pass over the darker sides of life.

C. Though closely connected with, yet distinctly different from, feeling is the basic psychological function of sensation (*saṁjñā*, Pali *saññā*) transmitting to consciousness the perceived image of an object as a whole or picking out the most salient sensuous attribute of the object, such as for instance, the blue colour of a deep lake, the loud peal of thunder, or the sweet smell of a flower. And it is through learning and knowledge (*abhiññā*) that it also operates effectively in the process of recognizing.[1]

Just as in the case of feeling, so as regards sensation, a distinction must be made between concrete or sensuous sensation and abstract sensation. The former is always mixed up with presentations, feelings, thoughts, etc. It means that in concrete sensation we have not only the perception of a flower itself, but also the perception of its stem, its leaves, its fragrance, its domicile, etc.; we also attach a certain value in the sense of like or dislike to it, and we may even harbour some ideas about its species and usefulness. This kind of sensation has been defined as "having the nature of general inclusion"[2]. In abstract sensation, however, a certain salient feature is singled out and made the sole content or, at least, the principal content of consciousness. This way of sensing is aptly illustrated by the well-known simile of the blind men 'seeing' an elephant. Each blind man touched a certain part of the elephant's body and formed his conclusions about the appearance of the elephant after it, so that he who had touched his leg said that an elephant was like a pillar, while he who had touched the tail declared that the animal was like a broom-handle. This kind of sensation is

being grounded in an attitude", and he adds that by this term the *kāyika-sukha* or that kind of pleasurable feeling which chimes in with sensation is excluded and that the pleasurable aspect of the mood excludes the sad or depressed aspect (*idāni cetasikaṁ sukhaṁ ti ādisu cetasikapadena kāyikasukham paṭikkhipati, sukhapadena cetasikaṁ dukkham*). The same distinction between *cetasika* 'abstract' and *kāyika* 'concrete' is found in Abhidharmasamuccaya, p. 4, and in Abhidharmakośa I 14; II 7; 8; 24.

1. Aṭṭhasālinī III 188; *yā pan'ettha abhiññāṇena saṁjānāti sā paccābhiññā-parasā nāma hotī ti*. In this way the Indian term is wider than our "sensation".

2. Aṭṭhasālinī III 189: *sabbasaṁgāhikavasena hi sañjānanalakkhaṇā saññā.*

termed "intentness on the image singled out"[1]. It is furthermore said that sensation is like a flash of lightning, inasmuch as it does not penetrate into the object (and like feeling relish it exhaustively) and that it starts from whatever object there may be, regardless of what the associations later may be which are formed by the individual. As an example a young deer seeing a scarecrow and forming the idea of a man, is given.[2] Sensation, which in accordance with its whole nature is concerned with the object and the object stimulus, undergoes considerable changes in obedience to the attitude of the individual. If the individual's attitude is directed toward and expecting the actual and concrete, sensation will automatically seize only the momentary and manifest existence of things and will always be on the look-out for the new which at once is made to serve as a guide to fresh sensations.[3] As soon as this has been accomplished everything essential has been said and done. However, since there is always a subject which senses, it is impossible to have merely objective sensation. The subject will always, and because of its presence, must contribute its subjective disposition to the sensation which thus becomes totally different from the so-called objective sensation as soon as the subjective factor in the process of sensation becomes predominant. Subjective I understand in a very wide sense

1. Aṭṭhasālinī III 189: *yathāgahitanimittavasena abhinivesakaraṇapaccupaṭṭhānā*. Similarly we read in Abhidharmakośa I 14: *saṁjñā nimittodgrahaṇātmikā*. According to Yaśomitra the meaning of *nimitta* is the specific condition of the object as for instance its blueness and *udgrahaṇa* means limitation, accurate boundary—*nimittaṁ vastuno 'vasthāviśeṣanīlatvādi, tasyodgrahaṇaṁ paricchedaḥ*. The same definition of *saṁjñā* as *nimittodgrahaṇa* is also found in Madhyamakavṛtti, p. 343.

The Abhidharmasamuccaya, p. 2 gives as a definition "having the nature of taking up (or, singling out) the image of the various dharmas, by which one expresses (i. e. represents) things seen, heard, thought, and discerned"—*saṁjñā nānādharmapratibimbodgrahaṇa (svabhāvā) yayā dṛṣṭaśrutamatavijñātān arthān vyavaharati*. The Tibetan translation combines both concrete and abstract sensation.

2. Aṭṭhasālinī III 189.

3. This succession of sensations and their being concerned with the surface only may also be gleaned from the above-mentioned character of "as not penetrating into the object" *ārammaṇe anogālhavuttitāya*. Aṭṭhasālinī III 189.

and not as 'merely' subjective. In this case sensation says more than the image of the object and it develops into the depth of the meaningful. It perceives not only the surface but also the background. That sensation obtains a definite shade in accordance with the general attitude of the individual and its connection with the subjective factor, has been clearly stated in various works.[1]

D. The functioning of an attitude, or generally speaking, of a mental set together with all the other psychic functions involved, be they basic functions or subsidiary functions, would not be possible if there were not something which arouses and sustains psychic activity. Our mind or whatever else we may call our non-physical side, is not merely reactive, an inert mental substance to be acted upon by material substances in order to be roused out of its lethargy and to project by some mysterious faculties a world of things and beings, but is something creative and autonomous in its own right which moulds the world after its own fashion. That which arouses and sustains activity on the part of the human psyche is called *cetanā*. Broadly speaking, it is a stimulus, and in a sense, may be considered as a motive and also as a drive. A drive is a stimulus that arouses persistent mass activity, and a motive is a stimulus that sustains activity until the stimulus is removed, as by eating in the case of hunger, or until the organism has moved out of range of the stimulus, as in the case of a pin-prick. Since *cetanā* and Karman are synonymous, as we shall see later on, this idea of motive and drive applied to Karman would mean that the individual is bound and fettered to Saṁsāra until he has reached Nirvāṇa and thereby moved out of the effective range of Karman, hence the equation of attainment of Nirvāṇa and cessation of all Karman. Practically speaking—and the Buddhists want their teaching to be understood as having practical importance—the attainment of Nirvāṇa is a spiritual adjustment. In this respect *cetanā* or Karman as a persistent stimulus requiring an adjusting response is a very basic motive.

1. Dhammasaṅgani 4. Especially Aṭṭhasālinī III 189: "But when it is associated with knowledge sensation follows knowledge (i.e., when the attitude is directed toward knowledge, sensation in obedience to the attitude will act in a way prescribed by this attitude)"—*yā pan' ettha ñāṇasampayuttā hoti sā saññā ñāṇam eva anuvattati.*

This character of *cetanā* as stimulus, motive or drive can be clearly seen from the definition given in the Aṭṭhasālinī[1] where we read that:—

"*cetanā* motivates. The meaning is that it aims at associated factors as objects to itself. It has the nature of a stimulus, the meaning of which is that it has the nature of motivation. Its function is [arranging and effecting]....Its function of arranging and effecting comes to pass in healthy or unhealthy effects.[2] In its arranging and effecting process which produces healthy or unhealthy actions the other factors of the psyche play only a restricted part. The *cetanā* alone is [exceedingly full of effort, exceedingly full of vigor,] that is, it makes a double effort, a double exertion".

The meaning of stimulus, motive or drive becomes still more obvious when we take into consideration the similes that have been used in order to point out the effective nature of *cetanā*. According to the Ancients, that is, the authors of the old Aṭṭhakathā which has been lost, it is said that "This *cetanā* has the nature of landowner, a cultivator, who having taken fiftyfive strong men, went down to the fields in order to reap. He is exceedingly energetic, exceedingly strenuous, he doubles his efforts, doubles his exertions and with the words, 'Take your sickles' and the like, he points out the portion to be harvested. He knows what they need of drink, food, scents, wreaths, and the like, and he takes an equal part in the work. In this way the simile is to be understood: the *cetanā* is like the landowner; the fifty-five factors whose functioning results in healthy

1. Aṭṭhasālinī III 190.

2. A third factor has been left out here, called *āneñja*, denoting that quality which is neither healthy nor unhealthy but beyond these two. See Visuddhimagga XVII 60. Aṭṭhasālinī III 430.

It has to be noted that the arranging and effecting (*āyūhana*) is the essential quality of cetanā. All schools of Buddhism are unanimous in this respect. Sthiramati in his Vṛtti on Triṁśikā 4, p. 21 declares: "*cetanā* is effecting an attitude, it is an excitatory centre of the psyche and it is because of its presence that the mental set moves, as it were, toward the object"—*cetanā cittābhisaṁskāro manasaś ceṣṭā yasyāṁ satyām ālambanam prati cetasaḥ praspanda iva hoti*. See also Abhidharmasamuccaya, pp. 2, 5. The definition of *cetanā* in the Abhidharmakośavyākhyā, ad Abhidh.-kośa II 24 tallies with Sthiramati's *cetanā cittābhisaṁskāra iti cittapraspandaḥ. praspanda iva praspanda ity arthaḥ.*

The same explanation is also given in Madhyamakavṛtti, p. 311: *cittābhisaṁskāramanaskarmalaksaṇā cetanā ceti.*

effects and which have arisen as parts of the whole attitude (*cittaṅgavasena*) are like the fifty-five strong men; the doubling of effort, the doubling of exertion by this *cetanā* which, in arranging and effecting, produces healthy or unhealthy effects, is like the time of the doubling of efforts, of doubling exertion by the landowner. Thus should its function of arranging and effecting be understood".[1]

There is still one other simile which is extremely relevant for ascertaining the actual meaning of *cetanā*. There it has been said that:

"Its actuality is directing properly, that is, it arises, directing (the associated psychic factors to work in a certain direction as indicated by the general attitude) like the chief disciple or a head carpenter and the like, who accomplish their own and other's duties. As the chief disciple, seeing the teacher coming from afar, himself recites his lesson and makes the other pupils recite each his own lesson—when he begins to recite the rest follows—, or as the head carpenter, himself cutting the wood, makes the other carpenters cut each his own portion of the wood—when he begins to work the rest follow—, or as a general, himself fighting, makes the other soldiers take part in the battle—when he begins to fight the others also fight without turning their back—, so this *cetanā* starting its own work on its object makes the associated factors do each its own work—when it begins to operate the associated factors also operate. Hence it has been said 'like the chief disciple, the head carpenter and so on, who accomplish their own and other's duties".[2]

In all those instances we see that *cetanā* not only arouses mass activity but also sustains it so that certain definite results appear. This shows beyond doubt that the translation of *cetanā* by 'volition is against all evidence and has probably been adopted only on account of the fact that the translators of the Abhidharma texts did not understand these texts, and also did not know the meaning of the English word volition.[3] In

1. Aṭṭhasālinī III 191.
2. Aṭṭhasālinī III 192.
3. As Gilbert Ryle, The Concept of Mind, p. 62 sq. points out, volition is a term covering a welter of confusion and should be dropped as quickly as possible. Louis de la Vallée Poussin in his translation of the Abhidharmakośa IV 2 has been the only scholar in Indian philosophy who was not quite satisfied with this translation.

its most sharply distinguished sense volition designates merely the act of making a choice or decision, but it rarely suggests the determination to put one's decision or choice into effect. Volition is thus the very reverse of *cetanā* which everywhere is said to put something into effect. There is still one other point in the nature of *cetanā* which makes its translation by 'volition' absolutely absurd. This is that "it is evident in working in such cases as recollecting an urgent business and the like, because it stimulates the associated factors to be effective".[1] Volition, however, can never aid in recollecting what has been forgotten, otherwise we would not need to rack our brains about something we have forgotten, neither would a situation ever arise, which despite our best intentions we simply cannot recollect a thing. *Cetanā*, to state it plainly, is something that corresponds to our idea of stimulus, motive, or drive. Especially this latter concept of drive, as a stimulus arousing persistent mass activity assists in explaining the origin of activity as well as that which is excitated and is forthwith active. That which is aroused to activity is the sum total of all potentialities,[2] it is the *ālayavijñāna* in the terminology of the Yogācāras or Vijñānavādins; the 'subtle *manovijñāna*' or *bhāvāṅga* in the terminology of the Sthaviravādins and symbolized by 'fifty-five strong men'. It has been unfortunate that a number should have been taken as absolute, as it initially must have been only meant as some indeterminate number, and although the various schools adopted various numbers, by insisting on their absolute number of factors they set themselves an artificial barrier which hampered further progress.

There is an intimate connection between *cetanā* and feeling (*vedanā*) and that which I have called the momentary total situation (*sparśa*). This intimate connection accounts for the fact that some stimuli act more as motive than others. It will be useful in this respect to make use of the term tension. Tension means primarily that something is tense. Just as in the motive of hunger the stimuli which arouse activity are the sen-

1. Aṭṭhasālinī III 192. Cf. Visuddhimagga XIV 137.

2. In the terminology of the Yogācāras it is the *ālayavijñāna*, which is "called endowed with all potentialities (*bīja*), because it is endowed with the power to produce all phenomena", Triṁśikāvijñapti, p. 36. See also Vijñaptimātratā-siddhi, p. 434.

sory reports of the stomach contractions constituting a persistent tense state of certain visceral muscles, so also, by way of simile, we might say that there is in the psyche a tense part, acting as stimulus. But to continue the physiological aspect, the inner physiological state which is a stimulus arousing activity, is apparent in all appetitive motives, of which hunger is typical. To this kind of stimulus the term appetitive tension may be applied. It is, furthermore, a well-known fact that a loud noise arouses activity in an infant and, what is most remarkable, this activity will be sustained for some time after the physical stimulus has ceased. The explanation of the difference between the knee-jerk reflex, in which activity is aroused but not sustained, and the persistence of response to a loud noise lies in the concept of emotion. Emotion is primarily a psychic state of feeling (*vedanā*), attributing a specific value to an existing content, and then also a physiological state of innervation; both these states together have a cumulative effect upon each other, that is, to an intense feeling there attaches a sensation of muscles or organs being innervated to contract, so that even an indifferent sensation has a specific emotional tone, viz., the tone of indifference, which itself is a valuation. Beside a state of feeling, therefore, a loud noise sets up an inner physiological and neutral state and, for this reason, the emotional tension persists after the noise stimulus has ceased, and is itself a stimulus to activity. Stimuli which arouse emotional tensions are, therefore, broad and persistent in their after-effects and consequently are motives. This concept to emotional tension, which later on will arouse specific associative selections, assists greatly in explaining the effect of *cetanā* or Karman, because *cetanā* 'projects', i.e., arouses the *vedanabījas* or potentialities to emotional manifestations and reactions. For where there is *cetanā* there also is *vedanā*, both of them lying in the power field as which the psyche may tentatively be conceived. *Vedanā*, of course, is at first characterized as 'indifference' (*upekṣā*), 'neutral' (*avyākṛta*), since unconscious processes, as we would say, are involved, while the specific value of acceptance (emotion of pleasure) or of rejection (emotion of displeasure) appears only in conscious experience, when an actual object arousing the specific emotion is encountered and judged. Since, however, tensions by their nature arouse only general activity they are spoken of as drives, a drive being a stimulus which arouses persistent mass activity. This concept fits well into the definition of *cetanā* which may be given graphically as

stimulus→drive→activity
(as emotional tension).

Activity in the psyche takes its origin, as we gather from various sources, with reference to some situation,[1] which means that there is always one part, so to say, of the psychic organization which is more easily aroused into functioning and toward which excitations are drawn. In this way *cetanā* may even be considered as a pattern or a gradient leading up to dominance. This concept of an excitation gradient belongs, properly speaking, to physiology where it refers to the fact that in the nervous system there is always one part which is more easily aroused into function than are other parts. For instance, in the main axis, the head tail or cephalocaudal axis which is seen in the adult as the brain and the spinal cord, there is, initially, some portion which is physiologically more active than some other part. This more active portion consumes oxygen at a greater rate than other parts, is of higher electrical potential and is more susceptible to certain stimuli. Between this more active point and other points there exists a difference in rate of development, this difference being called the 'physiological gradient'. By way of hypothesis we might say that the *manas* out of which the conscious experience develops, since the 'subjective factor' precedes the objective re-presentation, has a higher potential than the other factors.

E. As the last function-event which is concomitant with every-attitude, in the Pali texts *citta* is mentioned. The author of the Aṭṭhasālinī considers this to be a mere tautology. In his opinion the term *citta* in the opening sentence of the Dham-

1. Though the number of *cetanās* varies according to context, there are essentially six situations in which *cetanā* is most active. These are vision, audition, smelling, tasting, touching, and 'minding'. As such the six *cetanās* form the *saṁskāraskandha*. See Saṁyuttanikāya III 60 : Abhidharmakośa-vyākhyā ad Abhidh.-kośa I 15. Abhidharmasamuccaya, p. 5 adds that by its operation in such situations healthiness of attitude, aflectivity, or the termination of a certain state is brought about.

Of decisive importance is *manaḥsaṁcetanā*, because it 'projects' a new existence, because it is by nature Karman (activity). Abhidharmakośa-vyākhyā, p. 319.

masaṅgani, viz., "when a healthy attitude (*citta*), belonging to the realm of sensuous relatedness, has arisen", first of all specifies a certain time, and it is only natural that at this time there is also a certain attitude.[1] However, he makes an interesting remark about the nature of *citta*, which shows that he favours a Central Theory of Mind as is done by the Yogācāras, as we have seen above.[2] He says that "Such things as the sun and so on are only linguistic conveniences for grouping such occurrences as colors and so on, but there is no thing apart from and above its various states; so when the sun rises there is its heat. And although one speaks of the sun, it is nothing different from its occurrences. But with *citta* it is different. We speak of the states of mind such as a total situation (*phassa*) and so on but *citta* itself is different from these states".[3] Thus, as far as the material world is concerned the author of the Aṭṭhasālinī is a thoroughgoing nominalist, the "thing", in a word, is a metaphysical mistake, due to transference to the world-structure of a linguistic convenience. But as far as the mental world is concerned he is on the side of the realists who assume that a mind is different from its states. Unfortunately he does not say anything about the logical nature of this centre, whether it is existent or subsistent.

However, the term *citta* has so many meanings according to the Dhammasaṅgani[4] all of which are explained in the Aṭṭhasālinī, that the other schools of Buddhist thought who had an Abhidharma, singled out a certain function of mind and so avoided the tautology.[5] Since the various terms for what we call mind or specifically an attitude are extremely relevant for a proper understanding of complex psychic phenomena, they may be given here together with the explanation by the Aṭṭhasālinī.[6] It is called *citta*, because of the varieties of

1. Aṭṭhasālini III 197.
2. p. 12.
3. Aṭṭhasālini III 195: *yathā hi rūpādīni upādāya paññattā suriyādayo na atthato rūpādīhi aññe honti, teneva yasmiṁ samaye suriyo udeti tasmiṁ samaye tassa tejasaṅkhātaṁ rūpam paññāyati. evam vuccamāne pi na rūpādīhi añño suriyo nāma atthi. na tatha cittam; phassādayo dhamme upādeya paññāpiyati; atthato pan' etam tehi aññam eva.*
4. Dhammasaṅgani 6.
5. See above p. 13 note 2.
6. Aṭṭhasālinī III 274-276.

attitudes; *manas*, because of its measuring (i.e., taking stock of, interpreting) the sensed objects; *mānasa*, though identical with *manas*, because the functional aspect is stressed, *hadaya* ('heart'), because of inwardness; *paṇḍara* ("transparency"), because in every experience there partakes something of the indeterminate and ineffable luminous continuum, in and through, and out of which all experiences come to pass, and which in its purity and lucidity apart from the sensed and introspected differentiations, is more emotionally moving and spiritually satisfying than the sensed or introspected data, which only veil and limit the brightness and boundlessness of 'mind'. It is called *mano manaāyatana* in the sense of birth-place, inasmuch as such factors like *phassa* and the like originate in it; in the sense of a meeting-place, inasmuch as the data of the outer objects, visible, audible, olfactory, gustatory, and tangible, assemble here as objects of the *manas* (to be interpreted by it); and in the sense of cause inasmuch as it is the necessary antecedent for the co-existence of such functional patterns as *phassa* and the like. It is called *viññāṇa*, because of its discriminating nature, and *viññāṇakkhandha* with respect to the complexity of psychic processes among which the conscious attitude is a specific aspect; and finally it is termed *tajja manoviññāṇadhātu* in order to point out its readiness to act and to react in a definite way (*tajja*), to denote its character of giving meaning and order to the atomic data of the senses (*manas*) and its nature of discriminating between the manifold data of perception and introspection (*viññāṇa*), and above all to point out the fact that though general psychological laws (*sabhāva*) are operating in every individual, yet they cannot be said to have an individual nature of their own (*nissatta dhātu*), because there are too many factors which condition and influence the nature of mind.

Concomitant Function—Events in an Attitude II.

The various function-events which have been mentioned so far and which may be termed certain states of mind, are acknowledged in all schools of Buddhist thought as of primary importance, and are either called 'belonging to an extensive level' (*mahābhūmika*) or are said to be 'going everywhere (*sarvatraga*).[1] But it is from here on that the classification

1. The first term belongs to the Abhidharmakośa II 23 and Vyākbyā, the second to the Triṁśikāvijñapti, p. 25.

of function-events varies in the different schools. I shall begin with a discussion of the events mentioned in the Pāli Abhidhamma and then proceed to an analysis of the events mentioned in the Abhidharma works of the Vaibhāṣikas and Yogācāras each system having certain merits and certain defects.

In the Pāli Abhidhamma five function-events are mentioned which are found again as constituents of meditation. This is important, because in this way the practical side is again emphasized. A healthy attitude is the foundation for meditation, for only out of meditation results knowledge which leads to liberation. Knowledge is thus different from mere discursiveness.

The five function-events are : *vitarka* (Pāli *vitakka*), *vicāra*, *prīti* (Pāli *pīti*), *sukha*, and *cittāikāgratā* (Pāli *cittass' ekaggatā*).

The first of these terms can hardly be translated adequately. It is the initial stage of concentration, a process of positing, implying examination leading up to judgment and decision (*ūhana*) and it may also be regarded as a process mediating between the already present and prepared content of the particular or general attitude of the individual and the new content, inasmuch as it 'drags' (*takkana*), i.e., relates, the new content to be apperceived and to be meditated upon into the circle of interest.[1] As such *vitakka* is likened to a man who being a friend to or a relative of the king, establishes the connection between the king and the man who wants to meet the king.[2] Or, it has also been compared with the first beating on a drum or a bell, and in this way, is if we are allowed to use a new simile in ancient terms, a kind of diagnosis through auscultation (*āhanana-pariyāhananarasa*) by which subject and object approach

1. Aṭṭhasālinī III 198 : *vitakketī ti vitakko; vitakkanaṁ vā vitakko, ūhanaṁ ti vuttaṁ hoti. svāram ārammaṇe cittassa abhiniropaṇalakkhaṇo. so hi ārammaṇe cittaṁ āropeti.* See also Aṭṭhasālinī III 278 for the active aspect of *vitakka*. On *ūha* see Abhidharmakośa (Transl). I, p. 175 and 2.

2. Aṭṭhasālinī III 198; "Just like someone relying on a relative or a friend dear to the king ascends the royal palace, so *citta* relying on *vitakka* ascends the object. Therefore *vitakka* is said to have the nature of lifting *citta* on the object".

each other and become acquainted with each other.[1] It is by properly performing its function that *vitakka* develops into the second member of the Buddhist Eightfold Path: *sammāsaṁkappa* (Skt. *samyaksaṁkalpa*) which by acting in its true nature and proper way and by virtue of it leading man out of the confused mass of indeterminate ideas, makes man gain correct ideas—"to hit the mark", as it were.[2]

Insofar as *vitakka* precedes every act of the more subtle discursive reasoning, it is something robust (*oḷārika*), like the beating of the bell; ensuing subtler activity is called *vicāra* and denotes the steadily moving reflection, the quiet and serious consideration and study of that which has been brought into the circle of interest by the gross *vitakka*. It is by this activity that all details are taken in and that all the co-existent events and processes of the psyche are activated and involved.[3] Being subtle (*sukhuma*) and following every detail, *vicāra* is likened to the reverberations of the sound of a ball; and it is here by repeatedly going over and into the object that a close tie between the object and the investigating mind exists in the manner of an arrow fixed on the string of a bow.[4] It is the viewing of the object either by standing in front of it or by going over it[5]. The relation between *vitakka* and *vicāra*, which somehow are inseparable (*sante pi ca nesam katthaci aviyoge*),[6] is described by way of various similes : by a bird flapping its wings in order to ascend into the air and its subsequent calm moving of the wings while flying in the air; by a bee alighting in front of a lotus flower and its gyrating over the flower on which it has alighted. In the Aṭṭhakathā, which the author

1. Aṭṭhasālinī III 198.

2. Aṭṭhasālinī III 278: *sutthukappanavasena saṁkappo...yathāvatāya niyyānikatāya ca kusalabhāvappatto pasaṭṭho saṁkappo ti sammāsaṁkappo.*

3. Aṭṭhasālini III 199-200. The distinction between the gross *vitarka* and the *subtle vicāra* is also found in Abhidharmasamuccaya, p. 10; Abhidharmakośa II 33.

4. Aṭṭhasālinī III 279.

5. ibid.

6. In the Bhāṣya on Abhidharmakośa III 33 there is an interesting discussion as to how it is possible that grossness and subtlety are co-existent. Vasubandhu's answer is that this co-existence is one of succession but not of simultaneity and that the five members of the first meditation stage belong to the meditation sphere and not to one moment.

of the Aṭṭhasālinī had before him *vitakka* has been compared with the movement of a bird in the sky, taking the wind with both wings and keeping them steadily in a line, since it advances bent on a single definite object, while *vicāra* is the flapping of the wings in order to take the wind[1]. Or, it has been said that *vitakka* may be compared with the hand that takes a firm hold of a dirty copper bowl, while *vicāra* would correspond to the other hand which scrubs the bowl; or *vitakka* is like the hand of a potter pressing down clay, while *vicāra* is like the hand turning the clay to and fro; finally, *vitakka* is compared with the point of a drawing compass fixed in the middle of the paper and *vicāra* with the revolving point.[2] All these examples serve to illustrate the difference between *vitarka* as first taking hold of an object, and *vicāra* as its detailed investigation.

While *vitakka* and *vicāra* refer to the cognitive aspect in the process of concentration, the following two events, *prīti* and *sukha* point to the emotive aspect which is never absent in any of our mental processes, though we are apt to overlook and to underrate its importance because of the more intellectual orientation of our mental life. But it is precisely due to our having underrated the emotional factors, which in Western psychologies were not given even the status of secondary qualities, but were relegated to tertiary qualities—primary qualities being only those qualities possessed by material substances; colors, sounds, odors, and sensed space and time being secondary qualities-that the modern man has become divided against himself and everywhere meets with frustration. For the intellect tells him one thing and pushes him one way, and his emotions push him another way, all of which means that the 'enlightened' modern man is actually suffering from a very serious neurosis and that it will need hard labour on the part of the patient and of the physician to develop 'a healthy attitude'.

Abstractly speaking, *prīti* is a driving and even overwhelming emotion implying an agreeable sensation and as such is clearly distinguished from feeling by quite perceptible physical innervations. According to intensity *prīti* varies from

1. Aṭṭhasālinī III 200.
2. Aṭṭhasālinī III 201.

a slight thrill to transport. "It makes satisfied is the meaning of *prīti*; its nature is to make pleasant; its function is to make both the function patterns (*kāya*) and the mental outlook (feeling) satisfied or quivering with exultation. Its actuality is buoyant exultation. It is either a slight thrill or a momentary (electrifying) stimulation or a flooding emotion or an all-pervading ecstasy or even transport. The slight thrill is only able to raise the hairs on the body; the momentary electrifying stimulation is like flashes of lightning from moment to moment; the flooding emotion descends on the body and breaks like the waves of the ocean on the coast; transport is very powerful, it lifts the body up to the extent of launching it into the air,"[1] while by all-pervading ecstasy, as its name implies, "the whole body is fully charged and saturated like a full bladder or a mountain cave swept by a mighty flood of water".[2]

The emotive aspect of the process of concentration is rather a complex phenomenon, inasmuch as it is mixed up with other function elements, i.e., in it there is an almost inseparable blending of feeling with sensation. Thus, when *prīti-sukha* are mentioned together, as is often the case, we are entitled to translate this compound term by 'feeling-emotion', *prīti* referring to the sensation elements and *sukha* to feeling. It is this blending of feeling with sensation that has been pointed out in the analysis of *prīti*. Speaking of joyfulness (*pāmojja*) and the causing of delight and joy (*amodana*, *pamodana*) the author of the Aṭṭhasālinī informs us about the blending of the various elements in the emotive aspect of concentration in the following words: "Just as the mixing of medical herbs, or of oils or of hot and cold water is called blending (*modana*) so also this emotive aspect is a kind of blending, because it unites (harmonizes, makes one) the various elements."[3] Other manifestations of the emotive aspect which due to the healthy attitude is positively toned, is that one can laugh and laugh heartily.

The fact that the emotional value which attaches to things plays a more decisive role in our life than the merely cognitive aspect is brought out in a charming simile: "*prīti* is spoken of as

1. Aṭṭhasālinī III 202. In 203-205 several anecdotes are related as to the nature of these five kinds of *prīti*.

2. Aṭṭhasālinī III 206.

3. Aṭṭhasālinī III 280.

wealth, because of its being the condition for happiness and because of its similarity to wealth. For just as a rich man feels happy because of his riches, so also happiness arises in a man of a joyous temperament because of *prīti*; therefore it is spoken of as wealth".[1] It is because of this emotional component that we feel elated (*odagya*) and that our mind feels itself to be its own (*attamanata*):—"The mind of a man who does not feel delighted or pleased cannot be said to be its own mind; because it is the basis for the disturbing play of unpleasantness; but the mind of a man who feels delighted or pleased is its own mind, because it is the basis for pleasure".[2] There is hardly any other passage which so emphatically points out the positive character of Buddhism and this positive character is born out of direct experience. It is in direct experience that we know that that which in a judgment we term unpleasantness is something alien to us and from which we want to keep away, since it throws us out of our course and constrains us to actions whose blind one-sideness inevitably entails self-destruction, while bliss accompanies all those moments which have the character of flowing life and where it is not necessary to look around to find a way out of a hopelessly entangled situation.

There is one other point to be noted here. Within the psychic household the emotions play a most important role. Unlike the emotional outbursts which throw man out of his course, the emotions, of which joy (*prīti*) is one manifestation, not only give spiritual sustenance and warmness of feeling to the dry, abstract, cold, and excessively formal, cognitive component, they also act as restoratives to the disturbed equilibrium of the psyche, so essential for life. For they release the tension that accompanies every one-sideness. It is precisely this joy (*prīti*) that brings about the relaxation of tension that keeps the mind keyed up to the process of clear and prolonged thinking and the muscles taut and fit for work. So, at least, we are used to saying due to the fact that we have been brought up in an irreconcilable dualism of body and mind, and the temptation is great to read this dualism into the Buddhist texts, inasmuch as 'relaxation' is called *kāyapraśrabdhi* (Pāli *kāyapassabdhi*) and

1. Aṭṭhasālinī III 280.
2. Aṭṭhasālinī III 280.

cittapraśrabdhi (Pāli *cittapassaddhi*) which we cannot but wrongly translate by bodily and mental relaxation. Thus the author of the Aṭṭhasālinī tells us that "This fivefold joy becoming pregnant and bearing fruit produces the double relaxation—the *kāyapassaddhi* and the *cittapassaddhi*. This relaxation, in turn, becoming pregnant and bearing fruit produces the double kind of bliss—*kāyika* bliss and *cetasika* bliss".[1] However, the Buddhist term *kāya* and the adjective *kāyika* do not so much denote the physical body but an integrated organization and function pattern. *Kāya* comprises the function patterns of feeling, sensation, and motivation which in the ordinary human being who is torn by affects, are in a turmoil rather than in a state of being conducive to the realization of blissful peace and illuminating wisdom. The texts are quite explicit on the point that *kāya* does not mean the physical body as contrasted with some mental or spiritual substance. We are informed that "*kāya* here means the three *skandhas* beginning with feeling i.e., feeling (*vedanā*), sensation (*saññā*), motivation (*saṁskāra*). Taking the relaxation of *kāya* and the relaxation of *citta* together one speaks of relaxation of *kāya* and *citta* which have the nature of assuaging the turmoil of *kāya* and *citta*; which have the function of eradicating the turmoil of *kāya* and *citta*; and which have their basis in *kāya* and *citta* respectively. They are to be considered as a remedy against the emotive items such as agitatedness which does not admit of rest".[2]

1. Aṭṭhasālinī III 207.

2. Aṭṭhasālinī III 248. See also III 295, and Dhammasaṅgani 40, 41. Sthiramati in his commentary on Triṁśikā 11 : p. 27 is more explicit as to what is meant by *praśrabdhi* which I have tentatively translated by 'relaxation of tension'. He says : "*praśrabdhi* is the workability (also implying adaptableness) of *kāya* and *citta*, the remedy against *dauṣṭulya*. The *dauṣṭulya* is the non-workability as well as the latent potentialities of the affective items in our conscious life. When this *dauṣṭulya* disappears because of the actualization of *praśrabdhi*, then there is workability of *kāya* from which ensues its capacity of being set to work easily with respect to its proper functioning. The workability of *citta* is a special mental property in an attentive mind and its characteristic is delight and lightness, on account of which *citta* acts easily toward its objective; therefore one speaks of the workability of *citta*. The *kāyapraśrabdhi* is to be known as some perceptible bodily sensation produced by joy (i.e., a perceptible innervation), as has been said in a Sūtra:—'The *kāya* of him who experiences joy relaxes.' Since by its influence the whole

We have seen above in the explanation of the feeling function that feeling may be considered under two aspects, either as concrete feeling, feeling mixed up with other function elements such as those of sensation, or as abstract feeling which, by being raised above the differences of individual feeling-values, expresses itself in a mood or a state of feeling which has a more general and neutral character rather than an individual or personal one. Thus, while *prīti* stresses the perceptible bodily innervation and thus is approximated more to sensation, *sukha* is differentiated from it as a feeling (judgment) of pleasure which imparts itself to both the function patterns (*kāya*) and to the whole attitude of the individual (*cetasika*). Its definition runs as follows; "To make happy, is the meaning of *sukha*, that is, it makes him feel happy in whom happiness arises. Or, (etymologically speaking), *sukha* means to eat up properly or to dig out the afflictions of function patterns (*kāya*) and of an attitude (*citta*). It is a term for the feeling of serenity. Its characteristics are those of feeling (*vedanā*) as described above. However, another method of explanation is that it has the character of being agreeable, that it functions as expanding the associated processes, and that its actuality is beneficent effectiveness".[1]

foundation of our life is changed, it acts as a means eradicating all veiling obstacles in the form of emotional instability".

Though substantially the same, the Abhidharmasamuccaya is more concise: "What is *praśrabdhi*? It is the workableness of *kāya* and *citta*, because the non-workableness of *kāya* and *citta* has subsided. It eradicates all obstacles" (p. 6). Here not only the *kleśāvaraṇa*, the veil of emotional instability, is meant but also the *jñeyāvaraṇa*, the veil of our primitive beliefs about reality.

"Agitatedness" (*auddhatya*, Pali *uddhacca*) is explained in Dhammasaṅgani §§429, 1159, 1237 as agitatedness (*uddhacca*), restlessness (*avūpasama*), distractedness (*cetaso vikkhepa*), and delusiveness (*bhantattaṁ cittassa*). It is an affect because of its delusive character. See Dhammasaṅgani p. 429. Sthiramati in his above-mentioned commentary, p. 31 emphasizes restlessness: "*auddhatya* is restlessness of mind....It is the root if the restlessness of a mind which remembers former laughters, enjoyments, and funs, all of them favouring passionateness and it is an enemy of repose". Similarly Abhidharmasamuccaya, p. 9.

Yaśomitra on Abhidharmakośa II 26 emphasizes the erotic nature of agitatedness.

1. Aṭṭhasālinī III 208. The latter explanation is favored by the Vaibhāṣikas. See Abhidharmakośa II 7 and Yaśomitra's commentary on it.

In whatever sense feeling may be interpreted, either in the sense of extensiveness or in the sense of intensity, the one spreading and supporting a harmonious sociability, the other developing into the depth of a religiosity which has nothing in common with sectarian show-off and which is carefully shielded from profane eyes, it is a creative factor. Without feeling the harmonious atmosphere which is so essential for concentration (from the spiritual point of view) and for a sympathetic participation in all worldly affairs (from the practical point of view) is unthinkable. Therefore also it has been stated that "bliss becoming pregnant and bearing fruit produces the kinds of concentration—momentary concentration, approaching concentration, and accomplished concentration. Except in the latter kind of concentration the two other concentrative processes obtain here (i.e., in a healthy attitude belonging to the realm of sensuous relatedness; the accomplished concentration being possible only by means of repeated exercises and meditation)".[1]

Finally the clear distinction between the sensation component and the feeling state in the emotional aspect of mental processes must be referred to. Although both factors are intimately related to each other, each of them having a cumulative effect upon the other and thus leading up to an 'affect', yet they must be discriminated from each other. An 'affect' is marked by quite distinct bodily innervations to which is joined a reinforced feeling, while feeling itself for the most part is without these innervations or, if they are present they are so feeble that only by certain instruments can they be demonstrated. Therefore, while an affect is always accompanied by feeling, feeling must not necessarily be accompanied by sensation elements. The difference between *prīti* and *sukha* is given in the following words: "Although *prīti* (joy, marked by perceptible bodily innervations) and *sukha* (bliss, feeling-judgment) are somehow intimately connected, *prīti* denotes the (anticipatory and eager) delight one has in obtaining a desired object, while *sukha* denotes the relishing of the taste of the object obtained. Where there is *prīti* there also is *sukha*, but where there is *sukha* there is not necessarily *prīti*, *prīti* being classified under the *saṁskāraskandha* (comprising all motivating

1. Aṭṭhasālinī III 207.

and driving forces), *sukha* being classified under *vedanāskandha* (comprising the three feeling valuations of likes, dislikes, and indifference). *prīti* (makes itself perceptible) when a man exhausted by travelling through a desert sees or hears about a grove or water, *sukha* (is experienced) when this man enters the shade of the grove or relishes the water"[1].

It is out of the blending of the cognitive process as expressed by *vitarka* and *vicāra* and of the emotive process as pointed out by *prīti* and *sukha* that concentration in the proper sense of the word is possible. Concentration, thus combining the cognitive and emotive aspects of our mental processes, is called "one-objectness"[2] inasmuch as it does not allow of being distracted and torn away from its objective and also joins the other functions (involved in concentrative processes) to itself and has them operating on and toward the same object. Concentration is defined in the following way : "*cittass' ekaggatā* means that one's whole being and whole mental operation (*citta*) is directed toward one object (*ekagga*); thus it is another term for absorption through concentration (*samādhi*). About its nature we read in the Aṭṭhakathā that absorption through concentration has the nature of both leadership and non-distraction"[3]. This double nature is then explained by two similes. The one declares that "Just as the dome of a gabled house is the leader (of all the building material), because it binds all the other building materials to itself, so also absorption is the leader of all healthy processes involved, because all these healthy processes have been made to function properly by the influence of absorption".[4] and the second simile states that "Just as in a battle the king goes wherever the army is giving way, and the army wherever he goes becomes reinforced and follows the king, after the enemy's army has been crushed, so

1. Aṭṭhasālinī III 209. See also III 21n. This clear distinction has been obliterated by the Vaibhāṣikas who in Abhidharmakośa VIII 9 are said to regard *prīti* as serenity and *sukha* as relaxation: *prītir hi sa umanasyam praśrabdhiḥ sukham ādayaḥ.*

2. *agga*—Skt. *agra* means *ālambana*. See Abhidharmakośavyākhyā ad Abhidh.-kośa II 24 : *agram ālambanam ity eko 'rthaḥ. yadyogāc cittam prabandhena ekatrālambane vartate, sa samādhiḥ.*

3. Aṭṭhasālinī III 211.

4. Aṭṭhasālinī III 211.

also absorption has the nature of non-distraction (non-scattering) because it does not allow the co-existent processes to be distracted or to be scattered".[1]

This explanation of the nature and function of absorption through concentration is in accord with the conception of this state by the Vaibhāṣikas, for whom *samādhi* or *cittasyaikāgratā* was a special entity by whose efforts and efficiency all associated and co-existent processes became united towards one objective, the processes concentrated on one objective themselves not being what one has to understand by concentration.[2] This is one of the rare instances where the author of the Aṭṭhasālinī gives preference to the views of the Ābhidharmikas and not to those of the Yogācāras. However, he gives still another and more detailed definition of concentration which to judge from the whole mode of expression—inclines toward the one given by Asaṅga and Sthiramati. He says that "There is another explanation: This absorption (*samādhi*) which is called 'one-objectness' (*ekaggatā*) of the mental set (*citta*) has the nature of not dissolving and of not becoming scattered, has the function of welding the co-existent processes, as one kneads water and bath-powder into a paste, and has its actuality as becoming quiet and as knowing, as has been said (in the Sūtras, Dīghanikāya I 83, Aṅguttaranikāya V 3, etc.): 'He who is concentrated knows and sees things as they really are". In particular, concentration is based upon the feeling of bliss and the steadfastness of mind and should be understood as being like the steadiness of the flame of a lamp in the absence of wind".[3]

Concentration may be viewed from various angles.[4]

1. Aṭṭhasālinī III 211.

2. Abhidharmakośavyākhyā ad Abhidh.-kośa VIII 1 : *na cittāny eva samādhiḥ. yena tu tāny ekāgrāṇi vartante samāhitāni sa dharmaḥ samādhiḥ.*

3. Aṭṭhasālinī III 212. Asaṅga in his Abhidharmasamuccaya is very concise : "What is concentration ? One-objectness as regards the object to be scrutinized. It gives support to knowledge'.

Sthiramati, p. 26 is more detailed : "Absorption is concentratedness on one object to be scrutinized. An object is to be investigated according to its merits and defects. One-objectness means to have one object. It gives support to knowledge, because a concentrated mind sees things as they really are."

4. Dhammasaṅgaṇi § 11

Its most conspicuous feature is its steadfastness and its stabilizing effect (*ṭhiti, saṁṭhiti, avaṭṭhiti*). Unshaken and unshakable it stands on the object that has been selected. It also concentrates all the attendant functions on the very object it has taken its stand upon, and it even penetrates deeply into the subject matter. However, it is only in a healthy attitude that concentration and absorption are possible and actually come about with beneficent results, at the same time involving several other processes such as having confidence (*śraddhā*) which is the initial plunge into the matter, inspection (*smṛti*) which is the non-floating and non-drifting away from the problem at hand, absorption (*samādhi*) pointing out the firm stand on the subject selected, so that it may not slip away from the penetrating scrutiny of inspection, and finally the analytical appreciative understanding (*prajñā*), which means the thorough penetration into the problem and the absorbing of everything concerned. But when the attitude is not healthy and therefore unable to deal with anything in a proper manner concentration does not lead to a thorough understanding of the nature of our problems, because passionate desires (*tṛṣṇā*), preconceived ideas and unfounded beliefs (*dṛṣṭi*), and ignorance or the inability to see things in their correct perspective and to deal with them accordingly (*avidyā*), rush like a devastating flood upon man's mind and produce the morbid state of 'mental inflation', as we would say today, taking the analogy from the dire consequences of a monetary inflation in economics. "Just as by sprinkling a dusty place with water and smoothing it, the dust subsides only for a little while and wherever the water dries up the dust resumes its original condition, so also concentration in an unhealthy attitude is weak (and unable to rouse the positive factors, and jointly with them strives for a goal of permanent value)".[1]

Concentration, however, may also be defined by the method of negation (*avisāhāra, avikkhepa, avisāhaṭamānasatā*). Since concentration is the very reverse of agitatedness and uncertainty it is absence of distraction (*avisāhāra*), and since neither agitatedness nor uncertainty can scatter an attitude in

1. Aṭṭhasālinī III 281. Weakness of concentration is also referred to in Abhidharmakośa VIII 1.

which concentration is dominant it is also non-confusedness (*avikkhepa*), and since by way of concentration we are not pushed either this way or that and divided against ourselves, the whole attitude as the expression of our nature gains the quality of non-dividedness (*avisāhaṭamānasatā*).[1]

There is one other characteristic of concentration and absorption that has been emphasized correctly. This is the calmness and peace by which all the restlessness of a deliberating and scheming mind and all the jerkiness of an affect-ridden mind subsides. For reasons we are unable to account for, there may be, technically speaking, an influx of energy which leads concentration up to dominance and even give it the nature of an unshakable power, which finally will result in "right concentration" (*sammāsamādhi*, Skt. *samyaksamādhi*), which not only plays an important role in the meditative process but also is the irremissible condition for the attainment of the ultimate goal.[2]

Proper concentration and the state of absorption brought about by it, is, as we have just seen, not a completely isolated process but is connected with several other functions, and these functions may also gather such an amount of energy that they attain dominance over other processes and in this way contribute to a variety of psychological manifestations we meet in everyday life in every human psyche. Since the psyche is not merely re-active but is most active in its own right, we cannot do better than describe the changes that go on in it, by such abstract terms as energy if we want to be scientifically correct, although we are fully aware of the fact that no "explanation" of the phenomenon in its practical application has been given, nor will such an abstract term ever convey the emotionally moving richness which is inseparable from psychic processes. The concept of energy only gives a descriptive account of the fact that at certain times, and under certain circumstance certain processes are stronger and more decisive than others. Those functions, processes, or factors which may gain in strength and ability to work their proper course, thereby exerting dominance over other function events are: (I) *śraddhā*,

1. Aṭṭhasālinī III 282.
2. Aṭṭhasālinī III 282.

vīrya, *smṛti*, *samādhi*, *prajñā* (sometimes called *dhī*), (II) *manas*, *saumanasya*, *jīvita*.

Qualifying these functions by 'dominance' and some of them also by 'power', as we shall see later on, does not mean that a value, either moral or intellectual, has been imparted to them. It simply means the determining power which is manifest in the specific operations of these functions, i.e., their nature and 'effects'. The difference between 'dominance' and 'power' is that the former is variable in intensity and may subside as soon as other functions gain in strength and begin to exert their dominance, while the latter aspect, once the specific function has been established, will not subside or give way to other functions by way of a change in the energetic value.[1]

"Dominance' (*indriya*) is defined in a double way: (i) as the inherent power, characterizing the intrinsic nature of the particular function (*indaṭṭha*), and (ii) as sovereignty (*adhipatiyaṭṭha*), denoting the dominance over other factors. Only this latter aspect is met with in the definitions of other Buddhist schools of thought;[2] so the description of the functions and processes with respect also to their intrinsic energetic value, may be regarded as a unique contribution to Buddhist thought by the author of the Aṭṭhasālinī.

It is again difficult to give an adequate translation of the first term mentioned above. *Śraddhā* (Pāli *saddhā*) comprises all the conceptions we express by 'confidence', 'certitude', 'reverence', 'respect', and it is precisely the feeling of respect and devotedness, in addition to confidence and certitude, that distinguishes *śraddhā* from all other terms denoting similar qualities. It certainly is not mere belief or blind faith. It is described as that by which people have confidence and respect, or that by which we ourselves have confidence and respect or simply as confidence and respect. Inasmuch as it overcomes that which is not trustworthy and which does not deserve our respect, it is 'dominance' in the sense of exerting its sovereignty over its opponents, while it is 'dominance' in the sense of lordli-

1. For this difference see also Abhidharmakośa VI 69 and the Bhāṣya.
2. See for instance the long discussion as regards the derivation of *indriya* from the root *idi* by Yaśomitra on Abhidharmakośa, II.1.

ness with respect to its own nature determination and certitude.[1] Its nature is purifying that which is agitated as well as paving the way for the operation of other functions conducive to the attainment of the ultimate goal, or insofar as a healthy attitude in worldly matters only is concerned, for living the life of a respectable and respectful man. The former quality has been described in the following way: "Just as the water-purifying gem of a universal monarch, thrown into water, causes mud, moss, water-weeds, and filth to subside and makes the water transparent, clear and undisturbed, so also confidence-respect, when it arises, removes all obstacles, causes emotional instability (*kilesa*) to subside, and makes the whole outlook of the individual bright and clear. For it is with a pure mind that a man of noble family makes gifts,[2] observes the precepts for a decent and respectable life, performs the duties of fast days, and begins the way of spiritual "culture".[3] The

1. Aṭṭhasālinī III 213 : *sa ca assaddhiyassa athibhavanato abhipatiyaṭṭhena indriyam, adhimokkhalakkhaṇe vā indaṭṭhaṁ karotī ti indriyam.*

adhimokṣa is defined in III 254 as "having the nature of determination, the function of not dawdling along, the actuality of decidedness, and the basis on which it functions is the object that has been decided upon. Owing to its unshakableness in relation to this object it should be regarded as a stone pillar."

This is essentially the view of the Yogācāras. See the remarks of Yaśomitra commenting in Abhidharmakośa II 24 : "*adhimukti* is the determination or adherence to an object because of its merits. According to others it is liking. According to Yogācāras it is adherence to an object that has been decided upon."

Similarly Abhidharmasamuccaya, p. 6. Sthiramati, p. 25, making use of the definition of this work, declares : "*adhimokṣa* means adherence in this or that way to an object decided upon. The term 'decided upon' is used in order to reject everything that is not decided upon. A thing decided upon leaves no room for doubt, be it according to reason or be it according to the instruction by a competent person. When a thing has been decided upon, for instance with respect to its characteristics of impermanence or unpleasantness, then our mind will view the thing in this specific way, and the adherence to the decision made as to its so being and not otherwise, is determination (*adhimokṣa*). It acts in such a way as to make a withdrawal impossible. He who has gained this certitude cannot be made by his opponents to forsake his established view of a thing."

2. 'gift' is not so much the thing that is given, but the whole attitude out of which something is given. The gift, the giver, and the act of giving must be absolutely pure. Technically this is known as *trimaṇḍalapariśuddhi*.

3. Aṭṭhasālinī III 213.

second definition is elaborated in the following manner: "Just as a timid crowd standing on both banks of a great river full of and infested with all sorts of crocodiles, alligators, sharks, ogres and so on, being asked by a great warrior, hero of battles, why they were standing there, would answer that they do not cross for fear of danger, and the hero would grasp his sharp sword and with the words, 'follow me and do not fear', would go down into the river and wherever the monsters would come up he would repel them. And making it safe for the people he would lead them from the right bank to the left and from the left bank to the right in all safety. So also confidence-respect, precedes and is the forerunner of him who makes gifts, observes the precepts of a decent and respectable life, performs the duties of fast days, and begins the way to spiritual culture. Therefore it has been said that confidence-respect, has the nature of paving the way".[1]

To bring about clarity and perspicuity of mind, is according to all schools of Buddhist thought, the essential work of confidence. By its wholesome influence all passionate waves of egotism subside and leave the mind clear and transparent like a clear deep silent pool of water[2]. However, confidence and respect have still other effects as may be seen from a further explanation, which in many respects again reveals the inclination of the author of the Aṭṭhasālinī toward the views of the Yogācāras. He says that "*śraddhā* has the nature of having confidence and respect or the nature of decision as to the suitableness of the subject for further progress on the way. Its function is purifying like the water-purifying gem or paving the way like ferrying beings over a dangerous flood. Its actual manifestation is non-tarnishedness of mind by emotional instability or it is determination. The basis from which it functions is a trust-worthy subject or the 'entering-into the stream toward liberation; (*sotāpatti*).[3] It should be considered as a hand

1. Aṭṭhasālinī III 215.

2. See for instance Yaśomitra on Abhidharmakośa II 25: "*śraddhā* is purity of mind. It is by *śraddhā* that a mind made turbid by the major and minor egotistic passions, becomes pure just like water by bringing it into contact with the water-purifying gem." This is the view of the Vaibhāṣikas. The view of the Yogācāras will be dealt with later on.

3. This means that once we have decided upon a certain course, in

accepting that which is useful and helpful or as a valuable property or as a seed from which all healthy things will sprout".[1] And, "It is having confidence in, and respect for, as well as aspiring after the Three Jewels, the Buddha, the Dharma, and the Saṅgha.... It is the decision which one has made and follows by becoming deeply absorbed in the thought of the qualities of the Enlightened One, by dwelling on these qualities because one has, as it were, broken through (that which obstructs their realization). By *śraddhā* sentient beings have abundant certitude about the qualities of the Enlightened One, or *śraddhā* itself expresses itself by this abundant certitude".[2]

While confidence and respect pave the way toward our goal, it is only by energy (*vīrya*, Pāli *viriya*) that we are able to achieve the goal or actually set out for its attainment. Energy s thus the behavior of the energetic man as well as the activity displayed by him. Or, it denotes that which is to be effected or carried out methodically and by suitable means, where suitable is intended in the sense of bringing about beneficial results. It is 'dominance' in the sense of sovereignty by overpowering idleness, and it is 'dominance' in the sense of lordli-

the specific Buddhist sense, on viewing things from the Buddhist point of view, we shall follow this course which will lead us along like a sure current.

1. Aṭṭhasālinī III 216.

2. Aṭṭhasālinī III 283. This is in many respects that which the Yogācāras have to say about *śraddhā*. See Abhidharmakośa II 25 (Vyākhyā): "Adherence to the Truths, the Jewels, Karman, and its fruit. This is the opinion of others. The explanation of *śraddhā* then is : adherence to the doctrine that there are Four Truths, Three Jewels, Good and Bad Karman, Agreeable and Disagreeable Results".

Most explicit is Sthiramati, who in his Vṛtti, p. 26 enlarges on the definition in Abhidharmasamuccaya. p. 6, and declares : "*śraddhā* is the adherence to the doctrine that actions will have their results, to the Noble Truths, and to the Three Jewels: it is pellucidity of mind, yearning for the Noble. *śraddhā* operates in three ways : it is adherence to either a good or a bad thing, it is pellucidity only with respect to good and it is yearning for the attainment or production of good and so also pellucidity. *śraddhā* is opposed to and destructive of all tarnishes in one's attitude (and mental operations). Since through its influence the defects and stains of emotional instability in its grosser and subtler forms go away, one's whole outlook becomes clear. Therefore one speaks of the pellucidity of mind. It is the basis for will power (*chandas*)".

ness, by energetically taking hold of the problem at hand.[1] In this way energy is supporting as well as strengthening: "Just as an old house stands when supported by additional pillars, so also the aspirant (*yogāvacara*), when supported by energy, does not lose the healthy factors, be it some of them or all of them", and "Just as in an encounter between a small and a large army, the small army will fall back, and the king informed about this, will send a strong army corps, and reinforced by this, his army will defeat the hostile army. So also energy does not allow the co-existent and associated functions to fall back and to recede, but strengthens and reinforces them".[2] There is still one other explanation of energy, which is common to all schools of Buddhist thought and which corresponds to our concept of will power or perseverance.[3] It is said: "Energy has the nature of perseverance the function of supporting the co-existent functions, the actuality of not slackening, and the basis from which it operates is stimulation according to a statement in the Sūtra (Aṅguttaranikāya II 115), 'stimulated one puts one's shoulder to the task', or its basis is the initial putting of energy into an enterprise. For one must know that that which is rightly begun is the root of all achievements.[4]

This energy is not physical output, but is that which permeates the whole attitude or mental outlook of a man dealing with the problems of attaining spiritual maturity. It is itself graded according to the intensity of its manifestation. It may be simple cessation from idleness or simple rejection of sensuous and sensual enjoyments (*nikkama*), it may be viewed

1. Aṭṭhasālinī III 217.
2. Aṭṭhasālinī III 218.
3. This interpretation of will as perseverance is offered by Gilbert Ryle, The Concept of Mind, pp. 62 sq.
4. Aṭṭhasālinī III 219. It is interesting to note that the author of the Aṭṭhasālinī mentions the overcoming of idleness first and then points out the character of perseverance. This same order (which cannot be inverted, of course) is given by Sthiramati, p. 27 : "Energy is the opponent of laziness. It is perseverance in that which is healthy but not in that which is detrimental, perseverance in that which is laziness and indolence, because of its detestableness. Energy gives a firm basis for the fulfilment of that which is healthy and wholesome".

from its increasing intensity or as the cutting off of the ties that bind us to the world of relativity (*parakkama*), it may be seen in its progressive movement or its crossing the flood of desire (*uyyāma*), it may be the strong endeavour or the going to the other shore (*vāyāma*), it may be perseverance or that which precedes the solution of everything that is difficult (*ussāha*), it may be perseverance continually gaining strength (*ussolhi*), it may be firmness or the uprooting of the pillar of ignorance (*thāma*), or it may manifest itself as steadfastness because it carries (gives strength to) one's attitude and the functions operating in and according to it, and because it carries the continuous stream of healthy factors, and thus produces the firmness and resolution to go the way one has decided to be the best for one's spiritual welfare (*dhiti*). It is this firm resolution which will under no circumstances become weak and feeble (*asithilaparakkamatā*) that made the Buddha utter the proud words before he had attained enlightenment: "May my skin, my sinews, and my bones wither away, not until I have attained my goal shall I rise from this seat". And because this energy, this will power, does not throw off the earnest desire to do good and since it does not shirk the obligations involved in it, it is called, negatively expressed, "The manner of acting in which the desire for the sublime has not been discarded" (*anikkhittachandatā*) and "the manner of acting in which the obligations one has taken up are not shirked" (*anikkhittadhuratā*), and, positively stated, "the vigorous tackling of obligations" (*dhurasampaggāha*). It is out of proper employment of energy that right exertion for the attainment of the ultimate goal (*sammāvāyāma*) results.[1]

Just as it is necessary to have confidence in a thing one wants to achieve and just as it is necessary that one exerts oneself in order to achieve the desired end, without utilizing all experiences one has had in life and without directing them toward that which lies before one's eyes and ahead of oneself, all striving will be in vain. Therefore it is not enough to have confidence and to be energetic, one must also have and employ *smṛti* (Pāli *sati*). This term comprises two different ideas.

1. Aṭṭhasālinī III 283.

On the one hand, it is 'recollection', pointing to the past, while on the other, it is 'inspection'. Certainly, inspection itself is not memory, because it does not refer to the past but merely describes the apparent characteristic of its present objective constituent. But this objective constituent is very often the objective constituent of a co-existent memory-situation.[1] It has to be observed that the latter aspect of 'inspection' is emphasized in all texts. For it is not the futile running after fleeting memories and thereby losing sight of the present, but that function, by which one tries to keep the perceptual situation as constant as possible, in order to learn more about the objective constituent of the particular perceptual situation. Again it must be emphasized that a healthy attitude is meant for meditation and that inspection therefore is an important factor within this process. Its definition runs as follows: "By it people recollect, or it itself recollects, or it is just recollection. It is dominance in the sense of sovereignty because it overpowers confusion, and it is dominance in the sense of lordliness because it has the nature of being immediately present".[2] This definition makes it abundantly clear that *smṛti* implies and effects a non-floating away of the subject in mind and that it strongly takes hold of the material present by selecting and furthering that which is useful and healthy and by inhibiting all that which might impede the individual's spiritual progress. The former aspect is illustrated by the following simile : "Just as the treasurer of a king, who guards his tenfold treasure, both early and late makes the king take note of and remember the royal possessions, so also *smṛti* makes us take note of and remember that which is wholesome",[3] while the latter aspect mentioned above is described as follows : "Just as the counsellor of a universal monarch, who knows what is disadvantageous and what is advantageous, removes the disadvantageous and promotes the advantageous, so also *smṛti* scrutinizes the ways of the disadvantageous and advantageous factors and by deciding that misconduct in body (speech and mind) is disadvantageous it removes these disadvantageous factors and by deciding that

1. C. D. Broad, The Mind and its Place in Nature, p. 299.
2. Aṭṭhasālinī III 220.
3. Aṭṭhasālinī III 221.

good conduct in body (speech and mind) are advantageous factors, it firmly takes hold of these advantageous factors".[1]

Another explanation which the author of the Aṭṭhasālinī gives, tallies with the one given by the Yogācāras. This definition brings out the character of inspection particularly clearly: "*smṛti* has the nature of not letting the subject float away, the function of unerringness, the actuality of guarding that which has become the object of inspection or of facing the subject, the basis from which it operates being clear and firm perception of the objective constituents of the situation (*kāyādi-sati-paṭṭhāna*). Since *smṛti* is firmly standing on the object, it should be regarded as a door-post, or since it guards the senses from going astray, it should be regarded as a door-keeper".[2]

Thus *smṛti* comprises three aspects. It is recollecting and repeated recollection of past experiences and events (*sati, anussati, paṭissati, saraṇatā*); but above all it is the bearing in mind of what one has learned (*dhāraṇatā*), and unlike pumpkins and pots which float along the current of a river but do not sink under the water, *smṛti* does not let the subject drift away but takes hold of it in all its aspects (*apilāpanatā*), and finally, since one learns by inspection more about the nature of the subject it is non-obliviousness (*asammussanatā*) which adds to the character of dominance in shedding light on the present

1. Aṭṭhasālinī III 222.

2. Aṭṭhasālinī III 223. There is a curious connection between the Pali *apilāpanatā* and the Sanskrit *abhilapanatā*, the terms used by Yaśomitra in his commentary on Abhidharmakośa II 24 and by Sthiramati in his Vṛtti, p. 25 sq. Is *abhilapanatā* a Sanskritization of the Prakritic *apilāpanatā* ($\sqrt{}$*plu*) ? Although both terms characterize 'inspection' the former is the 'addressing' a known object, the later the not letting the object of inspection float away. Yaśomitra defines *smṛti* as follows : smṛti is non-obliviousness of an object. Through it mind does not forget an object and, as it were, addresses it". Sthiramati declares: '*smṛti* is unerringness as regards a known object, it is a mental address. A known thing is something formerly experienced. It is unerringness because it does not let go the hold on the object. The repeated recollection of an object formerly grasped, is addressing it. For when an object is addressed there is no distraction to another object or to another aspect, hence *smṛti* acts as not causing distraction." The simile of *smṛti* as door-keeper has been made use of by Śāntideva in his Bodhicaryāvatāra V 33.

and out of which right inspection as the preliminary step to knowledge (*sammāsati*) may result[1].

While these definitions make it quite clear that *smṛti* is above all 'inspection' and prove that the translation by 'memory' as found in most works is misleading if not even wrong, later authors have elaborated the difference between memory and inspection precisely and stated that in meditation memory is not suited.[2]

Inspection[3] is a necessary step. By it we learn more about the object and its nature and this assists us in becoming absorbed in the contemplation of the object. Therefore as the next factor operating in a healthy attitude, absorption by concentration (*samādhi*) is mentioned. By it mind is fixed upon the object that has been selected in inspection and it exerts its dominance by way of overpowering distraction and also by way of exercizing its lordliness in non-distractedness.[4] It is then from continued practice that absorption which is not uncommon in ordinary life, develops into proper absorption (*samyaksamādhi*, Pāli *sammāsamādhi*).

As will have been observed, the arrangement of the factors is not random, and it is from this gradual process, starting with confidence and leading up to absorption, that knowledge (*prajñā*, Pāli *paññā*) is attained. Knowledge, more properly speaking, analytical appreciative understanding, has a double aspect. The one is to know and the other is to make known. "Knowledge is so called because it knows. And what does it know? It knows the Four Noble Truths, beginning with the statement "that all this to which we are attached is transitory and unable to give lasting happiness and spiritual contentment and hence is miserable." According to the old Atthakathā, however, knowledge is so called because it makes known. And what does it make known? It makes known the verifiable fact of transitoriness, miserableness, and the absence of a persist-

1. Aṭṭhasālinī III 286.
2. Padma. dkar, po, Phyag, rgya. chen.poi. man. ṅag.gi bśad. sbyar. rgyal. bai. gan. mdzod, fol.88a. where 'inspection' is termed *yul. ṅes.kyi. dran. pa. khyad. par. can* "special kind of *smṛti* having a determinate object."
3. On this term see C.D. Broad, The Mind and its Place in Nature, pp. 299 sq.
4. Aṭṭhasālinī III 224.

ing personality or individuality.—Knowledge is dominance in the sense of sovereignty, because it overpowers ignorance, and it is dominance in the sense of lordliness, because it is by nature beholding reality.[1]

Knowledge is the light that spreads far and wide and dispels the darkness of mind, the inability to see things in their true nature and proper perspective. The light that knowledge sheds over all things is unparalleled. "Just as when a lamp burns at night in a four-walled house, the darkness disappears and light manifests itself, so also knowledge has as its nature the shedding of light. There is no light equal to the light which is knowledge."[2]

This knowledge is essentially analytical, but in its analysis it is certainly not destructive, but appreciative of all that is wholesome and furthers spiritual growth and development. It is not mere book-learning, it must be applied to life if it is of any value, and so it has a healing influence : "Just as a judicious physician knows which food is suitable for his patients and which is not, so also knowledge, when it arises, knows whether something is healthy or unhealthy, serviceable or unserviceable, low or exalted, dark or bright, similar or dissimilar."[3]

According to another explanation, knowledge is penetration into the real or true nature of a thing. This penetration is unfaltering like the penetrating effect of an arrow shot by a skilled archer. Like a lamp, knowledge spreads its light over the object and since knowledge is the opposite of delusion and operates where there is no delusion it is like a reliable guide in a dense jungle.[4]

Knowledge analyzes and in its analysis penetrates to the true nature of things. This true nature is their transitoriness, which means that all determinate things, whether they be sensed objects or postulated selves, are caught within the death-delivering ravages of time and that it is due to the fact that man cherishes the determinate factors and qualities of those who are dear to him, of himself and of all natural objects,

1. Aṭṭhasālinī III 225.
2. Aṭṭbasālinī III 226.
3. Aṭṭhasālinī III 227.
4. Aṭṭhasālinī III 228.

that he must of necessity suffer. Far from giving a pessimistic outlook, knowledge makes man see that whatever is determinate is not all and that there is something in the nature of the determinate which is inexpressible and yet can be experienced directly and immediately and in its direct experience offers lasting happiness. The realization and unequivocal acceptance of the fact that everything determinate is transitory, which we can verify by appealing to facts directly, and not to hazy ideas about them, is the first step to and the first sign of ethical practical wisdom.

Knowledge does not make man narrow, it achieves broadness of outlook, because due to its subtlety and amplitude it delights in the real meaning of things (*bhūte atthe ramatī ti bhūrī*). As lightning destroys stone pillars, so also knowledge annihilates emotional instability and quickly grasps and holds fast the real meaning of things. It is therefore a guide, who leads him who trusts knowledge, toward that which is good and wholesome and directs all associated functions in the psyche to the penetration of the real. Knowledge alone brings a mind which has gone off its tracks by believing things to be permanent, though they are so utterly transitory, back to the right course just as a whip brings horses that are running off the road back to the proper road.

Knowledge is the light by which we see and which sheds its illumination on everything knowable, not merely in the sense of intellectual knowledge, though intellectual acumen is an asset; but also in the sense of directly experiencing. It is this latter aspect that must never be lost sight of in Buddhist thought. In the darkness of ignorance, knowledge is an unshakable power, a sharp weapon to cut off the passions and affects that veil our view. Its sublimeness can only be inadequately compared with the lofty turret of a palace. Knowledge is a precious jewel, because it causes, gives, and produces delight, because through it wisdom is set up, because by it that which is difficult to understand is revealed, because it is incomparable, and because it is enjoyed by illustrious people.[1] It is by this knowledge which deeply penetrates into the nature of things, and is able to discriminate between the real and the seemingly

1. Aṭṭhasālinī III 290.

real, that man does not fall a prey to ignorance and becomes deluded to the real status of the world, including himself. This knowledge can never become distorted, though it may operate under certain limitations and hence is unable to shed its light unrestrictedly. To enable it to work free and unhampered, is the aim of developing a healthy attitude. Knowledge which is both analytical and appreciative and which is intimately related to direct experience and not merely discursive, is the irremissible condition for 'rightly viewing things' (*samyag-dṛṣṭi*, Pāli *sammādhiṭṭhi*),[1] the first step on the path toward liberation and the realization of ultimate reality.

All these 'dominances' (*indriya*) so far mentioned, in addition to their pre-eminent and lordly character, overpower their opponents and keep them subdued. In the constant flux and change of energetic values which characterize every living process they may acquire such an intensity or amount of energy that they become unshakable powers (*bala*). This 'charging' them with energy, so to say, is brought about by a systematic technique which is known as following the Eightfold Path, each step intensifying and increasing the potential of the essential factors in the attainment of the goal : enlightenment. However, there are in this connection three other 'dominances' mentioned. They are *indriyas* 'dominances' only by virtue of their lordliness.

The first of these 'dominances' in the sense of lordliness is the *manas*. Its function and intrinsic nature we have already discussed.[2]

The second is 'serenity of mind' (*saumanasya*, Pāli *somanassa*). It is, as we have already seen, a certain mood which gives a specific evaluation to the whole of the attitude without, however, interfering with the intrinsic nature of the psychic process. Serenity of mind, which is found in a healthy attitude, is because of its association with joy and enthusiasm (*pīti*) and the feeling of happiness and ease (*somanassa*) an embellishment to man's mental life.[3]

1. Aṭṭhasālinī III 290.
2. See pp. 16 sqq.
3. Aṭṭhasālinī III 230.

The third 'dominance' is life (*jīvita*). It is conceived by the author of the Aṭṭhasālinī much in the same way as by the Sautrāntikas and Yogācāras, insofar as it is, in modern terms, the kinetic energy of a process and not an entity or a substance (*dravya*) existing per se.[1] "Life is that by which the factors associated with it live. It is dominance because of its nature of guarding. It is the dominant force in the continuity of a process that is already going on. Life has the nature of guarding those processes which are not separated from it, the function of having them going on, the actuality of maintaining them, and the basis on which it operates is the very process which has to be kept going. Although life is specified as having the nature of guarding, life guards the processes only for the time of their existence, just as water does for lotus flowers; it guards them as soon as they have come into existence according to their own nature under the specific conditions of their origination, just as a nurse guards a child when it has been born. By virtue of its connection with what has been set going it causes this to continue going, just like a captain of a ship, but it does not cause it to continue going beyond the stoppage of the process, because it itself and that which is to be kept going do not exist any more; nor does life leave itself behind in the moment of stoppage, because it itself breaks up, just as the vanishing oil in a wick does not have the flame of the lamp remain.[2]

To include these three 'dominances' (*indriya*) here, has certainly been prompted by language which so often induces us to attribute to a metaphysical realm what really belongs to the 'logical projection'—to use a term of Susanne K. Langer—in which we conceive it. However, the fact should not be ignored that in meditative processes which are the cornerstone of Buddhism, there is a heightening of the intensity of certain processes and there we are not merely concerned with perception but also and much more so with conception. Conception is formulation, and formulation is the function of the *manas*.

1. Abhidharmakośa II 45 and Yaśomitra's Vyākhyā : *na dravyāntaram*.

2. Aṭṭhasālinī III 231. See also III 291 and the etymology of *āyu*, synonymous with *jīvita*, from the root 'to go'. According to Abhidharmakośa II 45 and the Bhāṣya and to Abhidharmasamuccaya, p. 11, life is a certain power in an event due to Karman.

Together with the dominance of formulation, of *Gestaltung*, there is a heightened feeling of ease and happiness and of free flowing life. In this respect the inclusion of factors or events which are 'lordly' and not 'overpowering' evinces a deep insight into the operations of certain functions within the boundaries of a healthy attitude, but to enumerate these factors as separate items is a fallacious trick of language.

It is with the intensification of analytical appreciative understanding (*prajñā*) that the correct view of the world and of ourselves is possible. It has to be emphasized over and again that right view (*samyakdṛṣṭi* Pāli *sammādiṭṭhi*) is not the acceptance of a doctrine based on hypotheses, but a view gained through continuous contemplation and direct experience. It is out of correctly viewing things that we are able to form a correct conception (*samyaksaṁkalpa*, Pāli *sammāsaṁkappa*) which, as we have seen above, is intimately related to the first occurrence in meditative concentration (*vitarka*, where we conceive of an object and then investigate it to the depth of its meaning. Then by exerting ourselves in a proper way (*samyagvyāyāma*, Pāli *sammāvāyāma*) and by right inspection (*samyaksmṛti*, Pāli *sammāsati*) we arrive at right absorption (*samyaksamādhi*, Pāli *sammāsamādhi*), out of which knowledge is born. At the same time this path which we traverse, helps to strengthen all that is 'lordly' and 'sovereign' so that it becomes an unshakable power (*bala*)[1].

But the power of knowledge, of discrimination and appreciation (*prajñābala*), is not given us for argumentation, for proving or disproving some metaphysical theory which is usually a pseudo-answer to a pseudo-question; it is in us that we may act in a manner which corresponds to the nature of our environment and of ourselves. Here we touch upon the problem of moral behavior. Two 'powers' are of decisive importance here. They are self-respect (*hrī*, Pāli *hiri*) and decorum (*apatrāpya*, Pāli *ottapa*). Each of these powers is analyzed according to four aspects: basis (*samuṭṭhāna*), decisive significance (*adhipati*), intrinsic nature (*sabhāva*), and general characteristic (*lakkhaṇa*).

1. Aṭṭhasālinī III 232: 233.

According to this schema, self-respect is grounded in one's self which also includes the immediate milieu (*jāti*), age (*vaya*), resoluteness (*sūrabhāva*), and learnedness (*bāhusacca*). Here one's self has been made sovereign over one's actions and is considered to be of decisive significance. Its intrinsic nature is the feeling of shame and disgust, "just as one is loath to touch an iron ball besmeared all over with excrement".[1] Its general characteristic is the careful evaluation or estimation of the worth of one's milieu, training, heritage and conduct in relation to one's fellow-beings. Thus it implies a show of deference, the measure of recognition which is due to oneself and to others.

Decorum is grounded in the opinion of the world; and what the world at large says and thinks about a thing or an action is of decisive significance. Its intrinsic nature is fear—fear of deviating from the accepted standard (*apāya*), and its general characteristic is to see the evil and formidable immediately.[2]

This analysis of moral conduct as depending on either an objective or a subjective standard deserves special attention, because it is liable to create considerable confusion if it is taken outside its connection with the general attitude of the individual. Certainly, the behavior of him who takes the opinion of the world as the decisive factor, coincides with the claims of society.

1. Aṭṭhasālinī III 239.

2. Aṭṭhasālinī III 224—240. Similar but more concise is Abhidharmasamuccaya, p. 6 : "What is self-respect ? To be ashamed of evil because of one's person. It affords the basis for restraint from evil actions. What is decorum ? To be ashamed of evil because of others. It has the same function (as self-respect, i.e., restraint from doing evil)". Sthiramati in his Vṛtti, pp. 26 sq. elaborates this statement much in the same way as the author of the Aṭṭhasālinī. He says : "Self-respect means the feeling of being ashamed of evil, because one has made oneself or the Dharma the decisive factor. Evil means the wrong and bad, because it has been blamed by virtuous people or because it yields undesired results. The humiliation one feels, because of evil done or not done, is the feeling of shame, and this is the meaning of self-respect, It affords the basis for restraint from evil actions. Decorum is the feeling of being ashamed of evil, because one has made the judgment of the world the decisive factor. 'Such action has been blamed in the world; if the world would know me to act in such a way they would blame me'—out of fear of reproach one feels ashamed of evil. This, too, affords the basis for restraint from evil deeds."

His morality is in accord with the moral viewpoint valid at that particular time he live in. What he tries to do and to be, is exactly what his environment needs and what it expects from him. However, it is by no means granted that the standpoint of objectively given facts remains the same for all times and under all circumstances. Objective conditions and objective values vary and only too often deteriorate and become the very reverse, sometimes even acquiring a definitely morbid character. An individual who is orientated by the outer standard, because it is from there that he expects the decisive value to come, must inevitably participate in the downfall as soon as the outer standard deteriorates. As a matter of fact, the incontestably moral thinking, feeling and action of a man who is orientated by outer standards, in no way hinder the evil and destructive from creeping in. On the contrary, they facilitate it, because due to his self-assurance, his unquestionable right-doing he overlooks what is new and valuable and forgets constantly that what once was good does not remain so eternally. Although decorum is meant to enable man from doing evil, if not balanced by self-respect, it is hardly able to achieve its own end. Buddhaghosa compares decorum aptly with a prostitute. "By having made another one's (standard) one's own norm one gives up evil by decorum, just like a harlot".[1] Indeed, a man who always conforms to the judgment of others and always is anxious to live up to expectations, acts like a prostitute who also must always be up to what her customers expect. Any reservation on her part will entail loss of business, which is definitely evil.

On the other hand, those who rely upon that which is group-patterned within them in their adaptation to life, very often create the impression of a reservation of the ego. But just as the objective conditions do not remain unaltered, so also the subjective factor is liable to change. The subjective factor, however, is not merely the ego, which in Buddhist conception is but a linguistic device for bundling certain occurrences together, it is the whole of the psychological background, the indispensable condition of psychological adaptation. This

1. Visuddhimagga XIV 142.

background, containing all the residua of experiences man has made throughout the millenia and through which he is able to make experiences, is ever present. This presence may lead to an exaggeration of the subjective factor in actual life, which because of the inflexibility of the subjective judgment creates the impression of strong ego-centredness. This reproach of ego-centredness, however, is wrongly applied; it only shows lack of understanding on the part of him who derives his conduct and morality from some outer standard. For he simply cannot understand that morality may consist also in not being at everybody's call. A proper evaluation of the subjective factor greatly contributes to the dignity of human nature, and by upholding the dignity of our own we are able to respect the dignity of others. Buddhaghosa, therefore, aptly compares self-respect with a respectable wife : "Having made one's self one's norm one gives up evil by self-respect, like a respectable wife".[1]

Self-respect and decorum are certainly not immortal laws, they are manifestations and expressions of a healthy attitude. It is by losing sight of their connection with and dependence upon an attitude, by allowing ourselves to be ruled by ignorance and its unescapable companion irritation, unnecessarily increasing the already amount of unpleasantness one experiences in everyday life, that self-respect and decorum are turned into the very opposite. *Āhrīkya* and *anapatrāpya* are not mere absence of *hrī* and *apatrāpya,* but the counteragents of all that self-respect and decorum stand for,[2] because instead of keeping men more at peace with each other they send them off on wild, impulsive, ill-considered and ill-grounded aggressive acts of either a personal, nationalistic, or religious character.

Although these forces which rule moral behavior are not imposed from somewhere in a way which we are supposedly not fitted to understand and which makes it impossible for man to have a say in a matter that concerns him vitally, this is not

1. Visuddhimagga XIV 142.

2. Abhidharmakośavyākhyā ad Abhidh.-kośa II 32. See also Abhidharmasamuccaya, p. 9. Sthiramati's Vṛtti, p. 31. Aṭṭhasālinī III 543. Visuddhimagga XIV 160.

to say that we should advocate moral relativism and sophistry. The insight into the nature of ourselves and of things and the awareness of the fallacy of the assumption that one side or the other must get the verdict, as if one-sideness could ever hold for both sides, makes for open-mindedness and an understanding of human nature which can hardly be surpassed. Buddhist morality derives from knowledge and not from blind belief. Knowledge is indispensable for understanding, and understanding expresses itself in sympathy and benevolence for all persons and things. Hence Buddhist ethics is free from the stain of thinking that it is one's moral and religious duty to force the prejudices and conventions of specific national, religious, and social groups on others and to punish and liquidate those who are not willing to accept these beliefs.[1]

Ethics belong to practice and not with theory, and, therefore, being expressive rather than discursive, self-respect and decorum are also called the guardians of the world (*lokapāla*)[2] as the Buddha has said : "These two bright factors' guard the world : self-respect and decorum. If these two factors did not guard the world there would be no recognition of one's mother, of one's mother's sister, of one's mother's brother's wife, of a teacher's wife, or of the wife of one's spiritual preceptors. The world would fall into promiscuity and act like goats and sheep, fowl and swine, cattle and wild beasts. But since these two bright factors guard the world, there is recognition of one's mother, of one's mother's sister, of one's mother's brother's wife, of a teacher's wife, and of the wives of spiritual preceptors".[3]

Thus far differentiations of a man's mind have been discussed from the viewpoint of function and the varying intensity of the various functions. And also so far this analysis may be called scientific, though not in the sense of emphasizing the most general results of science but in the sense of applying the scientific method of analysis to its particular province. There-

1. Ethical metaphysics as an attempt to legislate our own wishes, has been clearly pointed out by Bertrand Russel, Mysticism and Logic (Pelican Book), p. 104.

2. Aṭṭhasālinī III 247.

3. Aṅguttaranikāya I 51. Aṭṭhasālinī III 247.

fore, to introduce ethical ideas into a scientific study of mind and its functions seems to be a serious and, in the modern conception of philosophy, a deplorable deviation. However, as the above analysis of self-respect and decorum has shown, the inclusion of ethical factors does not mean that ethics is a topic of theoretizing discursiveness in which assertions are made about what is good and what is evil on the superstitious, though rarely admitted, assumption that one already knows the conclusions to be reached. Ethics is a function, a force in our mental life, our awareness and understanding, just as are cognition and feeling, and without this function man would cease to be man.[1] In this respect it becomes necessary to introduce a distinction between that which lends itself to and assists articulation and that which is the articulated expression. That which lends itself to and assists articulation is known as 'healthy roots' (*kusalamūla*), because any function or any event which is assisted by it, is strong and healthy, "just as trees which have firm roots are strong and well grounded".[2] These 'roots' which support and nourish a man's attitude are non-cupidity, non-antipathy, and non-delusion. This negative expression does not mean mere absence of cupidity, antipathy, and delusion, but attempts to convey the meaning of something absolutely positive, which in the final analysis is beyond affirmation and negation.

Non-cupidity (*alobha*) has the character of not being desirous for an object and not being attached to it, to the same extent that water will not cling to the leaves of a lotus flower. Its function is not caring for possessions, to the same extent that a man who has renounced worldliness does not care for the acquisition of possession. Its basis is the fact that it does not remain stuck, just as a man who has fallen into a dirty pit does not wallow in the dirt. It is the effective remedy against avarice and hence is the foundation and help of liberality.[3]

Through non-cupidity we remain modest and do not take more than is necessary, and non-cupidity also makes us

1. This does not mean that man is important in the scheme of things, it only means that ethics is expressive behavior and belongs to man's nature just as does his need to eat and drink.

2. Visuddhimagga XVII 70. Aṭṭhasālinī III 293.

3. Aṭṭhasālinī III 241.

see defects where there is a defect, while cupidity is always eager to cover and conceals defects, so that greediness may not be denied. Non-cupidity is essentially detachment and therefore it does not deliver us up to that feeling of misery which every parting from those who are dear to us entails, because knowledge informs us that everything which is determinate and composite is transitory and that our attachment to what is transitory and our undue attention to it makes us suffer. Nor does non-cupidity entangle us in the misery of rebirth, because it is craving that effects rebirth, and this craving is cut off at its very root by non-cupidity.[1]

Non-cupidity enables an ordinary person to live happily and should he be still subject to the law of rebirth he will not be reborn in the world of spirits, for it is through craving, the excessive desire to accumulate which no amount of accumulated wealth will ever stop, that we are made miserable and thus feel the pang of never being able to become satisfied.[2] Thus non-cupidity gives rise to the idea of renunciation (*nekkhammasaññā*) and the idea of impurity (*asubhasaññā*).[3] Of course, impurity is not an ultimate evaluation but a means to sever the ties of attachment, it certainly does not mean that there exists something to displease us. It would be difficult to reconcile such pessimism with the joyful and calm acceptance which characterizes the Buddhist outlook.

Non-cupidity makes us avoid a life addicted to sensual experiences as the sole aim of our existence and cuts all fetters of covetousness, thus becoming a condition for health. It also is a condition for the acquisition of wealth; for wealth comes to us when we do not hanker after it, when by renunciation (*cāga*) we have become free and so can enjoy whatever comes our way. Wealth never consists in its amount but in what we make out of it (*bhoga*). It is a condition of content.[4]

1. Aṭṭhasālinī III 242.
2. Aṭṭhasālinī III 243. The realistic schools of Buddhism believed in the concrete existence of spirits and hells, while the idealistic schools understood spirits and hells as symbolic representations of mind.
3. Aṭṭhasālinī III 243.
4. Aṭṭhasālinī III 244.

Finally, because of there being nothing to which we might become attached through non-cupidity our eyes are opened to the fact of transitoriness (*aniccadassana*). Only a greedy person in his futile hopes for lasting enjoyments fails to see the utter futility of a belief in permanency and so necessarily must suffer. In this way non-cupidity awakens the realization of the transitoriness of all that we encounter in our sense experiences, and this realization, in turn, facilitates the operation of non-cupidity; "who would become attached to that which he knows to be transitory !"[1]

Non-antipathy (*adveṣa*, Pāli *adosa*) has as its characteristic non-churlishness and non-obstructiveness and is like a helpful friend. Its function is to remove ill-will and worries and hence is soothing like sandal paste. Its basis is gentleness and pleasantness, and therefore is likened to the splendor of the full moon. It is a potent remedy against bad manners and unethical behavior and a solid foundation of ethics and manners[2].

By non-antipathy modesty is preserved in the sense that we do not take too little and thereby offend him who offers us something. Non-antipathy makes us acknowledge merits where there are merits, while a person ruled by antipathy will smear virtues and belittle merits. It also enables us not to feel miserable when we meet those who are not dear to us. Nor does non-antipathy entangle us in the misery of old age, while a person who is ruled by strong dislikes and aversions ages quickly,[3] because he is unable to bear a natural course and in his struggle to maintain youth wears himself out.

Non-antipathy enables everyone to live happily and protects a man from being reborn in hell. For it is antipathy that because of its fierceness produces hell according to its intensity. As the remedy against and opposite to antipathy and of all that antipathy entails, it instils in us the idea of non-malice (*abyāpādasaññā*) and the idea of the boundlessness (*appamāṇasaññā*) of love, compassion, joy which participates in all that is good, and benign equanimity.[4]

1. Aṭṭhasālinī III 245.
2. Aṭṭhasālinī III 241.
3. Aṭṭhasālinī III 242.
4. Aṭṭhasālinī III 243.

Non-antipathy makes us avoid self-mortification, the obsession of a sense of sin, which is but the aggrandisement of self-importance by inverted means. It cuts all the fetters that bind us to malevolence. It gives youth, for a person who is not governed by antipathy and therefore is not consumed by the fire of antipathy and hatred which causes wrinkles and makes the hair go grey, remains young for a long time. Non-antipathy is the condition for winning friends, because friends (*mitta*) are won by love (*mettā*) and are not lost through love.[1]

Just as non-cupidity does not make us enamoured of ourselves, so non-antipathy enables us to forsake enmity towards those who show us enmity. It makes us realize the miserableness of all that is transitory (*dukkhadassana*). And just as non-antipathy makes us see this miserableness, this realization reinforces non-antipathy, for "who would like to aggravate the existing miserableness he knows, by other violent outbursts of anger".[2]

Non-delusion non-bewilderment (*amoha*) is essentially identical with analytical appreciative understanding, as explained in the section on knowledge as a dominant factor. It is a sustaining power for the development of all that is healthy and therefore indispensable for the actual practice of all that leads to the goal of liberation.[3] Just as non-cupidity prevents us from taking too much and non-antipathy from taking too little, whether this be actual or figurative, non-delusion prevents us from taking the wrong thing, and in addition makes us realize what is possible and what is not, so that we do not feel miserable if we do not get that which our desire would like to make us get, because through knowledge we are restrained from futile hopes. So also there is no misery of death for him who does not suffer from delusion,[4] because it is a sign of delusion to assume optimistically that whatever we experience will not be subject to the ravages of time and death.

Non-delusion operates especially among those who have renounced a life of worldliness, and allows them to live happily. It prevents beings from being reborn as animals, a state which

1. Aṭṭhasālinī III 244.
2. Aṭṭhasālinī III 245.
3. Aṭṭhasālinī III 241. III 225-228.
4. Aṭṭhasālinī III 242.

is marked by the absence of judgments of various degrees of determinateness. It instils in us the idea of non-violence (*avihiṁsāsaññā*) and the idea of the impersonality of all events (*dhātusaññā*).[1]

Non-delusion or knowledge is the essential means to make us reach the Middle Path which avoids the extremes of existence and non-existence, of eternalism and nihilism, to mention only a few of the most formidable superstitions that beset the human mind and have a deadening effect on mental life. Therefore non-delusion makes man live long. It is also a condition for self-improvement, because a person who is not deluded by opinions about himself, but sees himself as he actually is, acts in such a way as is helpful and good for him in attaining the goal and so improves himself.[2] This may sound surprising to someone who has been brought up in the belief that Buddhism denies a self. First of all it has to be noted that Buddhism neither denies nor affirms a self, because ontological questions hardly play any role in Buddhism. The question about a self refers to the logical nature of what is conventionally termed a 'self' and here Buddhism declares it to subsist and not to exist. Moreover, without a concept which an individual has of himself no doctrine can operate, because on this concept (Mc Dougall's self-regarding sentiment) depends the development of character, the realization of goals, and the achievement of integration. What a person thinks about himself never fails to affect his level of aspiration at every turn. The important question is whether this concept of self is based on mere belief or on knowledge; Buddhism rejects any postulational belief and favors knowledge. Therefore also the statement that non-delusion leads to self-improvement is in no way contrary to the other statement that knowledge opens our eyes to the fact that there is no permanent self apart from the states of a self (*anatta-dassana*).[3]

While these three 'roots' lend themselves to and assist articulation, the articulated expression, the overt behavior, is non-covetousness (*anabhijjhā*), non-malevolence (*abyāpāda*),

1. Aṭṭhasālinī III 245.
2. Aṭṭhasālinī III 244.
3. Aṭṭhasālinī III 245.

and seeing things in their proper perspective as they are (*sammā-diṭṭhi*).[1] And intimately connected with this overt behavior is the nature of society which is governed individually by self-respect and decorum (but only where a healthy attitude and outlook of life prevail).[2]

A particular feature of a healthy attitude is functional ease. This the author of the Aṭṭhasālinī discusses from various points of view. This ease is found in what is termed *kāya* and *citta*. The term *kāya* admits of various interpretations and accordingly has been interpreted in various ways by those schools who acknowledge the Abhidharma. The author of the Aṭṭhasālinī subsumes under this term the function complexes of feeling, sensation, and motivation,[3] while Vasubandhu and Sthiramati understand by it some particular tactile element.[4] The term *citta* refers to perception and apperception.[5] This ease is first of all a relaxation of tension, the absence of strain (*passaddhi*, Skt. *praśrabdhi*), it overcomes distress and the tendency to make light of everything (*uddhacca*, Skt. *auddhatya*,) which are dangerous for meditation, which is, as has been pointed out before, the prerequisite for a healthy attitude. This absence of strain, is viewed from another aspect, functional lightness (*lahutā*)[6] which serves to overcome lassitude and, in particular, drowsiness and sluggishness (*thīnamiddha*) which are also dangers for meditation. Both these dangers, restlessness and drowsiness, being overcome, there is an adaptableness (*mudutā*) of all functions which serves to overcome the tendency to become fixed to a certain course (*thaddha*). It is a well known fact that in the course of life of an individual, inclinations, tendencies and interests grow stronger and in spite of better judgment cannot be shaken. Very often this is an endeavor to keep up the psychology of adolescence even in maturity. Everybody knows such persons, who are a nuisance to themselves and to others and who are called quite properly,

1. Aṭṭhasālinī III 246.
2. Aṭṭhasālinī III 247. See also above, p. 77.
3. Aṭṭhasālinī III 248, 295.
4. Abhidharmakośa II 25 and Bhāṣya, Vṛtti on Triṁśikā 11, p. 27
5. Aṭṭhasālinī III 295.
6. According to Sthiramati, loc. cit p. 27, out of the *praśrabdhi* there results the lightness with which one goes about one's work.

though not very flatteringly, 'opinionated asses'. It is this functional adaptableness that overcomes opinionatedness and the conceit resulting out of it (*diṭṭhimāna*).[1]

Absence of strain, lightness, and adaptability are the readiness to operate (*kammaññatā*), by which one applies oneself to one's work and persists tranquilly in it, just as the purity of gold remains the same regardless of the forms it adopts when moulded into ornaments. Seen from another angle, this readiness to work is vigor (*pāguññatā*) which overcomes any weakness and the dangers that lurk in weakness, the most dangerous being lack of confidence (*assaddhiya*). In its vigor this functional readiness to work follows its own law of 'straightness' (*ujukatā*). It overcomes all kinds of crookedness and in particular is the opponent of deceit and fraud (*māyāsāṭheyya*).[2]

Since a healthy attitude is the irremissible condition for meditative processes and since the whole systematic exposition of the functions that operate within a healthy attitude serves to facilitate the approach to and practice of meditation, certain factors are mentioned again according to the manner of their helpfulness and their combined activity. Particularly helpful are inspection (*sati*, Skt. *smṛti*) and an awareness (*sampajaññā*, Skt. *samprajanya*) which is viewed from its aspects of usefulness, expediency, scope, and non-delusiveness,[3] but essentially it is a form of analytical appreciative understanding.

So also tranquillity (*samatha*) and insight (*vipassanā*) are not different from the peace that settles over us when in meditation all restlessness and distress is overcome and our eyes are opened to the fact that everything we experience through our senses is transitory and hence no basis for lasting happiness, but they are mentioned here because it is a peculiar feature that tranquillity and insight come as pairs (*yuganaddha*).[4] Unfortunately our author does not explain the meaning of pairness, which Asaṅga[5] understands in the sense that the one leads to the other, unless both are present at once. It is in the Tantra aspect of Buddhism, which is based entirely on meditation, that

1. Aṭṭhasālinī III 248.
2. Aṭṭhasālinī III 249. Abhidharmasamuccaya, p. 8.
3. Aṭṭhasālinī III 250.
4. ibid.
5. Abhidharmasamuccaya, p. 75.

'pairness' was interpreted, not as co-existence but as the ineffable experience of that in which tranquillity and insight were singularly blended.[1]

Also intimately connected are energy and absorption, the one taking a firm hold of all co-nascent events (*paggāha*), the other preventing dissipation and distractedness (*avikkhepa*).[2]

It is, of course, impossible to make a complete list of all mental states or events; moreover, such an attempt as made in the Abhidharma, which listed certain occurrences in their intensity as separate items, has proved to be disastrous, inasmuch as it centred attention to the numerical definition and became oblivious to the spirit which laid down this analysis of mind and its functions as a guide within the larger scope of an attitude conducive to enlightenment. Even the addition of 'whatever other events there may be that arise in interdependence'[3] could not mitigate this defect, because they were limited to nine occurrences, viz., will (*chando*), decision (*adhimokkha*), attention (*manasikāra*), middle course (*tatramajjhattatā*), compassion (*karuṇā*), joy participating in the good whatever and wherever it may be (*muditā*), abstaining from misdemeanour in bodily acts (*kāya-duccaritavirati*), abstaining from misdemeanor in speech (*vācīduccaritavirati*), and abstaining from a wrong mode of life (*micchājīvavirati*).[4] Of these the four first occurrences are present in a single instant, the middle course implying the balancedness of these occurrences, all other occurrences may happen at different times of the psychic stream and on different levels.[5]

However, it would be a mistake to overlook in the presence of these obvious defects, the merits that this analysis offers. Its outstanding merit is that a man's mind is observed from a dynamic, rather than a static angle. It emphasizes the functions rather than the mere facts of mental phenomena and interprets mental phenomena with reference to the part they play

1. See for instance Rnal. hbyor. bzhii. bśad. pa. don. dam. mdzub. tshugs, fol. 5a, and Pañcakrama, chapter VI.
2. Aṭṭhasālinī III 250.
3. Dhammasaṅgani S·1; Aṭṭhasālinī III 251.
4. Aṭṭhasālinī III 252; Visuddhimagga XVI 150-155.
5. Aṭṭhasālinī III 253.

in the life of the individual. In this way the analysis starts from the living individual, from facts which can be observed by anybody without having recourse to any theory proposed *a priori* and verified only indirectly and *a posteriori*, and so liberates mind from any kind of absolutism. Though it seems that a teleological explanation of the functions found by analysis is paramount, this analysis makes it, by its very wording, quite clear that the conception of purpose is applicable within reality, not to reality as a whole. The same holds valid for any mechanistic explanation. This realization, it is true, is implicit in the Abhidharma literature. It has been made explicit by the Madhyamikas who did not acknowledge the Abhidharma canon.

It is only natural that in such a complex phenomenon as the human mind, with varying intensity, the various functions assume specific modifications[1] which it is permissible to treat as particular phenomena, though it is not permissible to conclude that such particulars represent absolute entities and evolve out of it a metaphysical system. Yet in no way are we justified in blaming the Buddhists for this, since the same has happened in Western philosophies and continues to lie at the bottom of many modern philosophies.

In conclusion it may be pointed out that the classification of healthy attitudes—there are eight in all—is made from three different points of view. Ranking foremost is the mood of an attitude, whether it is permeated by joyfulness (*somanassasahagata*) or by indifference (*upekkhāsahagata*), because no attitude is ever without a certain feeling tone, and joyfulness as well as indifference, which is not carelessness, are signs of a healthy outlook of life. The second aspect is whether an attitude contains a cognition (*ñāṇa*,. Skt. *jñāna*) or not[2] The third is whether a healthy attitude has come about by its own very healthy nature without any efforts on the part of him who has a healthy attitude (*asaṅkhārena*) or whether a healthy

1. Aṭṭhasālinī III 256-264.

2. Aṭṭhasālinī III 310. *prajñā* is explained by *paricchindana*. This reminds us of Dharmottara's statement in Nyāyabinduṭīkā 69 seq., that when something is cognized (*paricchidyate*) it is contrasted (*vyavacchidyate*) with its counterpart. While *prajñā* is a function, discriminating and selecting, *jñāna* is the ineffable, positivistic mystic knowledge by experience.

attitude has been set up by an effort of the individual, be this of his own account or by being admonitioned by others (*sasaṅkhārena*)[1] This latter aspect contains an element which has been of paramount importance in Mahāyāna Buddhism, viz., the formation of an attitude which is not merely healthy but is directed toward enlightenment (*bodhicittotpāda*). As Asaṅga informs us, such a formation is due to various reasons. It may be due to the inherent healthiness, to all that is good and wholesome, which would correspond to the 'effortless' attitude (*asaṅkhārena*) mentioned in the Pāli Abhidhamma; but it may also be due to the admonition of friends, which would correspond to the 'prompted' attitude (*sasaṅkhārena*).[2] This shows that Mahāyāna Buddhism continued the practical side of the Buddhist teaching, where a healthy attitude is of utmost importance.

Unhealthy Attitudes

The utter realism and positivism which is at the basis of Buddhist philosophy and psychology, becomes again evident in the recognition of the fact that there are not only healthy attitudes but also a variety of unhealthy (*akusala*) attitudes. Unlike healthy attitudes which are rooted in detached love and knowledge, unhealthy attitudes are incompatible with spiritual development, because their structural pattern is infected by various effective instabilities such as cupidity (*lobha*), antipathy (*dveṣa* Pāli *dosa*), and delusion-bewilderment (*moha*). Due to this diseasedness, as we might say, unhealthy attitudes are tied to the world of sensuous relatedness (*kāmāvacara*) where likes and dislikes and unwarranted assumptions occupy the arena most of the time, and therefore also they do not admit of any spiritual levels (*bhūmi*) which can be realized by detachment and not by attachment, by love and not by cupidity, by knowledge and not by ignorance.[3] A further characteristic of unhealthy attitudes is their association with opinionatedness (*diṭṭhigata*) on the one hand, and with conceitedness (*māna*)

1. Aṭṭhasālinī III 309. The same division, but with different terms, is found in Abhidharmaras, II 79.
2. Mahāyāna-sūtrālaṅkāra IV 7 and commentary.
3. Aṭṭhasālinī III 540.

on the other. Finally, while healthy attitudes have either a happy or indifferent mood, unhealthy attitudes have a sullen mood in addition.

Opinionatedness, as well as conceitedness, exclude any cognition (*ñāṇa*) in the sense that things, whether they be natural objects or personal selves, are not seen in their true nature. Whatever a person cognizes or knows he does so in the framework of pre-established ideas (*diṭṭhigata*). The explanation of the second term—*gata* in this technical term *diṭṭhigata* is rather illuminating, because it shows the limitations of all preconceived ideas and the dogmatism they entail. The first explanation is a literal one, namely, "that which has turned into (something)". In modern terminology this means that the immediate in awareness is used merely as the springboard for arriving at postulationally prescribed beliefs about three dimensional external objects or about internal principles called variously a soul or a self. In other words, all factual information is fitted into theories and assumptions and evaluated from this standpoint rather than its own. It follows that, from the Buddhist point of view, a common-sense man, a scientist, a philosophical or a religious man of the modern world would have to be considered as suffering from an unhealthy attitude because he does not use the immediate in his awareness and experience as something good in itself, but only as a means to aggravate an already unhealthy inclination which cuts off life from its riches and leads to emotional and spiritual starvation. Since such a procedure is doomed to failure and frustration and at the very beginning comes to a dead end the second interpretation of *gata* follows directly from it, viz., that it is 'unwalkable' in the sense of not being conducive to enlightenment and to the appreciation of virtues and merits.[1] Opinionatedness, the insistence on common-sense belief and confessional credulity, is a dangerous jungle, a barren desert killing the last vestige of life, a misrepresentation and falsification of facts. It is full of inconsistencies and oscillates mainly between such absurdities as eternalism and nihilism. It is a fetter which not only binds men but to which men cling most stubbornly.

1. Aṭṭhasālinī III 540.

In short, opinionatedness is the only and true perversion.[1]

Due to the fact that things are not seen in their proper perspective and their real nature, unhealthy attitudes are conspicuous by the absence of self-respect and decorum.[2] This absence must not be understood as a mere vacuum but as forces which have disastrous effects. For absence of self-respect leads to self-degradation which does not know of any limits and the absence of decorum is the ruthless disregard of others. Thus instead of preserving the world and society these forces of self-degradation and disregard destroy it (*lokanāsaka*),[3] because morality based on these forces and ultimately on ignorance, only serves as a cloak for almost everything : religious superstitions and their concomitant intolerance, national customs, psychological inhibitions, legal systems, personal dislikes, and political machinations.

Whether an attitude be grounded in cupidity or antipathy or delusion—cupidity and antipathy are mutually excluding, but go together with delusion—it has certain characteristic traits. Cupidity (*lobha*) makes the individual chase after the sensuous and sensual objects which he believes will satisfy his craving, but to the same extent that he obtains the desired objects, his craving also increases so that he is driven relentlessly from one object to the other, to let it go almost the same moment he has grasped it. His attachment to the objects of worldliness are compared with fresh meat put into a heated vessel, a sepa-

1. Aṭṭhasālinī III 552. *parāmarśa* which is explained as 'to set aside the true nature of things (*dhammasabhāva*) and to conceive of them as being eternal and so on in a way contrary to their nature (*parato āmāsati*)' consists of *dṛṣṭiparāmarśa* and *śīlavrataparāmarśa*. The former is according to the Abhidharmasamuccaya, p. 7, the view which considers the five psychosomatic constituents (*pañcopādānaskandha*) as having a most excellent nature (*paramatas*), the latter is the view which considers the same five constituents as being purity and liberation (*śuddhitas, muktitas*) on account of religo-superstitious observances.

According to Abhidharmakośa II 29 and Bhāṣya an unhealthy attitude is connected with wrong views (*mithyādṛṣṭi*, the denial of the relation between cause and effect), or with the two kinds of perversion, *dṛṣṭiparāmarśa* and *śīlavrataparāmarśa*. But an attitude which considers the five constituents as a Self (*satkāyadṛṣṭi*) or considers them from the viewpoint of eternalism or nihilism is *antagrāhadṛṣṭi*) is not unhealthy, though it is not very healthy.

2. Aṭṭhasālinī III 543. Abhidharmakośa II 26 cd.

3. Aṭṭhasālinī III 550

ration of the two not being possible, or since there is no check on his craving, no sense of renunciation, attachment spreads like an oil-ointment, all over the body. Craving, like a stream that increases continuously with its progress and turbulently rushes down to the ocean, carries the individual along with it into the abyss of low existences (*apāya*).[1]

In its overt form such an attitude is marked by covetousness and possessiveness (*abhijjhā*), the obsession to acquire that which others have and to invent all kinds of strategems to put this mania into practice.[2]

Where cupidity is at the basis of an attitude, two aspects become most prominent. The first as we have seen, is the association with opinionatedness in all its varied forms and where a person has certain 'strong views' about certain things and feels either happy in displaying them or gives vent to his opinions with cool indifference. The other is the association with conceitedness (*māna*), where a person is drunk with his own importance and in his exultation just 'shows off' (*ketukamyatā*).[3]

As the case may be, such unhealthy attitudes may be aggravated by indolence, the habitual love of ease and a settled dislike of activity, and by sluggishness (*thīnamiddha*), both of which are related to inattendance.[4]

1. Aṭṭhasālinī III 544.
2. ibid. III 545.
3. ibid. III 558. The author of the Aṭṭhasālinī derives the word *māna* from the root *mad* 'to get intoxicated, and gives as its characteristic *unnati* 'arrogance'. The Abhidharmakośa II 33b derives it from the root *mā* 'to measure' one's superiority over others by one's actual qualities or by those one imagines to have, and distinguishes *māna* from *mada* 'intoxication'. See also Vyākhyā ad Abhidh.-kośa II 33. The same distinction is found in Abhidharmasamuccaya, pp. 7, 9. Sthiramati's Vṛtti, pp. 28 sq., discussing the differences between *māna, atimāna, asmimāna, abhimāna, ūnamāna, mithyāmāna* p. 31. *mada*. Seven types of māna are also mentioned in Abhidharmasamuccaya, p. 45, Abhidharmakośa V, 10 and Bhāṣya.
4. Aṭṭhasālinī III 557. *thīna*, Skt. *styāna*, is according to the Aṭṭhasālinī the inability to make efforts, the expulsion of energy, a collapse. *middha* is the inability to operate, drowsiness.

According to the Abhidharmasamuccaya, p. 9 *styāna* is the inability to operate. The same definition in Sthiramati's Vṛtti, p. 31. Both these sources declare *styāna* to belong to delusion (*mohāṁśika*). The explanation of this term in Abhidharmakośa II 26 and the Bhāṣya on it, is similar to the one given by Asaṅga and Sthiramati.

When unhealthy attitudes are grounded in antipathy (*dosa*), the general mood is one of sullenness (*domanassa*) and one is easily shocked at everything, because one sees everywhere something offensive, distasteful, and contrary to one's principles (which after all are not much worth) (*paṭigha*); therefore one constantly selects the unpleasant side of life[1]. In their overt forms such attitudes are marked by hatred and malevolence. A person whose attitude is grounded in antipathy poisons the whole atmosphere with his maliciousness and at the same time undermines his own position. Wherever and whenever he finds a chance he rouses enmity.[2] This malevolence also finds its expression in the venomous remarks he is apt to make at any moment. His words lack courtesy and smoothness, and his speech is abrupt, for "at the moment of anger there is no coherent speech".[3] Worst of all such a person is unable to find contentedness.[4]

Just like unhealthy attitudes rooted in cupidity, unhealthy attitudes grounded in antipathy may be accompanied by indolence and sluggishness, and in addition may be qualified by envy (*īrṣyā*, Pāli *issā*), niggardliness (*mātsarya*, Pāli *macchariya*), and by regret (*kaukṛtya*, Pāli *kukkucca*). Envy means to regard another with varying degrees of jealousy and hatred, because the other possesses something we covet or feel should have come to ourselves. It is a fetter which binds a man to another person's possessions in a way that he has to turn his face away from it (*vimukhabhāva*).[5] Niggardliness means to conceal that which one has got or is to get. It is the inability

middha is according to Abhidharmasamuccaya, p. 10 and Sthiramati's Vṛtti, p. 32, a self-confinement of mind on a narrow point. Sthiramati then adds that *middha* induces a person to let go the chance of doing something. It also belongs to delusion. See also Abhidharmakośa II 30; V 47; VII 11.

1. Aṭṭhasālinī III 562. Abhidharmasamuccaya, p. 7. Sthiramati's Vṛtti, p. 28 very clearly brings out the idea of only selecting the unpleasant side of life (*asparśavihāra*).

2. Aṭṭhasālinī III 562.

3. ibid. III 564. The author brings a pun on *asuropita* 'unpolished, incoherent' in the spelling *assuropa* 'causing others to weep'.

4. ibid.

5. ibid. III 563. According to Abhidharmasamuccaya, p. 8, and Sthiramati's Vṛtti, p. 30, envy is part of antipathy (*dveṣa*) and produces sullenness and the peculiar feature of selecting the unpleasant.

to bear the thought of sharing with others, and it means to be so closefisted that one gives only grudgingly the smallest amount possible. It is a disfigurement of one's whole mental build-up.[1] Regret is the futile ruminating over past deeds, over something done or left undone. It is a state of slavery,[2] because it does not make man strong to act in a way he should act.

Unhealthy attitudes which are rooted in antipathy, like those grounded in cupidity, are either something natural in the sense that they operate without having been prompted, or they have been prompted by taking a person having an unhealthy attitude as an example for one's example or by being instigated to adopt such unhealthy attitudes.[3]

A third group of unhealthy attitudes are those rooted in delusion-bewilderment (*moha*). They are marked either by scepticism (*vicikitsā* Pāli *vicikicchā*) or by frivolity (*auddhatya*, Pāli *uddhacca*).[4] Scepticism, in the Buddhist sense, is not so much the attitude of a doubter who suspends judgment because he insists on the limitations of human reason, but of a person who wearies himself out (*kilamati*) by ruminating and cogitating about the nature of things without ever penetrating it. A person who is dominated by scepticism feels a doubt with respect to everything and is unable to reach a decision as to where the truth lies. Mind is weak and feeble in the sense that it cannot stay with one subject and through absorption penetrate into its very nature and so is torn between a multitude of topics. Yet this fluctuating does not prevent a hardened and obstinate attitude which is closed to every tenderness and pliability.[5]

1. ibid. III 563. According to Abhidharmasamuccya, p. 8 and Sthiramati's Vṛtti, p. 30 niggardliness is part of cupidity (*rāgāṁśika*). Since *dveṣa* and *rāga* (*lobha*) are mutually exclusive, as we are told by the Pāli sourc-es, niggardliness ought to belong to an unhealthy attitude rooted in cupidity.

2. ibid. III 563. According to Abhidharmasamuccaya, p. 10 regret is part of delusion and produces instability of mind. The same definition in Sthiramati's Vṛtti, p. 32. See also Abhidharmakośa II 28 and Bhāṣya, as well as Yaśomitra's Vyākhyā.

3. Aṭṭhasālinī III 565; 556.

4. ibid. III 566-568.

5. ibid. III 566-567. According to Abhidharmasamuccaya, p. 7, scepticism is doubt and divergence (*vimati*) from the Truths of Buddhism. Sthiramati in his Vṛtti, p. 29 adds doubt as to the relation between Karman and its effects and the doctrine of probability and improbability.

Another aspect of an unhealthy attitude rooted in delusion-bewilderment is frivolity. It does not allow the mind to come to rest, though it does not divide it against itself between a variety of topics. It is like a carriage over which one has lost control and which therefore lands in a ditch, or it is like cattle going astray and staying where they happen to be. Hence frivolity is engrossed with one topic and not with many at the same time.[1]

All unhealthy attitudes are marked by an absence of confidence, inspection, analytical appreciative understanding, and the ease, straightforwardness, and adaptability of all psychic functions.[2] "Where there is no confidence there is no lucidity of mind. But, it may be argued, do not those who have certain views trust their teachers. Certainly, they do so, but what they do has nothing to do with confidence, it is just taking their words at their face value. Actually it is non-investigation, a certain view one holds. Also where there is no confidence there is no inspection. But, it may be asked, do not those who have certain views remember something they have done. Certainly they do so, but this has nothing to do with inspection; it is just the course of an unhealthy mind which looks like this function. It may be asked why this function is called wrong inspection in the Sūtras. It is pointed out in order to make the number of wrong steps agree with the number of the right steps in the Eightfold Path, although everything unhealthy is devoid of inspection and opposed to inspection.[3] Actually wrong inspection does not exist.[4] Also in a dark and immature mind there is no analytical appreciative understanding. But it may be asked, do not those who hold certain views make use of discrimination in deluding others. Certainly they use discrimination. But this discrimination is not an analytical

1. Aṭṭhasālinī III 568. For the definition of *auddhatya* see Abhidharmakośavyākhyā ad II 26; Abhidharmasamuccaya, p. 9; Sthiramati's Vṛtti, p. 31.

2. ibid, III 546.

3. Inspection is a factor by which we try to learn more about the nature of the object we are studying. But when we hold certain views we automatically refuse to learn.

4. This is an interesting remark. The Vaibhāṣikas and Yogācāras considered 'wrong inspection' (muṣitasmṛti) as an existent entity. See Bhāṣya ad Abhidharmakośa II 26. Abhidharmasamuccaya, p. 9.

appreciative understanding (which produces knowledge), it is deceit (*māyā*). In reality it is craving. And so this (unhealthy) attitude is care-worn, heavy, oppressed, hardened, obdurate, unable to operate with ease, morbid, biased and crooked. Therefore it does not know of relaxation and so on".[1]

Conclusion

Due to its practical nature which points out a way that will lead man to his goal and also points out that which is not conducive to this, Buddhism has always been concerned with the immediately present and the immediately given : the disposition of the individual or, as I prefer to render the technical terms *citta*, the attitude of a person of a more or less stable set of opinion, interest, and purpose, involving expectancy of certain kinds of experience and readiness with an appropriate response. However, the highly technical language has often obscured this practical nature of Buddhism and has led scholars and philosophers to believe that Buddhism is as highly speculative as are the Western philosophical systems. Yet actually there is nothing in the teaching of Buddhism which our immediate experience does not contain. This and the absence of dogmas which induce the belief that we have knowledge where actually we have ignorance, certainly account for the appeal Buddhism has to the modern Western mind.

The discussion of the various attitudes which we can observe any time, is certainly not scientific in the sense that it provides the *a posteriori*, indirect test for the postulated *a priori* theory. But there can be no doubt that it is a descriptive type of science, the science of the human mind. Put more precisely, it is true phenomenology, the systematic investigation of our experiences as experiences, and it has succeeded in giving a true and realistic picture of our emotions and the role they play even in our cognitive processes, and it also has succeeded in setting up a true and realistic morality. A healthy attitude is one which broadens our outlook, while an unhealthy attitude makes us narrow, bigoted, and cuts us off from wider participation. But healthiness and unhealthiness are evaluative

1. Aṭṭhasālinī III 546.

judgments which form an essential aspect of all cognitions, and not functions which are the activity of the psychic structure or, since it is doubtful to speak of a psychic structure as contrasted with a physical structure, the activity of a living organism. This also the Buddhists have recognized from the very beginning and hence distinguished between merely functional processes and qualitatively differentiated processes. About these differentiations all schools of Buddhism agreed, but they differed from each other in what appears to us as the weak point, viz., the numerical classification of various attitudes and the numerical limitation of functions. Thus, for instance, the Theravādins recognized fifty-two to fifty-six functions, the Sarvāstivādins forty-six, and the Yogācāras fifty-one. Though there is a close resemblance between those which are considered to be functions of mind, the grouping of them has been done by the various schools from various points of view.[1]

1. See the tables at the end of the book.

MEDITATION

(*dhyāna*)

WORLDLINESS AND GESTALTUNG

The world of things and events which stimulates us sensuously and sensually and to which we react with our impulses, our apprehensions, with all that marks sentient life, begins and ends with our attitude—an emotional and intellectual pattern which governs all individual life.[1] According to its mode of being emotionally and intellectually toned an attitude is either healthy or unhealthy. But whether healthy or unhealthy, our attitude in this world of sensuous and sensual relatedness is something given; we find ourselves in the world with a certain disposition towards it, and only an insignificant part of its overt manifestation can be said to owe its presence to the intentions of the individual. Its roots lie before the beginning of an individual and lose themselves in the dim nebulosity of beginningless time.[2] Another characteristic of healthy and unhealthy attitudes is the fact that they do not give us a true and vivid picture of reality to which they profess to be related, though in a healthy attitude this fact is less apparent than in an unhealthy attitude. There is no denial of the fact that in either case the vivid experience which is the essence of that general human response called life, has been projected and translated into a system of entities and, in having become a 'thing' has lost its symbolic expressiveness. In worldly attitudes we are concerned with the termination of

1. See for instance the famous verse in Saṁyuttanikāya I 39; *cittena nīyati loko cittena parikissati.*

cittassa ekadhammassa sabbe va vasam anvagū ti

"The world is conducted by our attitude, the world is harassed by our attitude. Everything comes under the control of this unique power."

Further references p. 15, n. 2.

2. In the final analysis our present attitude has been brought about by Karman.

the symbolific activity of mind rather than with the symbol-forming process itself. Particularly where those attitudes are concerned which are considered to be unhealthy, the loss of vivid appreciation of all that is, the disregard of meaning which, if it has any life and health, must deepen at every turn, is most conspicuous. Utilitarian considerations are the predominant feature of such attitudes. To give only a few examples, taken at random from what is always before our eyes. We love things and covet them because they are a source of income and in considering them so, we turn them into counters for understanding and computing the course of prices in the market-place. Or, we enter into an armament race, at the same time, hypocritically, convening disarmament conferences, because, while projecting our delusion of persecution which in the language of politics means to think in terms of national security, towards others we want to be ready to be the first to strike the fatal blow, and we are not ashamed of indulging in hostile and subversive activities whose foundation in hatred is only too obvious. Under the power of delusion we make such behavior acceptable by calling it a duty we owe to ourselves or to our country, which is but another way of socializing the delusion of grandeur and of spreading the disease of righteousness. Thus there is a close connection between delusion and hatred and delusion and cupidity. But there is still another kind of unhealthy attitude in which delusion alone holds its undisputed sway—it is the attitude of the slogan-raiser who believes in all earnestness that any slogan—the sillier, the better—is the cure for all the evils in the world. Against this multiplicity of unhealthy attitudes, healthy attitudes almost fade into insignificance. Maybe the numerical difference between healthy and unhealthy attitudes, asserted in the Pāli Abhidhamma, has a deeper significance than just being a mere classification and listing of eight healthy and twelve unhealthy attitudes.

It remains a fact that unhealthy attitudes cannot be developed in any way; they move in a vicious circle, for cupidity breeds cupidity, hatred rouses and intensifies hatred, and deludedness unleashes a host of manias. But, although unhealthy attitudes are predominant and constitute worldliness in the narrower sense of the world, this does not mean that there is no way out of this calamity. An attitude is nothing rigid and permanent, at best it is persistent for some time, and while at one moment an unhealthy attitude may prevail at another moment a healthy one may operate. Man is too complex in his nature to restrict him to something or other. All that we can say is that the interplay between healthy and unhealthy attitudes may depend on the distribution of energy within the organized system called man, but certainly not through the presence of some supernatural entity, "soul" or "entelechy" or "mind-stuff".

While cupidity, antipathy, and delusion have never been constructive cultural elements, but have served only to destroy that which they themselves had erected and in this cataclysm, to put an end to all that is humane, cultural values have been produced by those who had a healthy attitude, in whom there was no cupidity, no antipathy, no deludedness, who realized that the world, at best, just is and in this acceptance possessed something which continued to live in them and which did not allow itself to be turned into a mere counter. The bearers of culture are the philosophers, artists and musicians. It is wrong to consider art as unintellectual and philosophy as unartistic and, under a misconception of what reason, intellect and so on has to be, to deny the value of the one or the other. The essential point is whether there is insight and direct knowledge (*ñāṇa*) or mere opinion (*diṭṭhi*), whether there is significant form and expressiveness or purposeful expression.[1]

To find the way back from a world of 'things' to a world of pure Gestalten, to expressive forms (*rūpa*).[2] Out of which

1. That intellectualism or rationalism is not hampered by an appreciativeness of art and vice versa, has also been insisted upon by Susanne K. Langer, Philosophy in a new key, p. 82.

2. There are three main interpretations of *rūpa* in Buddhist texts. The oldest one is found in Saṁyuttanikāya III 86 : *ruppatī ti kho bhikkhave tasmā rūpam iti vuccati* "it breaks down, oh Bhikṣus, therefore it is called *rūpa*". This definition emphasizes fragility in the sense of transformation and deterioration, as is pointed out in the Bhāṣya ad Abhidh.-kośa II 13. In this way *rūpa* might be said to be a term for grouping events which commonsense attributes to the physical world. The second explanation derives *rūpa* from *rūpaṇa* in the sense of *pratighāta* 'resistance', 'not allowing something else to occupy a certain space'. This is the commonsense view about a

we construe a world of things and events practically and objectively arranged, but in which we also find liberation from the oppressiveness of externally and internally fixed relations, has constituted a very special, if not the central, problem in Buddhist teachings. The solution of the problem is based on the recognition of certain fundamental human needs. Actually, the world of pure Gestalten is the starting point of all intellectual activity and it is more general than directive thinking and fancying, although this fact is readily overlooked in a world of 'things' where all life has been flattened out in discursiveness. But since life does not admit of any stoppage, Gestaltung is of the utmost importance as the formulative non-discursive understanding of sentient life.

That which leads to the world of Gestalten and to the experience of Gestaltung is called *cetanā* and all that is connected with a *cetanā*.[1] As we have seen[2] *cetanā* is essentially a drive, an impulse motivated by an inherent need rather than by a prospect of acquiring some useful tool for perpetrating some utilitarian design. At the same time this need is also the way or the seeking of the situation which will satisfy the need or *per contra*, the striving to avoid the situation which blocks satisfaction.[3] But there is a qualitative difference between *cetanā* on the level of sensuous and sensual relatedness and *cetanā* on the level of meditative practices. While we are born into the world of sensuous and sensual relatedness, to which we adjust and adapt ourselves with very little of what is in us,

material object.—The third explanation, in Madhyamakavṛtti, p. 456, understands *rūpaṇa* in the sense of indicativeness. None of these definitions, with the possible exception of the second one, guarantees the translation by 'matter'. Our merest sense-experience is a process of Gestaltung or formulation. The translation of *rūpa* by Gestalt, which I offer here, avoids the dualism of mind and matter, which does not exist in experience, and experience is the keynote of Buddhism.

1. Aṭṭhasālinī III 326.

2. pp. 43 sq. Here again the absurdity of the translation of *cetanā* by 'volition' becomes apparent. It is impossible to 'will' meditation. Unless a person feels the need for meditation he is unable to start with it.

3. Aṭṭhasālinī III 326 : '*maggo ti upāyo. vacanattho pan' ettha—tam upapattim maggati gavesati janeti nipphadetī ti maggo* "Way" has the meaning of 'means'. The literal meaning is : "he makes a way for this origination, seeks it, produces it, expands it."

with items which report or refer or mostly substitute direct experience, our needs are vegetative, to put it bluntly, and there is very little of the 'human' in us. But when we make an effort of some kind to find access to the world of Gestalten, to regain a direct experience, then we act in a way in which no other animal would act, because symbolific activity is a primary need of man. Therefore the section on meditation does not begin with an enumeration and classification of mental functions and processes, but with the words that 'he, the individual, seeks a way to the attainment of Gestaltung'.[1]

The Differences in Temperament

The essentially phenomenological approach to problems of psychology and of spiritual growth, which characterizes the whole of Buddhism throughout its historical development, is again evident in and helpful in the methodical elaboration and presentation of all that is necessary to and guarantees the attainment of Gestaltung (*rūpūpapatti*). The method itself is termed *dhyāna* (Pāli *jhāna*) and may be said to be a process of concentrated meditation and ensuing absorption.[2] This process starts from various objects and topics, all of them subsumed under the generic term *kammaṭṭhāna*, which may be rendered in English as 'a starting point for relevant processes'.[3] However, the selection of an object or a topic from which to start, depends upon the temperament of the individual. This is important to note because only on this basis does Buddhist meditation become intelligible and practicable. Moreover, it is only after a prolonged study of the aspirant by a competent teacher that an object or topic suited to the aspirant's tempera-

1. Aṭṭhasālinī III 326. Dhammasaṅgaṇi §160.

2. *dhyāna* is 'derived from the root *upanidhyai* 'to know directly and correctly' in Abhidharmakośa VIII 1. (Bhāṣya), 141c add Vyākhyā; Aṭṭhasālinī III 337, where the object of knowledge is divided into the object proper (*ārammaṇa*) and the intrinsic character (*lakkhaṇa*), Buddhaghosa in his Visuddhimagga IV 119 also gives the derivation from *upanidhyai*, but adds a popular etymology 'burning away obstacles' (*paccanīkajhāpana*). Similarly Aṭṭhasālinī III 337.

3. Visuddhimagga III 59. In III 60, 104-105 forty such starting points are mentioned, while Aṭṭhasālinī III 339 acknowledges only thirty-eight.

ment will be given to him. This has one other consequence. Meditation in the Buddhist sense is not some sort of panacea which anybody can make use of indiscriminately and without harm.

There are six basic temperaments, three of which emphasize the emotional aspect and three the intellectual aspect of man's nature. The former three find their characteristic expression in cupidity or possessiveness (*rāgacarita*), antipathy (*dosacarita*), and deludedness or a general state of bewilderment (*mohacarita*). The latter three are characterized by confidence (*saddhācarita*), critical intellectual acumen (*buddhicarita*), and the tendency to attend to all and everything (*vitakkacarita*), in plain words: woolgathering.[1] Confidence, as we have seen,[2] is pellucidity of mind, but it has also a strong religious connotation. However, we must guard ourselves against understanding Buddhist religiosity as something like a sectarian sentiment which, in Buddhist thought, would just fall under ignorance and opinionatedness, having nothing to do with or in common with knowledge and pellucidity of mind. All these basic temperaments can enter various combinations[3] and there is also a certain intimate relation between the emotional and intellectual aspects, which Buddhaghosa has described in the following way[4] :

"Since with a person in whom possessiveness prevails, confidence is strong when he turns to the good and wholesome, a person in whom confidence prevails is similar to a person in whom possessiveness dominates because of the affinity that exists between possessiveness and confidence. For, on the unwholesome side possessiveness is attachment and non-aversion, while confidence is this on the side of the good and wholesome, and just as possessiveness seeks for objects of sensuous and sensual satisfaction confidence searches for virtues to be found in ethics and so on, and just as possessiveness does not let go of evil, so confidence does not abandon good.

1. Visuddhimagga III 74.
2. pp. 61 sq.
3. Visuddhimagga III 74.
4. Visuddhimagga III 75-77.

"Since with a person in whom antipathy prevails, discrimination is strong when he turns to the good and wholesome, a person in whom discriminative intellectual acumen prevails is similar to a person in whom antipathy dominates because of the affinity that exists between antipathy and intellectual acumen. For, on the side of the unwholesome, antipathy has nothing of fondness or desire for an object, while discrimination operates in the same way on the side of the wholesome, and just as antipathy seeks for non-existent faults, so discrimination finds out the existing faults, and just as antipathy is manifest in misanthropy, so is discrimination in a rejection of motivations.

"Since in a person in whom bewilderment and delusions prevail, as a rule, destructive ideas crop up when he attempts to institute the good and wholesome that has not yet become manifest, a person who is a scatterbrain is similar to a person in whom bewilderment and delusions work because of the affinity that exists between the tendency to attend to all and everything and bewilderment. For just as bewilderment is something unfirm owing to its confusedness so also the tendency to attend to all and everything is something unfirm owing to its going here and there and just as delusion is something shaky because of its inability to penetrate to the real, so also the tendency to attend to all and everything is something unstable because of the easiness with which it produces ideas".[1]

Although in this description of the various temperaments a certain tendency to deny the value of the emotional aspects as against the intellectual ones is apparent, the intimate connexion between religiosity (*saddhā*) and possessiveness (*rāga*)—actually *rāga* is a term which oscillates between the ideas we associate with love, passion, desire, cupidity, lust, possessiveness and so on—reveals a very important feature. Religiosity is intimately connected with a consciousness of value, with a clear perception of merits (hence *saddhā* is pellucidity of mind), and opens our eyes to a 'Beyond' and 'More' filled with holiness which—and this is the decisive point—only love and the capacity to love is able to realize. But where love is absent nothing becomes possible. For absence of love is the rule of cupidity

1. In III 87-96 follows a long discussion on how to ascertain the respective temperaments.

and possessiveness, and this by its very nature excludes any pellucidity of mind.[1] However, it will be readily admitted that it is very difficult to decide where love ends and where cupidity begins, and this difficulty entails two errors which go hand in hand : (i) the confusion of love with cupidity and vice versa, and (ii) the rejection of everything that has the slightest resemblance to the emotion of love in order to adopt an almost incurable negative attitude toward life. Not only has this happened in earlier times, it still continues to happen. It is, therefore, more than plausible that the Tantric element in Buddhism, which goes back to a very early period of Buddhism and which has been a sore puzzle to scholars, was a healthy reaction against the negative attitude of being afraid of love, because this fear in the long run would have sterilized and blocked man's spiritual growth and development. Nāropa quite explicitly states that "Evil springs from the loss of love, because all compassionate tenderness has disappeared",[2] and Saraha advises us :

> "Paint all the three levels of the world
> In the unique color of Great Love".[3]

1. As has been pointed out in Aṭṭhasālinī III 546, unhealthy attitudes do not admit of saddhā, which is a purely healthy function.

2. Sekoddeśaṭikā, p. 66. The author further declares that *karuṇā*, compassion, sympathetic tenderness, has as its character the increase of love. The positive aspect of love, as the unique means of liberating beings from misery, has also been pointed out by Anaṅgavajra in his Prajñopāyaviniś-cayasiddhi I 15 :

"Because it makes beings cross the ocean of all misery and all that stems from misery,
Compassionate tenderness is called Love".

Love (*rāga*) is the unique means and the single moment in which the course of the world is decided. The moment love is born, the sense of self may be increased and possessiveness may assert itself whereby new fetters are forged, but the sense of self may also completely disappear and in this disappearance of all selfish and possessive thoughts freedom from all that narrows man and makes him unhappy and poor, is won. As is stated in the Cittaviśuddhiprakaraṇa 35.

"One becomes tainted by love thoughts, one becomes free through loving".

3. Dohākoṣa 28. In verse 29 the author refers to the fact that in true love we are lifted out of any dualism which we are accustomed to read into all and everything. He says :

"There is neither beginning nor middle nor end,
There is neither Saṁsāra nor Nirvāṇa;
In this supreme great bliss
There is neither an I nor a Thou".

As a natural consequence, the Tantrics advocating love and practising love were, and still are, considered as people of appalling wickedness.[1]

Similarly the critical intellect very often appears as 'cool', because its critique which lays bare any defect that may be found in the knowable, naturally destroys any attachment and warm feeling we may have for a given thing. But to point out defects is in itself nothing negative. On the contrary, it is something highly positive, for philosophical thinking, the pursuit of meanings, begins with discrimination. Only if we start from the premise that there is nothing but defects and that the world exists to annoy us, while actually there is no evidence that it is concerned with us in either way of pleasing or displeasing us, do we allow the intellect to overstep itself and to succumb to the undiscriminating activity of antipathy. The denunciation of the love of reason or of what we call rationalism and intellectualism is based on a misconception of the function of discrimination and on an unwarranted limitation of the knowable.[2] In other words, discrimination is understood as implying only discursiveness, while there are many other forms of discrimination which are not discursive. Without discrimination man would cease to be man and discrimination is the king of all the functions of mind.[3]

It is easy to understand why the temperament of a scatterbrain is related to delusion and bewilderment. Neither a deluded person nor a scatterbrain will ever attempt to penetrate to the nature of a problem, but will soon stop short in his inqui-

1. This Puritan prejudice against all that is connected with the Tantras is found everywhere, not only in India but also in the Western world. The ideal is obviously to produce and to recognize only a race that is physically and mentally impotent. However, against this ideal stands the irrefutable fact that neither the Hindu orders nor the Buddhist orders admit an impotent person into their ranks.

2. As is well known, the philosopher Locke thought that there must be some imperceptible substratum to which the sensibly perceptible characters of the thing belong and he believed this substratum to be unknowable. Similarly for Kant the thing in itself was unknowable. Following this trend of thought the Russian scholar Th. Stcherbatsky has read this assumption into the Buddhist texts which precisely assert the opposite.

3. Yaśomitra's Vyākhyā ad Abhidharmakośa I 2; *api tu dharmapravicayakāle prajñā caittasyāpi sarvasya kalāpasya rājāyate.*

ries, because he is content to accept things at their face value. In the strictly Buddhist sense of the word, delusion is the conviction of one's own importance.

Under such circumstances the starting point for meditation must vary individually. For, to give an example, it would be poison to a person affected by cupidity to start with an object or a topic which would rouse his passions and intensify attachment and addiction to a thing, because this very attachment has already led him into an impasse. For this reason the objects and topics to start with are according to the various temperaments as follows.[1]

In order to sever the ties that bind a person in whom cupidity is predominant, to an object which in most cases is a living person of either the opposite or the same sex, the contemplation of the various stages of decay in a corpse is a very effective means. Traditionally ten stages have been laid down as topics of contemplation and meditation.[2] Since cupidity does not operate singly, but is intimately connected with delusion, (where there is no delusion, i.e., where there is knowledge, discrimination both discursive and non-discursive (*prajñā*), cupidity and antipathy are absent), and since delusion is above all the idea of self, another effective means is the analysis of one's body as to its constituents.[3] However, it has to be observed that in all these exercises the aim is to sever attachment, not to convert attachment into its opposite, antipathy.

Since without love nothing is possible, it is essential that a person whose temperament is one of antipathy, hatred, malice, and ill-will, first of all should learn to love. To this effect the practice of the four 'divine behaviors' (*brahmavihāra*), also known as the four 'Immeasurables' (*apramāṇa*),[4] is of utmost impor-

1. Visuddhimagga III 121.

2. Technically they are known as the *daśa aśubha*. A detailed discussion of each point and of the means of practising this kind of contemplation is given in Visuddhimagga VI 1-94. See also Aṭṭhasālinī III 417-425. Abhidharmakośa VI 9.

3. Technically this is known as *kāyagatāsati*. Visuddhimagga VIII 42-144.

4. Visuddhimagga IX 1-124; Abhidharmakośa VIII 29. Aṭṭhasālinī III 399-416. They are called 'divine' because of their excellence and because those who possess them live like the Brahma-gods. Aṭṭhasālinī III 412; Abhidharmakośa IV 124 and Vyākhyā. They are 'immeasurable' because their field of operation is unlimited. Aṭṭhasālinī III 415. Abhidharmakośa VIII 29.

tance. The first 'divine behavior', without which all others are impossible, is *maitrī* (Pāli *mettā*). The term *maitrī* is explained by 'to love, to be fond of', particularly in the sense of being expressive of the state of feeling one finds in a friend or in the behavior of a friend.[1] Although it is permissible to say that this feeling is love, yet it is different from love insofar as it connotes a feeling which proceeds in a settled and regulated manner. It evokes the good and focuses interest on the good; and so it manifests itself in a way that all ill-will is removed. The basis of this feeling is to see the pleasant side of beings. However, this feeling has also a negative aspect which easily may overturn the positive character. While its positive character is the cessation of all hostility[2] and, since Buddhism has a thoroughly positive view of man and is convinced that good is always stronger than evil, hostility is, so to say, only the remote enemy of *maitrī* and need not be feared. But the proximate enemy of *maitrī* is passion (*rāga*) which leads to attachment and hence in the practice of *maitrī* the utmost attention has to be given to the danger that *maitrī* may not become a prey to passion.[3] While *maitrī* does not exclude love and affection in the best sense of the words, though it does not admit of passion, it is essentially benevolence, a natural kindliness and interest in others' happiness and well-being, which finds its expression in the desire : "May all beings be happy".[4]

It is only when there is benevolence and interest in others' happiness that the more active compassion (*karuṇā*) can operate,[5] although 'more active' does not mean that benevolence is a mere 'passive' sentiment. Compassion makes the heart of good people beat more quickly when they see the misery and plight of other fellow-beings, and so it attempts to dig out the roots of misery that it may be destroyed forever. In this way compassion is like a stream that turns to all who are afflicted

1. Aṭṭhasālinī III 401 :......*mitte vā bhavā, mittassa vā esā pavattatī ti ettā.*
2. ibid. III 402. See also Abhidharmakośa VIII 29 and Vyākhyā.
3. Aṭṭhasālinī III 404.
4. Visuddhimagga IX 9. Bhāṣya ad Abhidharmakośa VIII 30.
5. Aṭṭhasālinī III 414.

and like rain pours relief on them.[1] Compassion is therefore a steady current which carries all misery away with it. It is a feeling which is unable to bear the misery of others and it manifests itself in such a way that no annoyance can befall people. Thus the basis on which compassion operates for the well-being of sentient beings is an awareness of the helplessness and desolateness of all those who are afflicted by misery.[2] But compassion has also its negative side. While on the positive side through compassion all that annoys us is removed, on the negative side it is the futile crying and whimpering over the misery of the world.[3] Therefore the very fact that the misery and frustration we observe everywhere makes us sad and depressed, is the proximate enemy of compassion.[4] So depression is something we have to guard ourselves against and in spite of the saddening things we see we should strive to have all beings liberated from misery.[5]

Just as benevolence and compassion advance participation in others and decrease the sense of self-importance which is inseparable from a debasement of others, so also, and maybe in a still stronger manner, joy (*muditā*) helps to overcome inhibitions. As cheerfulness it manifests itself in overcoming unwillingness[6] and has as its basis the awareness of the happy and auspicious circumstances of the sentient beings[7] which have been brought about through benevolence which is well-wishing and through compassion which removes misery.[8] But joy has its pitfalls, too. While on the positive side joy overcomes and need not fear unwillingness, on the negative side it is mere jollity[9] which is unaware of, or forgets the conditions through which true joy can come about. Therefore a happy

1. Aṭṭhasālinī III 401 :......*kiṇāti vā paradukkham hiṁsati vināsetī ti karuṇā. kiriyati vā dukkhitesu karuṇāvasena pasāriyatī ti karuṇā.*
2. ibid. III 402. Abhidharmakośa VIII 29 and Vyākhyā.
3. Aṭṭhasālinī III 402.
4. ibid. III 405.
5. Abhidharmakośa VIII 30 and Bhāṣya.
6. Aṭṭhasālinī III 402. Abhidharmakośa VIII 29 and Vyākhyā.
7. Aṭṭhasālinī III 402.
8. ibid. 414.
9. ibid. 402 : *pahāsasambhava.*

mood in beholding the wealth we have at home is the proximate enemy to joy.[1]

Out of this joy then crystallizes[2] the highest divine behaviour, the impartial outlook (*upekkhā*, Skt. *upekṣā*) which realizes that one being is by nature the same as all others, and so its impartiality is due to the circumstance that it cannot be disturbed by either sympathies for or antipathies against someone. The basis of its operation is the realization of the fact that everybody reaps the results of his or her actions and views the whole world from this standpoint.[3]

It is unfortunate that such impartial behavior can be described only in negative terms which are apt to mislead the casual student. Not to be swayed by antipathies or sympathies is undoubtedly, a positive and highly valuable asset. To this many will agree. Yet at the same time the fact that this impartiality sees things and individuals in a way which makes it perfectly clear that nothing can be done,[4] seems to be in no way comforting. Yet this view is utmost realism and most sober reasonableness. Nobody can do another's task. All that can be done is to teach a person how to stand on his own feet. Once this has been done, whatever could be done has been accomplished. There is only the danger that in our immature minds we may take impartiality to mean indifference, which is the habitual attitude of him whose maxim is 'I couldn't care less'. Indifference is ignorance, because it does not discriminate between good and bad. But impartiality is born from knowledge and understanding. Therefore, not to strive for knowledge but to adopt a behavior rooted in ignorance and manifesting itself in indifference is the proximate enemy to impartiality, against which we have to guard ourselves.[5]

Since these four types of divine behavior have as their objects sentient beings, extending from a single individual to the totality of beings in the worlds, and since it is often tremend-

1. Aṭṭhasālinī 406.
2. "The outflow of the three preceding divine types of behavior is the divine behavior of impartiality", Aṭṭhasālinī III 410. Visuddhimagga IX 104.
3. Aṭṭhasālinī III 402.
4. ibid. III 414: *katabbābhāva*.
5. ibid. III 407.

ously difficult, if not impossible in the first moment, for a person who is ruled by ill-will, hatred, and antipathy, in brief, by all that alienates him from his surroundings, to establish a friendly relation with other individuals, an alternative to the practice and development of these four types of divine behavior are the color totalities (*varṇakṛtsnāyatana*, Pāli *vaṇṇakasina*). I shall discuss the various totalities in the next section. Here I only want to emphasize that in the entire process connected with the color totalities no reference to commonsense external objects is required. Essential is the capacity to grasp the immediately apprehended aesthetic factor in all its purity and it alone.[1]

Above it has been remarked that there exists a certain affinity between the intellect (*buddhi*) and the emotion of antipathy. Yet for a person in whom the intellect is of decisive importance, the approach to meditation is quite different.

The intellect may be said to be a function which enables us to understand descriptive phrases without knowing whether there is anything that is described by them, and to use such phrases significantly even if we believe that there is nothing to which these phrases apply or even before we are acquainted with the person or thing which is described by them. Intellectual knowledge is thus concerned with facts which are expressed in true propositions and with descriptions.[2] This constitutes most of our knowledge used in ordinary life.

Quite a different kind of knowledge we have when we are acquainted with a person or a thing. Acquaintance is considered to be an unanalysable relation in which a knower stands to something, and we are acquainted with that of which we are directly aware. And that is very little in ordinary life. Although knowledge by acquaintance does not admit of any degrees of knowledge as does knowledge by description with its distinction between determinate and indeterminate knowledge,[3] and although knowledge by acquaintance is of primary importance in Buddhism, yet the following distinction has to be taken into account. Ordinarily I am acquainted

1. Visuddhimagga V 12-20.
2. L. Susan Stebbing, A Modern Introduction to Logic, p. 22.
3. ibid., p. 24.

with a person to whom I have been introduced or with a thing of which I am directly aware. Yet this acquaintance may fail to mean anything to me. I may be introduced to Mr. X and I am entitled then to say that I am acquainted with Mr. X, but there the matter ends. This type of knowledge by acquaintance is of very little avail in meditation and in gaining access to the world of Gestalten. What is necessary is an emotionally moving acquaintance which does not operate on the premise that the knower and the known are mutually exclusive. For this type of knowledge which alone is effective I suggest the term 'knowledge by experience'.

In order to release the intellect from its habit of moving in descriptions and to make it directly aware of that which matters in individual development and by which human life becomes richer, it seems that only shock therapy is of any avail. Therefore to the intellectual type the contemplation of death is suggested as highly suitable. Buddhaghosa makes it quite clear that this contemplation must not move in descriptions, and that it is futile to think about death in a way in which death would be the subject of a proposition. His words are :[1]

"When one proceeds in an improper way it happens that we feel sorry when we think about the death of a beloved person, as a mother feels sorry when she thinks about the death of her newly born child; or we feel elated when we think about the death of a person we do not love, as do revengeful persons when they think about the death of their enemies; or we are not moved in the least when we think about the death of persons in whom we are not interested, just as the official burner of corpses is not moved at all when he sees a dead body; or we are driven into panic when we think about our own death, as is a timid person when he sees the murderer lift his sword.

"In all these cases there is no inspection (*sati*), by which we try to learn more about an object, there is nothing that moves us to the core (*saṁvega*), and there is no knowledge by experience (*ñāṇa*). Therefore we must make use of inspection, must allow ourselves to be moved to our innermost being and must gain knowledge by experience when we see persons who

1. Visuddhimagga VIII 5-6.

have just been killed and when we observed the death of those whose prosperity we have witnessed before".[1]

Buddhaghosa mentions three other practices as suitable for the intellectual temperament. Their connexion with the intellectual attitude is obvious when we bear in mind that the intellect, in Buddhist conception, partakes of the nature of the highest and most valuable function in man, viz., discrimination (*prajñā*), but with this difference that its way of functioning is trammeled by the veil of bewilderment—delusion (*moha*), and that bewilderment—delusion associates with the other emotive bases such as cupidity (*rāga*) and antipathy (*dveṣa*). As a remedy against the combined operation of bewilderment-delusion and the emotive bases, 'disgust of food' (*āhāre paṭikkūla-saññā*)[2] is supposed to be effective, because the analysis of food and the digestive process together with the consideration of the effects of food on health and disease is a means to release man from the ties that keep him to gluttony and other types of intemperance which all have their roots in cupidity. As Buddhaghosa informs us, usually we eat "being fond of food, being greedy for it, being rapacious for it, and being blinded by the desire for it".[3] A good illustration of such a type of man is Schopenhauer who combined intellectualism with misanthropy and the habit of dining well.

Another practice which involves as much the intellect as the emotions is the contemplation of the manner in which all that is divided into the conditioned and unconditioned, loses its affective hold over man (*upasamā*).[4] This cessation of affectively toned action and reaction (*virāga*) is the highest value, Nirvāṇa. It is interesting to note in this connexion that, from a philosophical point of view, Buddhaghosa shares the views of the Vaibhāṣikas who considered Nirvāṇa to be an entity in itself and opposed the view of the Sautrāntikas for whom Nirvāṇa was mere negation (absence of *rāga*). Buddhaghosa's words are : "Cessation of desire (*virāga*) is not mere

1. In VIII 8 sq. Buddhaghosa mentions other topics related to death. But here too the immediacy of experience and the vividness of the image is all important.
2. Visuddhimagga XI 4-26.
3. Visuddhimagga XI 22.
4. Visuddhimagga VIII 245-251.

absence of rāga (*na rāgābhāvamatta*), but the terms 'sobering from intoxication', 'Nirvāṇa' are names which the unconditioned receives".[1] However, it may be remarked that the view of the Vaibhāṣikas is as untenable as the view of the Sautrāntikas. For it is in no way necessary to assume that a certain experience must have an ontological correlate, whether this be positive as it is in the view of the Vaibhāṣikas, or negative as in the view of the Sautrāntikas. Such an assumption is likely to detract man from the immediacy of experience and involve him in intellectual descriptions which, as must be insisted upon, are not conducive to meditation in the Buddhist sense of the word. For this reason both the Vaibhāṣikas and Sautrāntikas have been severely criticized by the Mādhyamikas.[2] Moreover, the wording of the phrase in which this term 'cessation of affectively toned action and 'reaction' (*virāga*) occurs, certainly supports the Mādhyamika criticism.[3]

As the last alternative for the intellectual temperament, Buddhaghosa discusses the analysis of our individual existence on the basis of its constitutive elements (*catudhātuvavatthāna*).[4] The essential feature of this analysis is the realization that nowhere is the assumption of a self, ego, or creator necessitated. The whole of our existence can be understood as the interplay of functional dependence.

While Buddhaghosa connects this analysis which has

1. Visuddhimagga VIII 247 : *tattha virāgo ti na rāgābhāvamattam eva, atha kho yad idam madanimmadano...nibbānam ti yo so madanimaddano ti ādīni nāmāni labhati.*

2. Thus, for instance, Saraha declares in his Dohākoṣa-upadeśagīti (mi. zad. pai. gter. mdzod. man. ṅag.gi.glu), bs Tan. 'gyur, rgyud, vol. zhi, fol. 29a :

"Those who assume existence, I call similar to cattle;
Those who assume non-existence are still more stupid.
All who make use of the similes of kindling and extinguishing a lamp
Stay in the Mahāmudrā which by nature is indivisible."

Similarly Anaṅgavajra says in his Prajñopāyaviniścayasiddhi I 9 :

It is better to assume existence than non-existence;
A burning lamp may go out, but where does a dead flame go?

See also Candrakīrti's Prasannapadā, p. 525.

3. *virāga* applies to the conditioned as well as to the unconditioned (*dhammā saṅkhatā vā asaṅkhatā vā virāgo tesam dhammānam*, Aṅguttaranikāya II 34.).

4. Visuddhimagga XI 27-117.

found its profoundest formulation in the Pratītyasamutpāda, the Law of interdependent origination, with the intellectual type of man, Dvags.po.lha.rje. considers this analysis particularly suited to the type of man who is ruled by bewilderment-delusion (*moha*).[1] Bewilderment-delusion operates in the subjective disposition (*manas*) and, because of the unity of mind, engenders the idea of an Ātman or Pure Ego.[2] The analysis of our existence on the basis of its constitutive elements effectively destroys this belief which also in modern European philosophy has become very disreputable.[3]

Both Dvags.po.lha.rje and Buddhaghosa agree in this respect that breath control[4] is a suitable practice for a person whose temperament is such that he attends to all and everything without ever following one line of thought to its end.[5]

Finally we have to mention the religious temperament which Buddhaghosa asserts to have some resemblance to the possessive temperament. It is true, a person of this temperament has by nature a certain fervor which very often displays a marked similitude to the desire to possess. In theistic systems this fervor finds its expression in the love for God. Buddhism, however, is a thoroughly atheistic doctrine. The host of gods which appears on the stage of life are ethically inferior to man, superior only in their power and duration of life. In many cases these gods are symbols which have many significant functions and through which we are enabled to see 'meaning'. Atheism, to be sure, is in no way opposed to true religiosity. It is only dogmatism with its artificial restrictions and its thoroughgoing disorientation that prevents any true religious feeling from expressing itself and in this violation of a living process endangers mental health.

However, one can hardly refrain from remarking that

1. Dam. chos. yid. bzhin. gyi. nor. bu. thar. pa.rin. po. chei rgyan. zhes bya. ba theg. pa. chen. poi. lam. rim. gyi. bshad. pa, fol. 88b sq. See on this work my 'Dvags. po. lha. rje's "Ornament of Liberation" in JAOS 1955, pp. 90 sq.

2. Triṁśikā 6 and Vṛtti, p. 23. Vijñaptimātratāsiddhi, p. 255.

3. C. D. Broad, The Mind and its Place in Nature, p. 214.

4. Visuddhimagga VIII 145-244. Abhidharmakośa VI 12 and Bhāṣya.

5. Dvags. po. lha. rje. loc. cit. foll. 88b; 91 b.

Buddhaghosa has greatly underrated religious temperament. As particularly suited to this temperament he advocates the contemplation of The Buddha, in the first instance.[1] It is certainly an asset of religious life and essentially the outcome of the Buddhist conception of religiosity (*śraddhā*)[2] as pellucidity of mind (*prasāda*) that no defiling element of sin or the idea of being permanently in debt because of someone's sacrifice is present. But although the contemplation of the Buddha as the man who won enlightenment and subsequently was able to show the way to it as walkable to him who is ready to go, emphatically refers to the meaning of enlightenment, Buddhaghosa conceives it as moving in mere descriptions. Hence this contemplation can bring a man near a meditative mood, but not into a state of meditative absorption.[3] Another consequence of this underestimation of the religious temperament is that it becomes canalized into and remains fixed with conventionally formal elements instead of allowing a sobering expressiveness.

Mahāyāna Buddhism has made a better estimate of the religious temperament, which many writers on Buddhism mistook for an introduction of some theistic or pantheistic element. The fact, however, is that no phase of Buddhism ever had theistic or pantheistic[4] tendencies and that these writers, failing to grasp the essentials of Buddhism, conceived the grammatical gender of the nouns used in the representation of the ineffably vivid experience as a metaphysical assertion with an ontological admixture.

The various practices which have been discussed in their relation to individual temperaments, are essentially a preparatory stage to meditation. Only some of them admit of being

1. Visuddhimagga VII 2-67. Other topics are the Dharma (VII 68-83), the Saṅgha (VII 89-100), ethics (VII 101-106), liberality (VII 107-114), and popular deities (VII 115-118). This latter topic is essentially a comparison of oneself with others as regards one's ethical behavior.

2. See above, pp. 59 sq.

3. Visuddhimagga VII 66; III 106.

4. The term pantheistic is used very loosely in works dealing with Mahāyāna Buddhism, but certainly not in its proper meaning. What this term actually means has been pointed out by F. S. C. Northrop. The Meeting of East and West, p. 401.

taken as a Gestalt and therefore can be a content of meditation proper with its ensuing absorption.[1]

The Totalities (kṛtsnāyatana) And Meditation

'Totality' (*kṛtsnāyatana,* Pāli *Kasina*) is the name given to a particular content and experience in meditation. Properly speaking, it belongs to the final or fourth stage of the meditative process,[2] but its name extends also to the starting point from which a particular experience of wholeness can be gained. All texts, with slight variations in terms, agree on the wholeness of the experienced content and the experience itself. Vasubandhu explains this term by 'exclusive and total pervasiveness';[3] and Asaṅga adds that the deep absorption and the analytical appreciative understanding of the content together with the states of mind involved in this experience of wholeness are the 'totality'.[4] There are ten such totalities, eight of which belong to the world of Gestalten,[5] and two of which go beyond this realm.[6] The first eight derive their names from four elements : earth, water, fire, wind, all of them having symbolic significance, and from four colors : blue-green, yellow, red, white.[7]

In order to gain access to the world of Gestalten one or the other of these eight 'totalities' can be selected for meditation. As has been pointed out, this selection is done by the teacher of meditation, who instructs the disciple how to proceed with his exercises and who has made the selection according to the temperament of the disciple.[8] Since with slight variations due to the specific nature of each 'totality' the method of preparation and the beginning of meditation remains the same,

1. See Visuddhimagga III 106-107.
2. Abhidharmakośa VIII 36.
3. ibid. Abhidharmasamuccaya, p. 96. Buddhaghosa declares "in the sense of entirety" (*sakalaṭṭhena*) Visuddhimagga IV 119. Aṭṭhasālinī III 338.
4. Abhidharmasamuccaya, p. 96.
5. Abhidharmakośa VIII 36.
6. ibid.
7. The two remaining 'totalities' belonging to the Ārūpya realm bear different names and will be mentioned later on.
8. Visuddhimagga IV 24.

a description having as its center the 'earth totality' (*pṛthivīkṛtsnāyatana*, Pāli *paṭhavīkasina*) will suffice.

Out of clay which must not be strong colored, a circle is formed. This circle must have a very smooth surface and a definite outline to separate it from its surroundings. It is then placed at such a distance from the observer that though it is plainly visible to him the imperfections of the material do not appear. Both the smoothness of the surface and the even color of the circle serve as a help to minimize the idea of a three-dimensional external object as postulated by commonsense and to facilitate the transition from the perception of the object to pure sensation. Also the sharp outline of the circle is meant to avoid any chance that the meditative process remains a hazy affair. This purpose underlies all other 'totalities' as well. Thus, for instance, a color totality is prepared out of flowers having a color suitable to one's liking in such a way that the petals, pistals and stamens and other details of the flowers do not appear prominently.[1] An additional help in keeping attention on the object of meditation is the repetition of some name or epithet of this 'totality'. In the case of the 'earth totality' it is 'broad one, big one, fertile one, ground, mine of wealth, container of wealth'. Again it has to be observed that only one such epithet out of a large number of synonyms is used, because the use of several names at the same time would only lead to discursiveness. In this process we easily recognize the mantra which plays such an important role in Mahāyāna Buddhism. The etymology of this word, as given in authoritative texts, brings out the idea of keeping attention steadily on the object and of not allowing mind to become dissipated in discursiveness; for "mantra is called so because it protects mind".[2]

After all these preparations have been concluded the first stage is to acquire by practice and retain the power to call up an image which resembles that which we have seen repeatedly in the past. However, we must not confuse this capacity with memory, though it may be a condition for a genuine memory situation, because no judgment at all is involv-

1. Visuddhimagga V 13.
2. Sekoddeśaṭīkā, p. 33.

ed. Therefore also, in order to avoid the danger of arriving at judgments, it is insisted upon that neither the color nor other peculiarities of the object must be attended to. Without, however, ignoring the color property of the object, but keeping it the same as the original, one has to attend to the meaning (*paṇṇattidhamma*) which is supplied by the repetition of the mantra. The image which is thus called up is termed *uggahaṇimitta* and corresponds to the 'eidetic image' in Western psychology.[1]

The more attention is fixed on this 'eidetic image', the more we approach a state of deep concentration. Concentration itself is divided into two regions : deep concentration (*appanā-samādhi*) and border concentration (*upacāra-samādhi*), both are certain levels characterized by the presence of peace and insight on the one hand, and by the absence of disturbing influences, on the other, respectively.[2] For the meditative process itself the border concentration is of utmost importance, because it is here that the image contemplated loses its external reference whereby the perceptual situation melts into pure sensation or, at least, what is approximately pure sensation. The objective constituent of this situation is called *patibhāganimitta.*[3] Buddhaghosa describes it as follows : "The distinction between this objective constituent and the eidetic image is as follows. In the eidetic image any imperfections of the (material out of which the) totality (is made) are perceived. The *patibhāganimitta,* however, like a mirror taken from one's pocket, or like a polished conchshell, or like the disc of the moon coming out of the clouds, or like cranes against dark clouds, cleaves the eidetic image and issues forth a hundred, a thousandfold more clear. But it has no color and no shape. If it had it would be gross and discernible to the eye, tangible, and possessing the three characteristics (of origination, momentary duration, and annihilation). But it is not so; it is only

1. Visuddhimagga IV 29-30. This term has been completely misunderstood by those who translated the Visuddhimagga or parts of this work. Either they never practised meditation or thought it to be some physiological or pathological phenomenon. 'Sign, reflex image, mental reflex at the image' are the words used for a perfectly normal occurrence.

2. Visuddhimagga IV 32.

3. ibid. IV 31.

an objective constituent, a sensum, in him who attains concentration".[1]

Although meditation begins with the individual, as we have seen, this statement must not make us assume that meditation is, popularly speaking, an act of will. On the contrary, it is a process which must be allowed to grow by itself, as it were, with no interference from the individual practising meditation.[2] Interference means to read utilitarian ideas into it, to use meditation for what it is not meant to be used, namely for self-aggrandizement. Therefore meditation (*dhyāna*, Pāli *jhāna*) can be said to be practised and to be attained only when the sensuous and sensual relations have been cut off; in other words, when the external reference of the objective constituent in the perceptual situation has disappeared. Therefore also the formula of the first stage of meditation begins with the significant words : "Having become detached from the objects to which one is sensually related and having become detached from unwholesome elements".[3] This detachment is both physical and mental,[4] the former referring to the objects of sense, the latter to the emotional reactions to the objects.

The author of the Aṭṭhasālinī gives a further detailed interpretation of this classical formula. He points out that it essentially refers to the abolition of all obstacles to meditation, external as well as internal, though it must be noted that the distinction between external and internal is not so sharply marked as these terms seem to imply, but that the external and internal interpenetrate each other. There are five such obstacles : 'sensuality' (*kāmacchanda*), 'ill-will' (*vyāpāda*), 'indolence and sluggishness' (*styanamiddha*), 'frivolity and regret' (*auddhaccakaukṛtya*), and 'scepticism (*vicikitsā*).[5] The first part of the formula mentioned above is according to our author meant to refer to the abolition of sensuality, the second part to the abolition of the remaining obstacles. Similarly the first part refers to the eradication of cupidity as an unhealthy root of certain attitudes, while the second part refers to the extirpa-

1. Visuddhimagga IV 31.
2. ibid. IV 67-73.
3. Vibhaṅga 245.
4. Visuddhimagga IV 83; Aṭṭhasālinī III 331.
5. Abhidharmakośa V 58; 59 and Bhāṣya.

tion of antipathy and bewilderment. The formula further implies the necessary abolition of the latent possibilities for emotional outbursts and their effects which are subsumed under various headings, each of them picturesquely describing the situation in which a man swayed by emotions will find himself. Thus, emotional outbursts put man into awkward situations and push him down from any spiritual height he may have arisen to (*āsrava*); or like a torrent (*ogha*) they carry him along in uncontrollable fury; or, in a subtler way, they fetter (*yoga*) man to mere worldliness and so induce him to ascribe (*upādāna*) to himself all that which actually does not belong to him.[1] The author of the Aṭṭhasālinī adds two other headings which refer to particular features of the effects of emotional outbursts just described.[2] He sums up his discussion by stating that the formula under consideration is meant, in its first part, to refer to the eradication of craving (*taṇhā*) and of all that is connected with it and also to the abandoning of an attitude rooted in cupidity, while in its second part the formula refers to the destruction of unwisdom (*avidyā*) and of all that unwisdom entails and also to a liberation from other (unhealthy) attitudes.[3]

So far the classical formula for the initial step in meditation has given a negative account of what is necessary for and during concentration, because only in the absence of the 'obstacles' concentration becomes possible and the 'members' (*aṅga*) as the most characteristic features of the mental situation of meditation become prominent. The first step comprises five members:

vitarka, vicāra, prīti, sukha, samādhi (*cittasyaikāgratā*).[4]

Actually these five 'members' constitute the meditative concentrative process and are known as *dhyāna* which is just a convenient term to group the various aspects of meditation into

1. Aṭṭhasālinī III 334; Abhidharmakośa V 40 and Bhāṣya.
2. Aṭṭhasālinī III 334; *gantha* and *saṁyojana*. The former corresponds to the *bandhana* in Abhidh.-kośa V 41. Here five features are mentioned. See V 41-49b.
3. Aṭṭhasālinī III 334.
4. Abhidharmakośa VIII 7-8. Abhidharmasamuccaya, p. 68

a unity.[1] It may be noted that here we have one of the rare instances where a word is not taken as referring to an independent existence; where nominalism supersedes realism.[2] It has further to be noted that the prominence given to these five 'members' does not imply that all those mental functions which operate in healthy attitudes, are absent. On the contrary, they are all present[3] and interest is centred on the five members only because they act as strong opponents to the obstacles and hence are of primary importance and characteristic of the meditative attitude. As the author of the Aṭṭhasālinī points out,[4] *samādhi* counteracts sensuality; *prīti* ill-will; *vitarka* indolence and sluggishness; *sukha* frivolity and regret; and *vicāra* scepticism.[5]

The function of both *vitarka* and *vicāra* is the same as that in a healthy attitude with this difference, that the object is not a commonsense three-dimensional external object, but the 'eidetic image'.[6]

It is with respect to the meaning of *prīti* and *sukha* that the various schools disagreed. The author of the Aṭṭhasālinī understands by *prīti* an all-pervading ecstasy which fully charges the whole body, and by *sukha* a happy and contented mood.[7] The same view is shared by the Sautrāntikas.[8] The Vaibhāṣikas, however, understand by *prīti* a happy mood, and by *sukha* relaxation.[9] The arguments for their interpretations are not very convincing, since they are based on taking certain words in certain Sūtras as the basis rather than the actual experience which the author of the Aṭṭhasālinī so vividly describes by the words[10] : 'Ecstasy matures into functional and attitudinal relaxation; relaxation matures into functional and attitudinal pleasantness; and this pleasantness matures into the

1. Abhidharmakośa VIII 7-8, Bhāṣya, p. 148. Sāmantapasādikā I 146.
2. ibid., VIII 9 and Bhāṣya.
3. Aṭṭhasālinī III 340.
4. ibid. III 333.
5. A different interpretation is given in Abhidharmakośa VIII, p. 157 note 4.
6. Aṭṭhasālinī III 338.
7. ibid. III 202-210.
8. Abhidharmakośa, Bhāṣya ad VIII 9.
9. Abhidharmakośa VIII 9 and Bhāṣya.
10. Aṭṭhasālinī III 207.

types of concentration : momentary concentration, three borderline concentration, and full concentration.

With concentration having been achieved the first step in meditation has been taken. From here the process continues until it has reached its conclusion.

Meditation may be said to be a process by which an ordinarily diffused state of mind is brought into focus. The more the dispersion of mind's rays is gathered into a centre, it seems that more and more the mind's rays disappear. This is expressed in the texts that the number of 'mental factors' diminishes.[1] The focusing process can be viewed from various angles. It may be said to be a gradual descent into the calm depth of the sea from the shallowness of its shores; or it may be said to be a gradual ascent into the purer and more transparent air on a mountain peak from the suffocating and steamy heat of the valleys. Therefore, whenever meditation is referred to by similes, we find examples of the ocean or of the topmost height of existence. But it should be noted that such expressions are essentially symbolic, and insofar as they are comparisons they are imperfect, as are all comparisons.

Inasmuch as feelings and emotions are basic to all intellectual processes, meditation is also an approach to the basis of mental life. It proceeds from the more intellectual surface to the emotional substratum. Therefore the next step is characterized by the 'cessation of *vitarka* and *vicāra*',[2] *vitarka* and *vicāra*, as we have seen, being essentially intellectual functions. However, it is necessary to warn the reader of a possible and grave misunderstanding. When I say that the more intellectual processes, such as *vitarka* and *vicāra*, are passed over, this does not mean that the intellect is disparaged and that the best and easiest way to practise meditation is just to resort to some sort of wilful stupidity or affected ignorance (this has happened and still happens, mental indolence being made a show of as 'spiritual values'). Actually it means that the intellectual functions are freed from their restriction to the superficial and their restlessness and that these functions gain

1. Aṭṭhasālinī III 346.
2. ibid. III 341.

in depth and achieve a more translucent character. It also has to be noted that although we can make a distinction between the intellectual and the emotional, they operate in a unity. Therefore the new character is never the one or the other, but both. This new character is called 'individual clarity' (*adhyātmasamprasāda*, Pāli *ajjhattam sampasadanam*).[1] The interpretation of this new character has in many cases been marred by the dogmatism of a realistic conception. Clinging to a numerical schema is certainly a failure to comprehend the living process. The Sautrāntikas must be credited with not caring for a rigidly numerical schema and with having pointed out that this 'individual clarity' is a special characteristic and not an entity in itself.[2] But the Vaibhāṣikas and the Theravādins, advocating a numerical schema, understood this 'individual clarity' as an entity in itself and interpreted it as *śraddhā* 'confidence and conviction'.[3]

With this clarity the proper focus (*ekodi*) has been found. As the author of the Aṭṭhasālinī points out this term 'focus' refers to the fact that, on the one hand, due to the absence of *vitarka* and *vicāra* the best viewpoint has been found and that, on the other, the best viewpoint is only one point and reveals everything that has come into focus (*sampayuttadhamma*) to the best of its nature.[4]

While the subsiding of *vitarka* and *vicāra* leads to a state of lucidity (*samprasāda*) and to a penetration to the underlying emotive tone, it is necessary also that the emotional side becomes clarified, just as the intellectual side had to be released from its turbid and unclear operations. This clarification is brought about by allowing ecstasy and enthusiasm (*prīti*) (which in the beginning is tremendously helpful, because it keeps interest steady), to subside and thus to pave the way for seeing things with a balanced mind (*samam passati*) and for not falling prey to one-sidedness. This state is described by the technical

1. Aṭṭhasālinī III 342. Abhidharmakośa VIII 9 and Bhāṣya.
2. Bhāṣya ad Abhidharmakośa VIII 9, pp. 158 sq. Hsiuan-tsang's remark, quoted by L. de la Vallee Poussin in note 2 on p. 159, is significant: "Though this is reasonable it is not my system".
3. Aṭṭhasālinī III 342. Abhidharmakośa VIII 9 c.
4. Aṭṭhasālinī III 342.

term *upekṣā* (Pāli *upekkhā*), which is best translated by 'equanimity'[1]. It is, as it were, steering a middle course (*majjhatta*).[2]

With this equanimity achieved the peculiar and special features of meditative concentration can operate in proper form. Although these features were present in the earlier stages, yet their operation was obscured and labored, while now they operate freely just as a man can walk easily when he has no burden to carry. These peculiar features are 'inspection' (*smṛti*, Pāli *sati*) and 'full awareness' (*samprajanya*, Pāli *sampajañña*) and constitute the essential operation of the so-called third stage of *dhyāna*.

By 'inspection' we try to learn more about the objective constituent of the particular perceptual situation, i.e., the eidetic image, and we try to keep the object of our contemplation as steady as possible and guard it from becoming lost to our sight, while 'full awareness' aids us in not becoming bewildered by that which we see and is also a thorough analysis of the nature of the object of contemplation.[3] A further operation of 'inspection' and 'full awareness' is to prevent those who practise meditation and have proceeded up to this stage, from reverting to an ecstatic emotivity (*prīti*) and from succumbing to a blissful mood (*sukha*) which taken as an aim in itself would only stop any further progress and thereby falsify the purpose of meditation, viz. to attain enlightenment. As the author of the Aṭṭhasālinī points out in connection with this stage in meditation, the blissful mood in this stage is so subtle and so different from an ordinary blissful state of mind, that it almost amounts to an absence of blissful feeling.[4]

Although meditation is essentially of a cheerful character, this must not be understood in the sense that depressions and other unhappy moods will not appear or that difficulties will not be experienced. As in every other living process, medita-

1. Aṭṭhasālinī III 349; 354. Abhidharmakośa VIII 8 and Bhāṣya with identical terminology.
2. Aṭṭhasālinī III 354.
3. ibid. III 355.
4. ibid. III 355; 356. Abhidharmakośa VIII 9 and Bhāṣya, p. 152.

tion is something that fluctuates. But when the final consummation has been achieved, when all obstacles have been overcome, it is impossible to speak of that which is experienced in terms of ordinary parlance. Therefore also the fourth and final stage is described mainly in negative terms, as negative terms are less liable to make us commit ourselves to something, which on closer inspection would turn out to be invalid. In the course of the three preceding steps, both the pleasant feeling tone and the unpleasant feeling tone of the various functions within the meditative attitude, as well as the pleasant and unpleasant moods, are gradually overcome and equanimity in its purest form is brought about. This equanimity in turn produces a thorough lucidity and perspicuity of inspection (*upekkhāsatiparisuddhi*) and of all that is connected with it.[1] When this stage has been reached the transition from the 'thing' and its fragmentary aspects to the 'Gestalt' and its inherent totality has been completed.

Inasmuch as meditation is of utmost importance for leading man out of his fragmentary state of existence and diffused state of mind to spiritual maturity and fullness of being, it is only natural that it demands of man all that is in him. It demands that he 'does something' and that he applies intellectual acumen. 'Doing something' means that man actually walks a road (*pratipad*, Pāli *paṭipadā*), and this road begins with the first act of attention we bestow on some thing and extends to the moment when the borderline and borderstate of full concentration has been reached. At this moment when we are about to cross the borderline to enter full concentration, intellectual acumen and appreciative analytical understanding (*prajñā*) must be used. Technically this intellectual acumen is known as *abhijñā* (Pāli *abhiññā*).[2]

But not everyone is gifted in the same way. 'Doing something' may be extremely painful (*dukkhapaṭipadā*), because it is no easy task to bring into operation all those elements which

1. Aṭṭhasālinī III 366. Abhidharmakośa VIII 8 and Bhāṣya, p. 144.

2. Aṭṭhasālinī III 376. Abhidharmakośa VI 66 and Bhāṣya, which stresses *śamatha* and *vipaśyana* as equilibrating factors. See also Aṭṭhasālinī III 378.

counteract the obstacles that beset the road to spiritual maturity. Also intellectual acumen may be lacking, so that for a long time we fail to take the final step into full concentration (*dandhābhiññā*). On the other hand, others may have no difficulty in removing the obstacles and achieving full concentration (*sukhapaṭipadā, khippābhiññā*). Out of the combination of these factors there results quite a variety of human types.[1] The recognition of this variety of human types again emphasizes the thoroughly practical character of the Buddhist discipline which dealt with man as he is and not as he should or might be.

The Infinitudes

While the 'totalities' of the basic elements earth, water, fire, and air, and the principal colors blue-green, yellow, red, and white, were designed to lead man out of a world of 'things' into a world of formulative meaningful Gestalten, these 'totalities' by their very nature intimated that they were nothing ultimate, but if one be allowed to use the term, formulated energies capable of further formulations by which they become progressively articulated as 'things' and 'events'. They thus represent a transitional stage, pointing to world of things, on the one hand, and to a world of no-things, on the other. In any case it is necessary to go to the very source from which these formulated energies have sprung and to fathom the actual nature of formulativeness. This source lies beyond the world of Gestalten (*rūpāvacara*), though 'beyond' must not be understood in a spatial sense. Language easily misleads us by the linear successive order in which words are employed and is therefore most deceptive in many respects. Moreover, there also is no need to assume a world which is not in our space-time world. The statement that "The Ārūpyadhātu is without place but fourfold as to its practice of realization",[2] can be easily understood (and apparently was meant to be understood) that in this world of our experience there are things and events which do not fit the discursive mode of linguistic expression

1. Aṭṭhasālinī III 376-380. Cp. also Abhidharmasamuccaya, p. 75.
2. Abhidharmakośa III 3.

which involves space and time, and which nevertheless are factors to be taken into account. The general term is Ārūpya-dhātu. Literally this means 'the sphere of non-Gestalt'. Other terms referring to this world are subsumed under the 'infinitudes' of which there are three related to the method of realization, viz. 'infinitude of space' (*ākāśānantya*, Pāli *ākāsānañca*), 'infinitude of perception' (*vijñānānantya*, Pāli *viññāṇañca*), and 'infinitude of nothing whatsoever' (*akiṁcanya*, Pāli *ākiñcañña*). A fourth descriptive term is 'neither-perception-formulation nor non-perception-formulation' (*naivasaṁjñānāsaṁjñā*, Pāli *nevasaññāna-saññā*), which refers to the nature of the psychological process.

As to the intrinsic meaning of the term *ārūpya* various conceptions have been prevalent. The Vaibhāṣikas and Theravādins conceived *ārūpya* as a purely negative term denoting non-existence of Gestalt (*a-rūpabhava*).[1] Other schools, however, such as the Andhakas, Mahāsāṁghikas, and Mahīśāsakas, realized the difficulty that remains as to how it is that we can think and speak about that which in no sense is. This difficulty induced them to hold the view that there are 'different modes of existence'. They thought that there is a little *rūpa* (*īṣadrūpa*).[2] In modern terminology this would mean that in the Ārūpya world *rūpa* subsists. However, there is no necessity to assume special modes of existence, because the statement that there is no *rūpa* is equivalent to the statement that *rūpa* is unreal and 'being unreal' is not a property which can belong to something in the same way as the property, say, 'being blue.' *arūpa* and its other names do not stand for any conception at all. This is clearly brought out by Vasubandhu in his Abhidharmakośa : "The infinitudes of space, the infinitude of perception, and the infinitude of nothing whatsoever are termed after the method of realization".[3] The same idea is voiced by the author of the Aṭṭhasālinī when he declares that "The idea of a sphere of infinite space is synonymous with space as separated from a 'totality object"[4] and that "The

1. Aṭṭhasālinī III 427. Abhidharmakośa VIII 3c, p. 135.
2. Bhāṣya ad Abhidh.-kośa VIII 3c, p. 136.
3. i.e., not after an object that corresponds to the description. Abhidharmakośa VIII 4.
4. Aṭṭhasālinī III 437 : *kasinugghāṭim ākāsass etam adhivacanam.*

words 'space is infinite' are not used in this connection because of the co-implication of infinite with limited. For when something is infinite it cannot be limited and when it is limited it cannot be infinite".[1] We easily recognize here the Law of Contradiction which, dealing with real entities, states that a thing cannot both be and not be so and so; but since space is not a real entity in this connection, what our author wants to say is in terms of Logical Analysis the following : "There is no entity *c* such that '*x* is spacious and infinite' is true when x is *c*, but not otherwise."[2] Thus, when a person is thinking of the infinitude of space or of the infinitude of perception or of the infinitude of nothing whatsoever, what happens is that the property of being space-infinitude is present to his mind, not in the sense that he is conceiving the property of being space-infinitude, but in the sense that the complex of properties connoted by 'space-infinitude' is present to his mind. To be present to the mind must be taken in a very wide sense, extending, as it were, into all directions of mental action, as is evident from the statement that "Infinitude of space is a sphere in the sense that it is a basis for a meditative experience with all its attendant psychological functions".[3] This has far reaching consequences; it means nothing less but that our mental life is not restricted to what we call logical conceptions and to certain fundamental perceptual forms through which ordinary sense experience is understood, but also comprises that which does not allow itself to be cast into a mould of discursive thought whereby it assumes the character of the real, and yet participates in knowledge and understanding.

Although 'infinitude of space' as a description of *arūpya* which does not stand for any conception at all, as the explanation of this term by the Vaibhāṣikas and Theravādins has made quite clear, may be legitimately said to exist, as a property it is different in important respects from individual objects, for properties can be thought of and experienced, even if there

1. Aṭṭhasālinī. III 438.
2. See Bertrand Russell, History of Western Philosophy, The philosophy of logical analysis, Chapter XXXI.
3. Aṭṭhasālinī III 437 : *āyatanam assa sasampayuttadhammassa.*

are no objects which possess these properties.[1] In spite of this the Vaibhāṣikas in particular smuggled in the idea of space as something real (*vastu*) back into their system, which aroused severe criticism from both the Sautrāntikas and Mādhyamikas. Both the Sarvāstivādins and Theravādins divided space into 'sensed space' (*ākāśadhātu*)[2] and 'space as such' (*asaṁskṛta ākāśa*).[3] It has to be observed, however, that this differentiation does not correspond to the distinction Newton introduced between 'relative,....apparent' space and 'absolute... true....mathematical' space. 'Sensed space' (*ākāśadhātu*) is cavities and holes and other openings[4] if this type of space is made a meditation object, a 'totality' (*kṛtsnāyatana*, Pāli *kasiṇa*), it does not lead beyond or go past the world of Gestalten (*rūpāvacara*), because space in this sense as a Gestalt remains a perceptual fundamental form.[5] It is 'space as such' (*asaṁskṛta ākāśa*) that becomes the 'object' (*ālambana*, Pāli *ārammaṇa*) of meditation, although this object itself is logically non-existent (*arūpa*).[6] Though this 'space as such' cannot be demonstrated in the 'material mode' which alone is considered to be real and scientific (*actually* pseudo-scientific), it can be described, as is done by the author of the Aṭṭhasālinī in his long explanation of how to go about attaining this 'unreality experience'. This space experience is attained when all Gestalt impressions have been transcended, due to the fact that the emotional response to them has ceased (*virāga*), and that they have faded out of the sphere of interest of a person in meditation (*nirodha*);[7] also because all ideas of 'thing-ness' (*paṭigha*) have ceased to operate,[8] and finally, because no attention is paid to the

1. Reference may be made to the so-called 'unreality feeling', which is mostly branded as pathological, although this feeling occurs when in artistic and creative moods we take to the deep and go beyond the limits of conceptions.
2. Abhidharmakośa I 28; Vibhaṅga, p. 84.
3. Abhidharmakośa I 5b.
4. ibid. I 28; Vibhaṅga, p. 84.
5. Aṭṭhasālinī III 387.
6. Bhāṣya ad Abidh.-kośa VIII 3; Aṭṭhasālinī III 440.
7. Aṭṭhasālinī III 428.
8. ibid. III 429.

pandemonium of sheer impressions which are found on different levels and with different contents (*nānattasaññā*).[1]

While this meditative experience 'accompanied by a perception of the sphere of the infinitude of space', as it is described in the original texts, and which is also termed 'space (realized by) breaking through space-Gestalt',[2] may be said to be an experience in which the complex connoted 'space infinitude' is present to somebody's mind, it is essentially another aspect of the same experience, when there is a shift from the 'objective' to the 'subjective' and an experience comes about in which the 'being present to the mind' itself becomes the 'object' of mind and which is described as "the meditative experience accompanied by the perception of the sphere of the infinitude of perceiving (*vijñānānantya*, Pāli *viññāṇañcāyatana-saññāsahagata*)".[3]

The terms 'subjective' and 'objective' employed in this discussion of the problem, must not be allowed to lead us astray. Actually there is neither a subject nor an object in that which in no sense is. Therefore, the shift from the 'objective' or the perception of space infinitude to the 'subjective' or the perception of the becoming-aware-infinitude, and from there to the perception of the sphere of nothing whatsoever, should be considered as nothing more than a kind of description which becomes more pertinent and meaningful by progressing from problem to problem rather than from premise to consequence. Moreover, every perception is by nature formulation, and formulation is interpretation.

The most important and central experience, however, is the one which follows after the perception of the infinitude of becoming immediately aware has faded away and which is significantly termed as "accompanied by the perception of the sphere of nothing whatsoever" (*ākiṁcanya*, Pāli *ākiñcaññāyatana-saññāsahagata*), because "perception in the sense of 'being present to the mind' with reference to its object of infinitude of space has gone".[4] This experience may be said to be the energetic

1. Aṭṭhasālinī III 431.
2. ibid. III 437.
3. ibid. III 441.
4. ibid. III 443.

point which may dissolve into perceptivity and perceptibility in a process of transformation into Gestalten and their interpretation in terms of things and events or the "material mode".[1] It is from this point that the statement "*rūpa* is born from mind"[2] becomes intelligible, providing that we do not concretize mind into an entity. Mind actually is both real and unreal.

So far the *ārūpya* or the world of non-Gestalt has been dealt with from the viewpoint of the various techniques employed in breaking through the barriers of limited reality. Each of them appeared different due to the difference in discursive symbolism, language, which is then 'projected' on the *ārūpya* so that the one realm appears as comprising various levels. Therefore, language is responsible for a 'fourth' aspect being enumerated. This fourth aspect has as its object the "attainment of the sphere of nothing whatsoever"[3] and is described as being "accompanied by what is neither perception nor non-perception" (*naivasaṁjñānāsaṁjña*, Pāli *nevasaññānāsaññāsahagata*).[4] It has received this designation not from the technique of realization but from the nature (*sabhāvato*) of the psychological process.

Its nature is such that perception is involved in the whole of mental life (*cittacetasika dhamma*), but this perception also is such that it cannot be called perception in the ordinary sense of the word.[5] This means that it is not an isolated phenomenon but is in interplay with all other psychological factors. Another interpretation the author of the Aṭṭhasālinī gives, tallies with the one found with the Vaibhāṣikas, viz. that the perception formulation-process is so feeble that it is unable to function clearly (*paṭu*). Hence it is legitimate to say that it is non-perception. But since there is still formulation—formulation in the sense of active mental life—though not in a gross form (*saṁkhārāvasesasukhumabhāvena*) it is not possible to speak of non-perception in the literal sense of the word.[6]

1. cp. Abhidharmakośa VIII p. 143 n. 3.
2. Abhidharmakośa VIII 3d.
3. Aṭṭhasālinī III 452 : *ākiñcaññā yatanasamāpatti-ārammaṇassa jhānassa.*
4. ibid. III 445.
5. ibid. III 447.
6. ibid. III 448. Cp. also III 449 and 451. Bhāṣya ad adhidh.-kośa VIII 4c-d.

That which is 'perceived' (in the loose sense of the word) is the sphere of nothing whatsoever, since there is nothing else that could be perceived or into which the living process could transform itself,[1] though this 'object' is liable to be upsetting because it may formulate itself into the 'present to the mind' to the perceiving individual. This obviously means that every living process may terminate in a kind of discursive symbolism and thereby lose the character of liveliness. Moreover, the transformation which factual experiences undergo when they are cast into propositions when we want to communicate them, is that the relationships in them are turned into something like objects. When the author of the Aṭṭhasālinī illustrates the experience by the proverbial resignation of a population to a bad government,[2] he wants to tell of a way in which the population and the bad government are unfortunately and unhappily combined, but not of a succession of acts. There is no entity 'perceiving' in the complex of subject and object combined in such a way as to represent a structure of a state of affairs.

The author of the Aṭṭhasālinī is at pains to point out how this nature is grasped. He refers to Vibhaṅga 263 where it is stated that "one attends to the sphere of nothing whatsoever as something settled and achieves the attainment of that which is left of subtle formulativeness (*saṁkhārāvasesa*)". He explains the sentence as meaning that "The attainment is something settled, inasmuch as non-existence (*natthibhāva*) finds here its place as object (of contemplation)".[3] This is but another way of stating that in one sense we can say that something is, while in another sense it is true to say that it is not. It is when we understand what 'existence' and 'non-existence' respectively mean, that there is no further need to attend to anything (*anāvajjitukāmatayā*). Hence it becomes possible to say that the state of neither perception nor non-perception, being the nature of rather than the assertion about the experience, is more settled (*santatara*) and more sublime than the sphere of nothing whatsoever.[4]

1. Aṭṭhasālinī III 459.
2. ibid.
3. ibid. III 445.
4. ibid.

Knowledge and understanding are the essence of mental life. Formulation is its elementary process. Indeed, every experience is formulation, whether it be at the level of merest sense experience where seeing and hearing (as our most outstanding sense-experience) are themselves a process of formulation,[1] or whether it is at the level of meditation. Perception-formulation is therefore the keynote of all mental life. But mental life is not such that in it something remains static at all levels. The whole is transformed and disciplined through its interplay with all the other elements in the whole. Thus it is that not only perceiving as the knowledge-giving function of mind is in a state described as neither perception nor non-perception, but also feeling and the rest of mental factors; in other words, everything that we designate by mind and mental processes is involved.[2]

Formulation by way of transformation as the expression of mental life is a rather recent conception in Western philosophy,[3] yet it is the basic conception of the Vijñānavādins who in their critique of the Sarvāstivādins' conception of 'space as such' (*asaṁskṛta ākāśā*) which actually does not stand for any conception at all but was attributed existence (*vastu*), pointed out that it could be called existent only in the sense of being a description; a description, however, begins and ends with language which has the habit of making us 'conceive' objects where there are none, all this being included in the ceaseless transformation of mental life (*vijñānapariṇāma*).[4]

The author of the Aṭṭhasālinī, who is, as many passages in his work reveal, much indebted to the intellectual and spiritual acumen of the Vijñānavādins, is well aware of the deceptiveness of language which cannot but name one word first and then another. Certainly, that which in no sense is, the Ārūpya, cannot be said to have different levels. Description alone may vary. Thus he says: "Just as in the lowest storey of a four-storeyed palace there may be found the highest perfection

1. S. K. Langer, Philosophy in a New Key, p. 73. (Mentor).
2. Aṭṭhasālinī III 448.
3. It is indeed so new that Susanne K. Langer could rightly call her book "Philosophy in a New Key".
4. See Vijñaptimātratāsiddhi, p. 75.

of the five sensual pleasures in the form of heavenly dancing, singing, music, perfumes, garlands, sweet drink and food, couches, canopies and other luxuries; in the second storey these luxuries may be still more refined; and those in the third and fourth may be still more sublime than those in the preceding storeys, although these four are all palace storeys and there is no difference in them as such, it is only due to the difference in the display of sensual pleasures and luxuries that the higher storeys are more excellent than the lower ones"[1]

This should suffice to make us aware of the fact that the Ārūpya is no metaphysical thesis in the traditional sense of the word. Its recognition, however, widens the scope of mind, inasmuch as it points out that knowledge is not only found there where discursive projectibility reigns. It is found also in that which is beyond propositional thought and which is not necessarily blind, non-rational, and unknowable.[2]

Masteries and Freedoms

Meditation which encompasses all that which is commonly held to be real and unreal, but does not make use of either concept for propounding metaphysical assertions or producing 'proofs' of postulated theories, is a continual pursuit of meaning. As such it forms an integral part of human life which derives its meaning precisely from this pursuit of meaning and not from some final meaning, because final meanings about which the authorities on eternal verities are so cocksure, have mostly no meaning at all. Life becomes meaningless only when this pursuit of meaning comes to a dead end. Such a dead end is represented by fixations in the sense of emotionally entrenched, or even obsessive ideas exemplifying an inability to develop further interests and to arrive at a deeper, wider, and clearer understanding of experience. Mostly throughout our lives we remain static and only under rare circumstances we try to overcome such fixations, because they have been socially approved. Such a fixation is the mass man value with his suspicion of poetry, his distrust of art, and his contempt of philosophy. For even when we pay lip-service to the value of artists,

1. Aṭṭhasālinī III 455.
2. S. K. Langer, loc. cit., p. 71.

philosophers, and other creative geniuses for the advancement of cultural life, at heart we consider them as slippery customers, because they upset the familiar static pattern. But if life is to remain meaningful in the sense indicated above, it is imperative that such fixations and other stoppages are overcome and that the current can go on, freed from all obstacles which throw man back to lower levels of mental life and finally relegate him to intellectual dullness and emotional starvation. This removal of obstacles is important also in meditation, because, since it forms part of the greater stream called life, any disturbance in this section is likely to produce serious effects in the form of mental derangements and attendant physical ailments, which are all the more dangerous because meditation properly pursued is a gradual increase of an energetic potential. Interference with it is like touching a live wire, the higher the voltage the greater the danger.

It is not to be wondered at that Buddhism by virtue of its practical value in achieving spiritual maturation, should pay special attention to what is necessary in order to assure an unobstructed course. Two topics, indicative of a technique and of an unimpeded process, are pointed out as most intimately connected with meditation. They are termed 'masteries' (*abhibhvāyatana*, Pāli *abhibhāyatana*) and 'freedoms' (*vimokṣa*, Pāli *vimokkha*) respectively. Each group comprises eight sections, of which the two first masteries are related to the first freedom, the following two masteries to the second freedom, and the remaining four masteries to the third freedom.[1]

According to Vasubandhu the 'freedoms' are so called, because they turn away from lower levels,[2] or because they free a person from the obstacles on the way to meditative absorption,[3] or because they mean 'just freedom and nothing more',[4] while the 'masteries' refer to a command over the object one has chosen, so that as a consequence as it were,

1. Abhidharmakośa VIII 35b-d and Bhāṣya; Abhidharmasamuccaya, p. 96. See also Aṭṭhasālinī III 390-398.

2. Bhāṣya ad Abhidh.-kośa VIII 32d : *adharabhūmivaimukhyāt*.

3. Bhāṣya ad Abhidh.-kośa VIII 33a. See also note by L. de la Vallee Poussin.

4. Bhāṣya ad Abhidh.-kośa VIII 35b-d : *vimokṣamātra*.

emotional instability cannot interfere.[1] The explanation by the author of the Aṭṭhasālinī is similar to the one given in Abhidharmasamuccaya. He interprets 'freedom' (*vimokkha*) as meaning 'freedom in the operation of a feeling of worth-whileness' (*adhimuccana*) which, in its turn, denotes a proper freeing from opposing elements and a proper interest in the chosen object by taking delight in it. Its operation is said to be unrestricted and unhesitating, as free and abandoned as a small boy lying sprawled on his father's lap.[2] He further informs us that the 'masteries' and 'freedoms' are certain aspects of a meditational process which is also known as the 'totalities', and he states that the 'totality' instruction belongs to the Abhidharma, while the instruction in the 'masteries' and 'freedoms' belongs to the Sūtras.[3] This statement is of tremendous importance, because it irrefutably shows that there have always been two distinct modes of teaching, an esoteric one for those who had a deeper understanding and were from the outset particularly gifted to grasp the meaning of reality, and an exoteric one which dealt with generalities and was addressed to those who had to be prepared slowly for developing an understanding of the meaning of reality. This latter feature we find in the Sūtras, while the former is preserved in the Abhidharma which, as has been pointed out,[4] is the realm of the Buddhas, of those who are spiritually awake. This statement as to the double mode of teaching gives full validity to the Mahāyānic claim that the Sūtras presenting a general idea of Buddhism, and the Tantras embodying the psychological details of practising a philosophy (an idea to which the Western world is rather unaccustomed as the discrepancy between the lives and teachings of their philosophers visibly demonstrates), went side by side. The statement by the author of the Aṭṭhasālinī is all the more valuable, since it has been uttered by a man who is a recognized authority on Hīnayāna. It is the followers of the Hīnayāna, who nowadays, contrary to what is laid down in their own authoritative texts, violently oppose the idea of a double teaching by the Buddha.

1. Bhāṣya ad Abhidh.-kośa VIII 35 b-d : *vimokṣamātra*.
2. Aṭṭhasālinī III 395. See also Abhidharmasamuccaya, p. 96.
3. Aṭṭhasālinī III 398.
4. See above, p. 3, note 2.

The author of the Aṭṭhasālinī substantiates his statement by commenting on the fact that the formula of the 'masteries' is different in the Abhidharma from the one given in the Sūtras. In all instances of the 'masteries' in the Abhidharma[1] it is said that the 'masteries' are attended to while one does not include oneself in this practice, in other words, that one does not attend to one's body image which refers to the whole person constituted of body and mind, (*ajjhattam arūpasaññī*),[2] because in the practice of the 'masteries' the point is not to gain mastery over the body image but over those things which are believed to be external objects, by viewing them without the primitive beliefs about their 'material' nature, but solely in their aesthetic immediacy, in grasping and understanding the visual structure in one act of cognizing vision (*jānāmi passāmi*).[3]

Proportions and colors play an important role in the practice of the 'masteries', not only to the extent that that it is possible to attend to proportions separate from colors and vice versa, but also by an aesthetic evaluation of beauty and ugliness. These varieties are intimately related to the temperament of the meditating person. An object of small proportions is particularly well suited for a person who habitually is inclined to attend to all and everything (*vitakkacarita*), because an object of large proportions, extending to infinity as it were, would only reinforce his habit of attending to particular items within this extensive object whereby he would not succeed in gaining the necessary 'mastery' of grasping the whole in one act.[4] An object of large proportions, on the other hand, is suited for him who is overcome by bewilderment (*mohacarita*), because it has the effect of freeing him from the narrow suffocating world of small objects and events which make him feel imprisoned.[5] A person who sees faults everywhere and has a natural aversion towards anything that does not come up to perfection (*dosacarita*), can gain mastery only by attending to that which is beautiful, in particular, to a color

1. In his Bhaṣya ad Abhidh. -kośa VIII 35a Vasubandhu follows the Sūtra formulae.
2. Aṭṭhasālinī III 392.
3. ibid. III 390.
4. ibid. III 392. Visuddhimagga III 102.
5. ibid. III 392. Visuddhimagga III 101.

in all its radiance and stainless brilliance,[1] while a person who is dominated by possessiveness (*rāgacarita*) will be able to gain mastery by attending to that which is ugly, to a color which is dull and may be repulsive to him, because this is a means to sever the ties that fetter him to the object.[2]

'Mastery', however, is achieved only when we have become free; free in the sense of being able to attend to an object in a way we like, without meeting with frustration which comes about by our reading utilitarian ideas into the object, in other words, when we are able to grasp an object in its sensed and felt immediacy, dropping as far as possible the suggestion of a three-dimensional external object. An object is not only another person or an inanimate piece of nature, it is also our own person which is given to our mind as an image (*rūpa, nimitta*) that we fill with our beliefs about three-dimensional external objects and our importance. However, in order to gain the experience of immediacy we may start with any 'part' of our body such as the hair, the pupils of the eyes, the skin, the hands and feet, whether we view and experience them according to our temperament in their aesthetic beauty of shape and color, or in their hideousness of continuous decay. But just as we can see ourselves before we interpret and fill the image of ourselves, we also can see things and persons outside ourselves with the same immediacy of aesthetic appreciation. Thus to become able to see ourselves and others in and through a Gestalt, is the first 'freedom', which Asaṅga in his Abhidharmasamuccaya describes as follows[3] : "In practising meditation, by not allowing the experience of a Gestalt as to ourselves, the observer, to disappear or, positively stated, by bringing about in the observer the experience of Gestalt, it is that he sees visual structures. In this state where one is well versed in the practice there are found concentrated absorption, appreciative analytical understanding, all the attitudinal and functional patterns connected with this understanding, as well as freedom from the power that veils spiritual creativity".[4]

1. Aṭṭhasālinī III 392. Visuddhimagga III 100.
2. ibid. III 392. Visuddhimagga III 97.
3. Abhidharmasamuccaya, p. 95.
4. As to *nirmāṇa* see Abhidharmakośa VII 50.

Similarly the second 'freedom' is characterized as the ability to see visual structures in the external objects, without experiencing the same as to one's own person. This, at least, is the interpretation of the technical term (*adhyātmam arūpasaṁjñī*) given by Vasubandhu and by the author of the Aṭṭhasālinī who expressly states that the Gestalt-experience is not brought about by attending to the 'parts' or our body but only to the external objects.[1] Another interpretation which reflects a different psychological attitude, is given by Asaṅga. He declares: It is in the practice of meditation, by making the experience of Gestalt with reference to the observer disappear or, positively stated, by bringing about in the observer the experience of unreality (*arūpasaṁjñā*), it is that he sees visual structures. Just as in the first 'freedom' so also here there is concentrated absorption and appreciative analytical understanding".[2] There is here a marked difference in orientation. With Vasubandhu and the author of the Aṭṭhasālinī emphasis is laid on the experience of outer objects as Gestalten, obviously because the outer objects in their interpretation as three-dimensional material things had the strongest hold on them. But with Asaṅga the experience of oneself as unreal gains in importance, because the subjective factor in meditation is just as important. To become free from the self-concept as something solid and real is most decisive, because this freedom facilitates the experience of visual structures in a more deeply moving form. When Vasubandhu even goes so far as to identify these two types of 'freedom' with the practice of meditating on the progressive deterioration of corpses (*aśubhabhāvanā*),[3] which is but related to a certain temperament and not universal, he restricts the meaning of 'freedom' in a manner which is certainly not guaranteed by the formula itself, since its wording admits of a much wider interpretation.

The psychological difference in attitude—one is almost tempted to speak of extraverted and introverted types—is still

1. Bhaṣya ad Abhidh. -kośa VIII 32a. Aṭṭhasālinī III 397.

2. Abhidharmasamuccaya, p. 95. This interpretation tallies with the one given by Harivarman. See Abhidharmakośa VIII, p. 204 note 2c by L. de la Vallee Poussin.

3. Abhidharmakośa VIII 32ab. Cp. also Bhāṣya ad VIII 34.

more obvious in the interpretation of the third 'freedom', by which the observer is physically aware[1] of that which is termed the 'beautiful' (*śubha*, Pāli *subha*). According to Vasubandhu[2] this 'freedom' is related to the fourth stage of the meditative process exclusively, while the author of the Aṭṭhasālinī[3] allows this 'freedom' with every stage in meditation and relegates it to the color 'totalities'. Again it is Asaṅga who brings out the depth and scope of this experience which is so strong that it does not remain a mental image but innervates the whole of our physical existence. He states[4] : "In practising meditation, by gaining the experience of the relativity of the beautiful and the ugly as to and within ourselves, of the mutual conformity of the beautiful and ugly, and of the sameness of the emotional feeling tone and value of the beautiful and ugly, there is in the mastery of this practice concentrated absorption, appreciative analytical understanding, and freedom from the production of what is beautiful and what is ugly and from the veiling power of the rise of emotional instability (introducing a difference of values)". In passing it may be noted that 'sameness of emotional feeling tone and value' (*ekarasa, samarasa*) applied to the arbitrary division of life into a part called Saṁsāra and another part called Nirvāṇa, is the keynote of the Tantras which, just as the Abhidharma, embody the esoteric teaching as to psychological experiences.

The fourth to the seventh freedoms are related to the Ārūpya-world, each freedom referring to a particular mastery in that which is described in four different ways (infinitude of space, infinitude of perception, sphere of nothing whatsoever, and state of neither perception nor non-perception). Since the Ārūpya-world does not comprise levels, the four corresponding 'freedoms' owe their existence to the logical projection by language, in which we conceive our world, real or unreal. The eighth 'freedom' is the mastery which frees us from that which is described as neither perception nor non-perception, and

1. *kāyena sākṣātkṛtvā.* See Bhāṣya ad Abhidh.-kośa VIII 34 and Vyākhyā, Abhidharmasamuccaya, p. 95.
2. Abhidharmakośa VIII 32c; Bhāṣya ad VIII 34.
3. Aṭṭhasālinī III 397.
4. Abhidharmasamuccaya, p.95.

through which we realize the deep peace of the cessation of formulation by perception and feeling (*saṁjñāveditanirodhasamāpatti*).[1]

Conclusion

In discussing meditation as an integral part in Buddhist discipline the limitations of language are particularly obvious and troublesome. Meditation is not only a certain practice, it is also a unique experience which does not allow itself to be projected into discursive forms. Certainly, there are different stages in meditation, each of them leading to a deeper, wider, and more intense realization and all of them forming one integral whole. Therefore the 'freedoms' (*vimokṣa*), 'masteries' (*abhibhvāyatana*), 'totalities' (*kṛtsnāyatana*) and 'meditative stages' (*dhyāna*) are not isolated phenomena. They are so intimately interrelated that not only the one leads to the other but also that the one is not without the other.[2] Another and very important feature of Buddhist meditation is the fact that to concentrate on an object of one's choice is not the main aim or an end in itself. To become free from all ties that fetter us intellectually and emotionally is the aim, and this also implies that freedom has to be gained even from the object on which concentrated attention has been bestowed. In this respect Buddhist meditation is diametrically opposed to the meditation practices of Ignatius of Loyola in his *exercitia*, where the object of meditation is kept constant and not transcended.

The outcome of meditation cannot be specified just because it also encompasses that which reason as the instrument of discursive thinking would brand as unreal. Any description of it remains inadequate. Reality is not a well-defined or definable entity but something which expands the deeper we dive into it. Each dive reveals new aspects. Being concerned with gaining knowledge which is comprehensive rather than fragmentary, meditation aims at making man able to walk the

1. Abhidharmasamuccaya, p. 95. Bhāṣya ad Abhidh.-kośa VIII 32a and 33a.

2. According to the Bhāṣya ad Abhidh.-kośa VIII 36cd the topics mentioned follow this order, each one leading to the other.

Path[1] which will finally lead to enlightenment and spiritual maturity. Since spiritual maturity is rarely found in the world, although this our world is perhaps the only one where we may find meaning, the Path belongs to that which is termed 'super-worldly' (*lokottara*). Again it must not be assumed that 'super-worldly' has any spatial connotations.

The pursuit of meaning leads into realms from which a better understanding of Reality becomes possible. Better understanding means a clearer view and more enduring emotional satisfaction. This is already achieved on the first level of the meditative process (*dhyāna*) and is technically termed *dṛṣṭa-dharmasukhavihāra* and means that we have passed from a diffused state of mind into a concentrated and integrated state in which we experience the satisfaction and happiness of having become free from emotional instability.[2] Although this feeling of satisfaction and happiness also obtains in the following stages each successive stage is characterized in addition by deeper knowledge and a wider view. Thus at the second stage a superior knowledge and wider outlook is attained so that the incessant coming and going of being is realized.[3] While on the third stage the analytical appreciative understanding becomes more and more penetrating[4] until in the fourth

1. Abhidharmakośa VIII 34. All types of meditation belong to the 'worldly' (*laukika*) sphere. See Aṭṭhasālinī III 466.

2. Abhidharmakośa VIII 27c-28; II 4.

3. Bhāṣya ad Abhidh.-kośa VIII 27c-28. This wider view has its root in the 'superior knowledge in the form of divine vision' (*divyacakṣura-bhijñā*).

4. ibid. *prajñāprabheda*. By it the 'nature' or the properties' (*guṇa*) of the three world spheres are understood, viz, *aśubhā* (horrid), *ānāpānasmṛt* (attention to breathing), *araṇā* (knowledge as to emotional outburst on the level of the world of sensuality. Abhidh.-kośa VII 36; Abhidharmasa-muccaya, p. 96; Aṭṭhasālinī II 52), *praṇidhijñāna* (knowledge by resolution attending to all the knowable, Abhidh.-kośa VII 37; Abhidharmasamuccaya, p. 96), *pratisaṁvid* (exact knowledge, Abhidh.-kośa VII 37-38; Abhidharma-samuccaya, p. 96; further references with L. de la Vallee Poussin's transla-tion of Abhidharmakośa VII, p. 89 note), *abhijñā* (superior knowledge, Abhidh.-kośa VII 42; Abhidharmasamuccaya, p. 97), *vimokṣa* (freedom, see above p. 141), *abhibhvāyatana*, etc. See in particular, Abhidharma-samuccaya, pp. 97-102. All of them have a double nature according to their being 'worldly' or 'superworldly'.

stage all fetters are thrown off and an unshakable integration has been achieved which is significantly termed Vajropama, 'similar to a Vajra'[1], the Vajra being the symbol of indestructibility and unshakableness.[2]

1. Bhāṣya ad Abhidh.-kośa VIII 27c-28.

2. A similar gradation is found in Aṭṭhasālinī III 387. Here the meditation with 'sensed space' is said to lead to *diṭṭhadhammasukhavihāra* and to be the basis of *abhiññā, vipassanā* and *nirodha*. In this passage *vipassanā* corresponds approximately to *prajñāprabheda* and *nirodha* to *Vajropama*.

THE INTERPRETATION OF THE WORLD WE LIVE IN

(*rūpa*)

The World As We Perceive It

The interest in man as he appears to himself and the way in which it becomes possible for him to develop spiritually, have dominated the whole of Buddhist thought to such a degree that the external physical world, as we are wont to say, has more or less completely been lost sight of. This statement is valid with the proviso that mind and matter are two entities that can be clearly and easily divided from each other, have nothing in common with each other, and do not overlap at any point. However, the preceding analysis of 'mind' and 'mental states' has shown that 'mind' is but a convenient and conventional term for grouping a variety of events in a unity. Properly speaking, it is the centre of this unity that receives the name 'mind', whose logical nature is considered to be either existent or subsistent, although it has to be noted that there is no need to assume subsistence. As the critique of the various views held about 'mind' by the Mādhyamikas has shown, 'mental states' are for all practical purposes real, but 'mind' is a fiction. In analyzing matter we are forced to a similar conception not only by what modern experimental and theoretical physics has found, but also by an analysis of perceptual situations. When modern science, which has succeeded in making 'matter' less material and 'mind' less mental, declares that the observer is part of his observation, this means that a person who has experience of anything is part of that experience; the thought is part of the thing thought of. So we are thrown back to a perceptual situation and are forced to analyse it from the viewpoint of experience, because experience is the central theme of Buddhism, not theoretical postulation and deductive verification. Since no experience occurs more than once and all repeated experiences actually are only analogous occurrences, it follows that a 'thing' or material substance can only be said to be a series of events interpreted as a thing, having no more substantiality than any other series of events we may arbitrarily single out. Thus the distinction between 'mental' and 'material' becomes irrelevant and it is a matter of taste to speak of physical objects. In other words, although we shall continue to speak about matter and mind, we must bear in mind that it is but a figure of speech as untrue as the statement that the sun rises or sets.

What Buddhism asserts and what everyone will be agreed upon, is that there are perceptual situations, in which we claim to be in cognitive contact with something other than our states. Such situations are intuitive and sensuous, to use the terminology of C. D. Broad,[1] and have an epistemological object. However, as delusive perceptual situations, which do not show any relevant difference from a veridical perceptual situation, make abundantly clear the existence or presence of an epistemological object does not guarantee that there exists an ontological object which corresponds accurately to the epistemological object. We believe that there are trees, mountains, tables and other objects, but we do not believe that there are pink rats. Furthermore, the epistemological object is a complex whole. In addition to a spatio-temporally extended particular, a certain quality of which is sensuously manifested in a perceptual situation, there is the belief that this particular something is not completely revealed in all its qualities, that it is part of a longer strand of history than the momentary situation, and that this spatially larger and temporally longer whole is a certain 'thing'. In other words, every perceptual situation possesses an objective constituent of a characteristic kind and an external reference beyond the objective constituent. It is this external reference which we believe to be a 'physical' object. In order that a certain quality may reveal itself to the mind it is necessary that appropriate sense-organs exist. Since we have at least five senses we also have at least five different perceptual situations : *e.g.*, color reveals itself to sight, sound to hearing, flavor to taste, fragrance to smell, and hardness to touch.

These qualities or objective constituents of a perceptual

1. C. D. Broad, The Mind and its Place in Nature, pp. 144 sqq.

situation are referred to by the term *sarvaṁ rūpam.*[1] Since there is no reason to believe that the objective constituent of a perceptual situation is literally a spatio-temporal part of a physical object, because the idea of a physical object cannot be abstracted from the data of sense but is a hypothesis and is defined by postulates, the translation of *rūpa* by 'matter', contrasting it with mind in the manner of Descartes (whether this is openly admitted or not), is downright silly.[2] All that we can say about *rūpa* is that it is a name for an objective constituent in a perceptual situation. But since the objective constituent is mixed up with the external reference it is a loose way of speaking when *rūpa* is also used for an object, a 'thing'.

Certain of the qualities which reveal themselves to a mind, are regarded as more elementary or primary and hence basic, than others. These more elementary qualities are termed *mahābhūta*, usually translated as 'great elements' or 'great essentials', although the proper translation should have been 'great elementary qualities'. There are four such 'great elementary qualities' : earth-, water-, fire-, and air-basis.[3] Their names have been derived from the 'objects' which common-sense assumes, although the Buddhists never had the association of objects in our sense of the word. 'Earth' is the symbolic expression for all that is solid and able to carry a load, 'water' for all that is fluid and cohesive, 'fire' for all that is warm or has temperature, and 'air' for all that is light and moving.[4]

Vasubandhu and Yaśomitra explain the name of the four great elementary qualities in this way that their greatness (*mahatva*) is due to the fact that they are the basis of all secondary qualities and that it is from the 'physical' objects which have emerged from these primary qualities, that we learn

1. Abhidharmasamuccaya, p. 3; 41. Aṭṭhasālinī IV 2; 3 etc.

2. The translations of the Pali Text Society have completely failed to grasp the Buddhist meaning of *rūpa* and made a distinction not guaranteed by the texts into 'matter' and 'attenuated matter'. Unfortunately also the translators do not tell us how 'matter' is 'attenuated' and what 'matter' is.

3. Aṭṭhasālinī IV 3. Abhidharmakośa I 12; Abhidharmasamuccaya, p. 3.

4. Abhidharmakośa I 12; Abhidharmasamuccaya, p. 3. Aṭṭhasālinī IV 93, here 'being light' belongs to 'earth'.

their mode of operation,[1] while their elementariness and existence is due to the fact that they knit together the whole of that which exists[2]. Yaśomitra gives as examples of their mode of operation the following: "In rocks and other terrestrial objects we find cohesion (*saṁgraha*), temperature (*pakti*), extension (*vyūhana*), and so the existence of the other elements (beside the ability to carry things, *dhṛti*) is inferred. Similarly we see that water carries ships (*saṁdhāraṇa*), has temperature, and movement, so that in it there is also earth (the ability to carry things), fire (temperature), and air (movement) (beside its own property of cohesion). In a flame we observe continuance, compactness, movement, so that in it there is earth (solidity), water (cohesion), and air (movement). In wind we see that it is able to carry things, has temperature warm or cold, and possesses tangibility, so that in it there are present earth (ability to carry), water (continuity and tangibility), and fire (temperature)."[3]

Since qualities, in Buddhism, are dynamic, each property is defined from a dynamic point of view. 'Extension' (*vyūhana*) is both 'growth' (*vṛddhi*) and 'transition' (*prasarpaṇa*). 'Growth' means that within a given series certain factors appear, as for instance the limbs of a body or the shoots of plants, while 'transition' means the appearance in another place of that which constitutes a series of events forming an object. However, 'transition', the moving from place to place, represents rather a complicated problem because of the momentariness of the whole of reality. Just as an experience is a momentary event and cannot be repeated, every repetition being essentially an analogous experience, so also due to the momentariness of the objective constituent in our perceptual situation, it is impossible that one moment should move from here to there. The continuity we observe is actually a series of analogous moments. So Yaśomitra declares: "That which is momentary cannot go from one place to another. That which is momentary disappears on the spot where it has appeared. Hence it is said : 'Movement or the stream of elementary properties whose nature

1. Bhāṣya and Vyākhyā ad Abhidharmakośa I 12.
2. Vyākhyā, ibid. : *bhūtaṁ tanvantīti bhūtāni.*
3. ibid.

is such that it appears in successive places, is like a flame because of its momentariness. The momentary elementary qualities are like a flame because of their nature of being objective constituents of perceptual situations. The comparison with a flame is given because the momentary character of a flame is an established fact."[1]

The author of the Aṭṭhasālinī gives rather a different explanation of the term 'great elementary qualities'. He states that their greatness is manifest in the continuity of our environmental world (*anupādinnakasantāna*) as well as in the continuity of organisms (*upādinnakasantāna*) living in this world.[2]

In this connection it may not be out of place to discuss the meaning of 'organism', because the two technical terms *upādinna* 'organized' and *anupādinna* 'unorganized' are ever recurring in Abhidharma literature. Popularly speaking, an organism is a body animated by a mind,[3] or in purely Buddhistic terms, it is that which a mind and its states have taken up, appropriated as operational basis[4], so that a peculiarly intimate connexion obtains in which there is two-sided interaction.[5] But it should be noted that nowhere has anything been said about the nature of mind and matter and the nature of the origin of this connexion. In the narrower sense, however, 'organism' is but a conventional term for grouping biologically organized structures, of which the five senses are most prominent. Hence the statement that the five senses are always and without exception 'organized structures' (*upādinna*), but only as far as the present moment is concerned; the past and the future—the one no longer existing and the other not yet having come into existence—cannot be said to be so 'organized'.[6] Inasmuch as according to the doctrine of the Vaibhāṣikas it is not mind that sees by using the eye as its instrument, as is the conception of the Vijñānavādins, but the organized

1. ibid.
2. Aṭṭhasālinī IV 4-7.
3. Vyākhyā ad Abhidharmakośa I 34 : *yal loke sacetanam iti sajīvam ity arthaḥ.*
4. Bhāṣya ad Abhidh.-kośa I 34.
5. ibid. Vyākhyā : *anyonyānuvidhānād*
6. Bhāṣya ad Abhidh.-kośa I 34d.

structure 'eye' (again this word must not be understood anatomically, but functionally as the term *cakṣuḥprasāda* suggests),[1] the conception of an organism approaches a thoroughly behavioristic theory of mind and matter : any organized structure, insofar as it behaves in a certain way, *is* this mind (which popularly is supposed to animate something apart from it). Further, since any organized structure is said to contain other qualities than those derived from the elementary qualities and forming the particular organized structure, and since these other qualities partake of the organization, they are 'organized' (*upādinna*) in contrast to all other qualities which are not so organized (*anupādinna*).[2] This somewhat loose use of a certain technical term has led the Theravādins and their modern interpreters into a welter of confusion. It has prompted them to fail to mark the important distinction between organized structure (*upādinna*) and physical object which is but the conception of something not biologically organized.[3]

After this digression let us return to the explanation of the 'great elementary qualities' used by the author of the Aṭṭhasālinī. He continues to point out their greatness by referring to the tremendous changes that occur at the time of the dissolution of the world and when other deteriorating circumstances appear in organisms.[4] Of particular interest and importance, however, is the following description, because it suggests that there are no veridical perceptual situations but only delusive ones and that the four elementary qualities are not something existent but just names for certain events and their interrelations. With this conception the author shows his acquaintance with the ideas of Mahāyāna Buddhism of which he was in favour, as other passages have made evident. He says : "Just as a magician shows water which is not a gem as a gem, or clay which is not gold as gold, or himself not being an ogre or a bird, makes himself appear as an ogre or a bird, so also the

1. Vyākhyā and Bhāṣya ad Abhidh.-kośa I 42.

2. Aṭṭhasālinī IV 104 : *yasmā pana rūpāyatanādīni upādinnāni pi ahtti anupādinnāni pi......*

3. See also note 1 on p. 63 of the first volume of L. de la Vallee Poussin's translation of Abhidharmakośa.

4. Aṭṭhasālinī IV 10.

four great elementary qualities, themselves not being either blue or yellow or red or white, show themselves as the secondary qualities blue, yellow, red and white. Thus, because of their resemblance to the great feats of magicians (*mahābhūta*) they are termed 'great elementary qualities', (*mahābhūta*).—Or, just as such great beings (*mahābhūta*) as demons, are not found inside or outside a person whom they have attacked, and yet exist in relation to that person, so also these elementary qualities are not found inside or outside each other, and yet exist in relation to each other. Thus, because of their resemblance to such great beings as demons, due to the fact that their location is unthinkable, they are termed 'great elementary qualities'.—Or, just as such great beings (*mahābhūta*) as Yakṣiṇīs hide their fearful nature by graceful deportment, by fair complexion and shape, and deceive sentient beings, so also these great elementary qualities hide their true characteristics of hardness and other properties; in their appearance as woman and men, by lovely complexion, by graceful shapes of limbs, by seductive movements of hands and feet, fingers and eyebrows, they deceive simple people and do not allow them to see their real nature. Therefore, because of their resemblance to such great beings as Yakṣiṇīs, due to their deceptiveness they are termed 'great elementary qualities'."[1]

It is a great pity that the author does not elaborate this statement, because it is the very idea which is so important in the Tantra literature embodying the account of the psychological processes and experiences in course of spiritual development, viz., the doctrine of appearance which leaves the existence of physical objects merely hypothetical and which actually is the keynote of Mahāyāna Buddhism as a practical discipline rather than as a philosophical hypothesis. This conception is referred to by the technical term 'Śūnyatā in its aspect of possessing all excellent Gestalten' (*rnam. pa. kun. gyi. mchog. daṅ. ldan. pai. stoṅ. pa.ñid*).[2] This term reveals a very

1. Aṭṭhasālinī IV 8.

2. See for instance Rnal. hbyor. bzhii. bśad. pa. don. dam. mdzub. tshugs.su.bstan.pa, fol. 8b. Phyag. rgya. chen. p. p. lṅa. ldan. gyi. khrid. dmigs. yid. kyi. sñe. ma. fol. 5a. Rten. ḥbrel. kho. bo. lugs. kyi. khrd. chos. thams. cad. kynsñiṅ. po. len. pa. fol. 3a. Phyag. rgya. chen. poi. man. ṅag.

important aspect of Buddhism, namely, that the problem of Reality was closely connected with perception. In modern terminology this might be expressed in the following way : 'There is a certain sense field with an outstanding sensum, of which it is impossible to predicate existence or non-existence and which is hence termed Sūnyatā. This outstanding sensum has a certain characteristic (*rnam.pa=ākāra*) of which I believe that there is a physical object corresponding to it and to which it has a certain relation that it has to no other object. By virtue of this relation the characteristic sensum is an appearance of a physical object so that it is true to say that 'there is appearance without any existence (or non-existence)' (*med. bzhin. du. snaṅ.ba.*)[1] The similarity to what C.D. Broad calls 'The Sensum Theory' is obvious. It is this theory to which he gives preference over all other theories.[2] There are, of course, certain differences but they need not be dealt with in detail here.

While all schools of Buddhism agree that there are neither more nor less than four elementary qualities, from which all other qualities have been derived, although nothing is said of how, to give an example, color may be derived from solidity or the other elementary qualities, there is considerable divergence of opinion as to these secondary qualities (*upadārūpa, upādāyarūpa*). The Theravādins[3] recognized twenty-three categories, while the Sarvāstivādins and Vijñānavādins[4] admitted only eleven. Certainly, some of the twenty-three categories of the Theravādins are also found in the other schools, but as sub-categories rather than full categories, while others are not found in them and seem to owe their origin to a transference from the 'mental' to the 'physical', so that a physical

gi. bśad. sbyar. rgyal. bai. gan. mdzod, fol. 31 1a. Bsre. hphoi. lam. skor. gyi. thog. mar. lam. dbye. bsdu, fol. 60a; 45a. Rygal. ba. khyab. bdag. rdo. rje. ḥchan. chen. poi. lam. gyis. rim. pa. gsaṅ. ba. kun. gyi. gnad. rnam. par. phye. ba. fol. 270b.

1. See for instance Bsre. ḥphoi. lam. skor. gyi, thog. mar. lam. dbye. bsdu, foll. 66b; 72b; 77b.

2. C. D. Broad. The Mind and its Place in Nature, pp. 182 sq.

3. Aṭṭhasālinī IV 12; 25. Abhidhammatthasaṁgaha VI 4 increases this artificial system by another category, the heart (*hadayavatthu*).

4. Abhidharmakośa I 9 ; Abhidharmasamuccaya, p. 3.

object was halfway between an organized structure with its peculiar function and an unorganized something called a 'thing'. It is certain that the analysis has not been carried out sufficiently deeply by the Theravādins and Sarvāstivādins, because they were prevented from doing so by their clinging to the numerical dogmatism of their respective schools. On the whole it can be said that the secondary qualities (*upādāyarūpa*) comprise the objective constituents of perceptual situations (colors, sounds, etc.) and the 'sensitivities' (*rūpaprasāda*) of the sense organs which are manifested to a person himself by a mass of bodily feeling and to others through certain visual and tactual sensa.[1] However, the Theravādins alone held the view, which was challenged by Saṅghabhadra, that the objective constituents of tactile situations were not secondary qualities but the three elementary qualities of solidity, temperature, and movement, with the exception of the fourth elementary quality of cohesion.[2] The Vaibhāṣikas, on the other hand, thought that the objective constituents of tactile situations did comprise both the four elementary qualities and seven secondary qualities.[3] They also recognized a double nature of the elementary quality 'air', insofar as 'movement' was said to be a primary and elementary quality, while the property 'being light' (*laghu*) was a secondary quality.[4] The Theravādins, on the other hand, considered the property 'being light' as a metaphor for the primary quality of solidity (earth).[5]

Apart from these differences, the Theravādins and Sarvāstivādins agreed that the ability to perceive (*rūpaprasāda*) was itself 'invisible' (*anidarśana*, Pāli *anidassana*)[6] This means that this property of being able to perceive, manifested itself to the persons perceiving, as a mass of bodily feeling and thus it belongs more to the tactile group,[7] while it would fall under the visible group, when because of the intermingling of

1. Bhāṣya ad Abhidh.-kośa I 9 ; Abhidharmasamuccaya, p. 3; Aṭṭhasālinī IV 29.
2. Aṭṭhasālinī IV 93-97.
3. Abhidharmakośa I 35 and Bhāṣya.
4. Abhidharmakośa I 12 and Bhāṣya.
5. Aṭṭhasālinī IV 93.
6. Aṭṭhasālinī IV 29; Abhidharmakośa I 28 (Bhāṣya).
7. Cp. Bhāṣya ad Abhidh.-kośa I 28.

objective constituents and external references, it would be made an object of inspection. Although the texts do not say so, this is implicit in the fact that the capacity to perceive is referred to by anatomical terms and physiological processes.[1] Though invisible, as the texts say, it is active-reactive (*sapratigha*, Pāli *sappaṭigha*),[2] insofar as the organized structure 'proceeds in the direction of', i.e., acts on the object which, in turn, stops its further progress or even 'proceeds into the direction' of the perceiving structure or organ, as the author of the Aṭṭhasālinī describes : "When lightning flashes, this event (*rūpa*) acts on the eye, even if one should not want to see" and "When someone who wants to see, adjusts his eyes, the eyes act on the object.[3]

This two-sided interaction as it were, between the perceived object and the perceiving organ has raised the problem as to how these two entities 'reach' (*prāp*) each other. Vasubandhu and the author of the Aṭṭhasālinī declare that in the case of hearing and seeing this 'reaching' can be but a figurative mode of speech, while in the case of the other sense perceptions there is an intimate connection between the object and the organ, a state of non-separatedness in the sense that nothing else can come in between.[4] It is plain that this problem owes its origin to the ambiguity of language which uses one and the same word for a sensum and for the belief about it. To refer to this conception of the Theravādins and Sarvāstivādins as a philosophical problem is perhaps much too generous, it is better listed as the naivest view of 'I can see the distant sun without any trouble, but I can taste sugar only when I put it on my tongue'. There is nothing new or astonishing in the fact that our senses have different ranges of operation (*gocara*).

For the Vijñānavādins, naturally, this 'problem' remained meaningless, because that which was termed *rūpa* did not exist apart from the psychological process (*vijñāna*) which alone is real and which transforms itself into a *darśanabhāga* 'perceiving process' and a *nimittabhāga* 'perceived image'. Both these

1. Aṭṭhasālinī IV 28; 35.
2. Aṭṭhasālinī IV 29; Abhidharmakośa I 29 and Bhāṣya.
3. Aṭṭhasālinī 32; 33.
4. Aṭṭhasālinī IV 43; Abhidharmakośa I 43 and Bhāṣya: *nirantaratra*.

transformations find their integration in the *svasaṁvittibhāga* 'the direct experience'.[1] Formulated in this way, the view expressed by the Vijñānavādins avoids the constant confusion between the form sensed and the postulated external object, a confusion to which the Theravādins and Sarvāstivādins were particularly prone. It is obvious that the view of the Vijñānavādins raises the problem to a purely psychological level. However, the term *svasaṁvitti* is ambiguous, inasmuch as it may be interpreted as 'cognizing itself'. This interpretation was moreover prompted by considering the *svasaṁvitti* as the 'result' (*phala*) of the cognizing process[2] which, being mind itself, could not do otherwise but cognize itself. This interpretation provoked the severe criticism of the Mādhyamikas who declared that mind does not cognize itself, just as little as the edge of a knife cannot cut itself or the tip of a finger cannot touch itself.[3] This criticism led to a different interpretation of the term *svasaṁvitti* by the Tantriks who used this same term merely as a name for the unanalysable quality of being conscious. It thus was a term of experience and not of theory, and as everyone can verify for himself, in experience the postulated premise of the unresolvability of the gulf between the 'knower' and the 'known' does not obtain.[4]

In giving an account of what appears as an objective constituent of a perceptual situation all schools who admit an Abhidharma, show great similarity in terms and definitions. The numerical system is very much emphasized. Strictest in the limitation of the number of possible objective constituents of perceptual situations, were the Vaibhāṣikas, who admitted twenty or twenty-one varieties at the utmost.[5] The Vijñānavādins admitted a slightly greater number (twenty-three),[6] while the Theravādins started with recognizing twenty-one

1. Vijñaptimātratāsiddhi of Hiuan-tsang, p. 131.
2. ibid.
3. Madhyamakavṛtti, pp. 62 sq. ; Madhyamakāvatāra, p. 166.
4. Phyag.rgya. chen. poi. man. ṅag. gi. bśad. sbyar. rgyal. bai. gan. mdzod. foll. 42a sqq.
6. Abhidharmakośa I 10 and Bhāṣya.
5. Abhidharmasamuccaya, p. 3.

varieties and then broke up this limitation by admitting an almost indefinite number (*ye-vā-panaka*).[1]

The objective constituents of a visual situation comprise two types : color (*varṇa*) and shape (*saṁsthāna*).[2] Color is according to the Sarvāstivādins and Vijñānavādins fourfold : blue, yellow, red, and white. All other colors stem from these four primary colors. The Theravādins add to these four colors five others. Their distinction of colors is between colors per se (*sabhāva*) and colors found in particular objects (*vatthu*). The former are blue, yellow, red, white, black, crimson, and dark green, the latter leaf-green and mango-shoot-green.[3]

There is also another set of eight items which are considered to be colors. They are glare (*ātapa*), shade (*chāyā*), light (*āloka*), particularly the light of the moon, the stars, and of fire, plants, and jewels, darkness (*andhakāra*), clouds (*abhra*), fog (*mahikā*),[4] smoke (*dhūma*) and dust (*rajas*).[5] These latter two 'colors' are not mentioned by the Theravādins who, obviously in order to make up for this oversight, elaborate the colors of natural phenomena endlessly.[6] There seems to have been a controversy about the inclusion of such items as clouds etc. into the list of colors. As Yaśomitra points out:[7] "Because of their delusive appearance clouds and other phenomena have been mentioned separately, although they possess different colors such as blue and so on. From afar they look like walls, but when one approaches them they are not seen. In order to destroy erroneous conceptions and doubts about them—someone might say, 'there is nothing; to believe in them

1. Aṭṭhasālinī IV 52-55.

2. Abhidharmakośa I 10. The same division also in the otherAbhidharma-texts, though not referred to by name.

3. Aṭṭhasālinī IV 52.

4. According to the Vyākhyā *mahika* is the fog that rises over water and earth. The Aṭṭhasālinī gives as synonym *himā* which is translated by snow or frost'." This is certainly wrong, and the interpretation of the Vyākhyā has to be accepted, because it refers to a particular phenomenon one can watch in tropical countries during the cold season.

5. Bhāṣya ad Abhidh.-kośa I 10, Abhidharmasamuccaya, p. 3; Aṭṭhasālinī IV 53.

4. Aṭṭhasālinī IV 54-55.

7. Vyākhyā ad Abhidh.-kośa I 10.

is foolishness; what should it be but only a delusion'—clouds and other phenomena have been mentioned. They are real objective constituents of visual situation".

Shape (*saṁsthāna*) is according to the Vaibhāṣikas eightfold, according to the Vijñānavādins tenfold, and according to the Theravādins twelvefold.[1] The last named sub-divided shape into that which exists by co-implication (*aññamaññam upanidhāya*) and that which has a particular distribution of geometrical elements (*saṁnivesavisesa*).[2] As examples of the former class long and short, thick and thin are given; as examples of the second group : round, oval, quadrangular, hexagonal, sloping, and ascending. Since shape may also be known from tactile situations, the author of the Aṭṭhasālinī is loath to recognize shape as a proper objective constituent of a visual situation. A similar list, omitting thick, thin, oval, and hexagonal and adding 'even' and 'uneven' is given by the Vaibhāṣikas. They also make reference to the 'sky' (*nabhas*) which was recognized as a 'color' by the Vijñānavādins, "because from afar it looks like a wall of beryl".[3]

The Vaibhāṣikas also discussed at length the relationship between color and shape. According to them, blue, yellow, red, white, glare, shade, light and darkness could be colors without shape; while that aspect of long and short or even and uneven which is termed 'gesture' (*kāyavijñapti*) could be shape without color. All other qualities could be both color and shape,—a conception which was challenged by the Sautrāntikas who did not recognize the difference between color and shape. Their charge against the Vaibhāṣikas, however, was that the latter conceived color and shape as two distinct substances (*dravya*), but two distinct substances cannot occupy the same place. The retort of the Vaibhāṣikas that color and shape are

1. Bhāṣya ad Abhidh.-kośa I 10 ; Abhidharmasamuccaya, p. 3; Aṭṭhasālinī IV 53.

2. The translation of *saṁniveśa* by 'juxtaposition' in the Pali Text Society's translation of the Aṭṭhasālinī not only misses the import of this passage, but there is also no supporting evidence for it.

3. Vyākhyā ad Abhidh.-kośa I 10. On *nabhas* as a color see Abhidharmasamuccaya, p. 3.

perceived in one and the same thing actually evades the point in question and therefore cannot be considered as an answer.[1]

The conception of 'gesture' (*kāyavijñapti*) as a certain shape (*saṁsthāna*) and distinct from color has also been criticised by the Sautrāntikas, who refused to consider shape as a constituent of a truly visual situation and acknowledged it only as an 'interpretation' (*mānasa*, *parikalpita*),[2] because according to them 'long' and other geometrical forms are abstracted from a particular distribution of color points.[3]

While thus the Vaibhāṣikas contended that 'gesture' (*kāyavijñapti*) was a certain shape (*saṁsthāna*) apart from color, and while the Sautrāntikas denied the existence of 'gesture' as a particular substance (*dravya*), though they recognized it as having a nominal existence by being an interpretation, the Theravādins did not wrangle about the logical nature of 'gesture', but simply accepted it as that which makes known a certain state of ours to others or that of others to ourselves.[4] Prompted by the operation of healthy and unhealthy attitudes and by certain subliminal processes,[5] it resulted and became apparent in advancing or withdrawing the body, in looking straight ahead or glancing around, in bending or stretching the body,[6] while its nature was a stiffening of the bodily organization in various degrees.[7] Obviously the many features involved in gestures led the Theravādins to consider gesture as a category of its own rather than as a particular constituent in a visual situation. It also should be noted that in explaining gesture by 'movement of body and limbs' the Theravādins offended against the basic tenet of Buddhism, viz., the momentariness of everything conditioned. As has been pointed out above, that which is momentary does not move from one place to another, but appears and disappears on the spot. To consider

1. Bhāṣya and Vyākhyā ad Abhidh.-kośa I 10.
2. ibid. : *na hi cākṣusam etat saṁsthānagrahaṇam, mānasaṁ tv etat parikalpitam.*
3. Bhāṣya and Vyākhyā ad Abhidh.-kośa IV 2.
4. Aṭṭhasālinī IV 68.
5. ibid. IV 69.
6. ibid. IV 70.
7. ibid. IV 71.

gesture as movement from one place to another has also been the view of the Vātsīputriyas, this was criticized by the Vaibhāṣikas.[1]

The numerical limitation is met with again in the discussion of sound, the objective constituent of an auditive situation. According to the Vaibhāṣikas sound (*śabda*) is eightfold, inasmuch as the four main categories 'caused by organized great elementary qualities' (*upāttamahābhūtahetuka*), 'caused by unorganized great elementary qualities' (*anūpāttamahābhūtahetuka*), 'belonging to sentient beings' (*sattvākhya*), and 'belonging to others than sentient beings (*asattvākhya*) were either pleasant or unpleasant. The first category comprises sounds produced by the hand and by the organs of speech; the second by the whistling of the wind, of the rustling of the leaves of trees, and the murmuring of water; the third is articulate speech (*vāgvijñapti*); and the fourth comprises all other sounds.[2] What these sounds are, is not stated, but it may be surmised that they are those which are not audible under ordinary conditions.

The Theravādins do not limit the types of sound. Although they do not say so, on the whole they follow the same classification we found with the Vaibhāṣikas. Thus they mention sounds produced by the clapping of hands, the sounds of a huge assembly of people where words and sentences cannot be understood but submerge in the general hum, the sound of trees rubbing against each other or of bells and gongs, the whistling of the wind, and the roaring of the sea. To the last two categories of the Vaibhāṣikas correspond the sound of articulate conversation of people and the sound of non-human beings, both types considered to be sufficient to account for all kinds of sound. In addition they mention the sounds of big drums, tabors, tom-toms, the splitting of bamboo and the tearing of cloth.[3] But while the Vaibhāṣikas considered communication (*vāgvijñapti*, Pāli *vacīviññatti*) as a sub-division of the general category of sound, the Theravādins recognised it as a category of its own. It seems that they felt prompted to do so, because communication is not any odd sound, but a specific kind of

1. Bhāṣya and Vyākhyā ad Abhidh.-kośa IV 2.
2. Bhāṣya ad Abhidh.-kośa I 10.
3. Aṭṭhasālinī IV 56-57.

vibration to which accrues meaning and significance. As a noise it certainly is an objective constituent of an auditive situation (*rūpa*), but this does not exhaust the nature of communication. Their definition of communication is that it makes known a certain state of ours to others or that of others to ourselves and that in the course of language understood this particular state we want to be known is actually cognized.[1]

The Vijñānavādins also acknowledge eight types of sound, but their definition is with but two exceptions totally different from the one given by the other schools who acknowledge the Abhidharma. According to the Vijñānavādins sound is 'caused by organized great elementary qualities', 'caused by unorganized great elementary qualities', or it is caused by both types together. This distinguishes them from the Vaibhāṣikas who did not accept this double origination, viz., a sound produced by a hand beating a drum, the hand being 'organized' and the drum being 'unorganized'.[2] Further sound or, better said, words and topics expressed by speech are for example those that are recognized by the world, those for which proof is forthcoming, those that are merely imaginative, those that are used in instructions by saints (Buddhist saints, of course) and those that are used by heterodox people. All these sounds, words, verbal topics, may be pleasant, unpleasant or indifferent in their emotionally toned quality.[3]

Odour (*gandha*) is according to the Vaibhāsikas fourfold : good smelling, bad-smelling, strong-smelling, and weak-smelling; but it may also be threefold: good, bad, indifferent.[4]

The Vijñānavādins recognize odour as being good-smelling, bad-smelling, and indifferent. They add natural odour (*sahajagandha*), accidental odour (*sāṁyogikagandha*), and changing odour (*pāriṇāmikagandha*).[5] These three latter types refer to the fact that certain things have an innate odour, others adopt a certain odour by coming into contact with other

1. Aṭṭhasālinī IV 72-75.
2. Bhāṣya ad Abhidh.-kośa I 10.
3. Abhidharmasamuccaya, p. 4.
4. Abhidharmakośa I 10 and Bhāṣya.
5. Abhidharmasamuccaya, p. 4.

things, and still other things change their odour in course of time.

The Theravādins recognize as two main divisions, which suffice to list all types of odours as good or bad. But then to enlarge upon this topic they mention the smell of roots and of sap, which might be associated with the innate smell of the Vijñānavādins. Similarly as smell which turns out in course of preparation they mention the smell of as yet uncooked and badly cooked vegetables, and to the changing smell may be referred their list of smells found in fish, shell fish, rotten fish, and stale butter. Other examples they give is the smell of mildew and of clothes.[1]

Taste (*rasa*) is according to the Vaibhāṣikas six fold: sweet, sour, saline, pungent, bitter and astringent.[2] According to the Vijñānavādins it is sub-divided in such a way that these six types of taste may be pleasant, unpleasant, neither the one nor the other, innate, accidental, and changing.[3] The conception of taste with the Theravādins again resembles that of the Vijñānavādins, though additional tastes have been added. The author of the Aṭṭhasālinī declares that all types of taste have been abstracted from certain things and he exemplifies his statement by saying that 'sour' is derived from buttermilk, 'sweet' from cow's ghee which does not lose its sweet taste even if it is kept standing for a very long time, while honey though sweet, after some time becomes astringent, and raw sugar though also sweet, turns after some time alkaline, 'bitter' from the leaves of the neem tree, 'pungent' from ginger and pepper, 'saline' from sea-salt, 'alkaline' from brinjal sprouts and certain fruits, 'acrid' from the jujube, and 'astringent' from the myrobalan. Other tastes mentioned are those of clay, of walls, and of clothes.[4]

As has been pointed out above, the tangible (*spraṣṭavya*, Pāli *phoṭṭhabba*) is according to the Theravādins not made up of secondary qualities, but comprises only the three great elementary qualities of solidity, temperature, and motion, all other

1. Aṭṭhasālinī IV 58.
2. Abhidharmakośa I 10 and Bhāṣya.
3. Abhidharmasamuccaya, p. 4.
4. Aṭṭhasālinī IV 59-60.

tangibles being 'metaphors' for these elementary qualities. According to the Vaibhāṣikas it is of eleven types. They are the four great elementary qualities to which are added the seven secondary qualities: soft, hard, heavy, light, cold, hunger, and thirst.[1]

Vijñānavādins added to this list the following properties: slipperiness, feebleness, violence, warmth, satiation, strength, weakness, swoon, itching, putrefaction, disease, aging, death, fatigue, repose, and nourishment, all of them referring to some visceral sensation. In addition to this long list of objective constituents of tactual situations (in the broadest sense of the word), there is counted as something tangible a particular form of *rūpa* which does not form part of the *rūpāyatana* or field of objective constituents of sense perceptions, but of the *dharmāyatana* or reality field.[2] To understand what is meant by this constituent it is necessary to refer to the fact that in the ancient texts[3] three types of *rūpa* are mentioned, the former two being the objective constituents of perceptual situations and in the wider sense of the word, the epistemological object in perception, on the one hand, and the organized structure termed senses on the other, while the third was said to be neither visible nor active-reactive (*anidassana, appaṭigha*). Vijñānavādins interpreted this third type of *rūpa* in the sense pointed out above and declared that it was set up and realized in meditation[4]. The remarkable statement that this *rūpa* is something

1. Abhidharmakośa I 10 and Bhāṣya.

2. Abhidharmasamuccaya, p. 4. It is said to be of five kinds. It belongs to concentratedness (*ābhisaṁkṣepika*) (cp. Bhāṣya ad Abhidh.-kośa IV 4 'object of absorption' *samādher ālambanam* and Bhāṣya ad VII); it is *ābhyavakāśika* 'openness'. Does it mean that it does not occupy ordinary space? Bhāṣya ad IV 4. Or has this term to be understood in the sense given by Buddhaghosa in Visuddhimagga II 62; 'breaking with the obstacles a fixed abode offers (for meditation), and abolition of sluggishness and drowsiness'? It is further connected with taking upon oneself certain restrictions, *sāmādānika*, cp. Bhāṣya ad Abhidh.-kośa IV 49. It is a construct of mind (*parikalpita*), being a transformation of the sole reality mind, and it is all-pervasive, *vaibhutvika*.

3. Dīghanikāya III 217; Vibhaṅga, pp. 13; 64.

4. Bhāṣya ad Abhidh.-kośa IV 4. Hiuan-tsang's Vijñaptimātratāsiddhi, p. 140.

'tangible' sheds light on another aspect of Buddhist meditation which is likely to be overlooked owing to the importance that attaches to the visualization of forms. In Buddhist thought, reality is not something intangible and unattainable, lying for ever unknown and unperceived behind an impenetrable wall, but is something that can be realized through and in us and is sensibly felt, whereby feeling must be understood as feeling something and not merely as feeling somehow. (The English verb 'to feel' is rather ambiguous as it can be interpreted either way, while Buddhist terminology is more precise, denoting the feeling tone by *vedanā*, and the sensible aspect of the process by *sparśa*). Therefore it is thoroughly permissible to include this *rūpa* which is realized in meditation and which in a previous chapter has been referred to as Gestalt in its visual aspect, in the field of the tangible. Because it is being 'felt', it is an experience which is so strong that the whole of what we are accustomed to call our physical existence is innervated and permeated by it.

Vaibhāṣikas gave rather a different interpretation to the third type of *rūpa* mentioned in the ancient texts. They termed it *avijñapti* and considered it as the eleventh category of *sarvaṁ rūpam.*[1] Literally translated *avijñapti* means 'that which does not make known'. According to the Vaibhāṣikas—Theravādins also know this term but attach no philosophical import to it[2]—it is a serial continuity, the counterpart of any *vijñapti* (information, gesture, communication), which is set up immediately after a communicative act has been performed, and continues to set up itself by taking its stand on the four great elementary qualities organized into a sentient being, while the *avijñapti* itself does not partake of this organization (*avijñaptir anupāttikā*). In meditation the *avijñapti* derives from those elementary qualities which are not organized into a sentient being,[3] the idea behind this statement being obviously the fact, that in meditation the subjectivity of the individual is

1. See above p. 139. Abhidharmakośa I 9; IV 4.
2. See Aṭṭhasālinī III 584.
3. Abhidharmakośa IV 5-6 and Bhāṣya.

overcome and a wider relationship with that which lies outside the subjective and personal is established. The upshot of the long discussion the Vaibhāṣikas devote to this topic, seems to be that our actions, overt, symbolic, and covert, do not operate a vacuum and that there is integral unity. The rejection of the *avijñapti* by the Sautrāntikas and Vijñānavādins is not so much a rejection as such, but the fact that by their conception of the continuous transformation of the psychic process (*santati-pariṇāma*) they had something which accounted for a gapless continuity. Hence their controversy was verbal (and verbose) rather than substantial

The Interpretation of the Perceived World

As the preceding analysis has shown the technical term *rūpa* comprises a variety of concepts such as the objective constituent of a perceptual situation, the specific external reference of a situation, the fact that immediate experiences come organized as wholes, the organized structure of the senses, and that there is continuity and not randomness. On the other hand, the fact that this *rūpa* is said to possess lightness (*lahutā*), whereby the rapid change of all that is termed *rūpa* becomes manifest, pliability (*mudutā*), whereby in all operations no obstacles are encountered, and workability (*kammaññatā*), whereby a certain 'strength' is manifest,[1] and above all that it has a life of its own (*jīvita*)[2] in the sense of the kinetic energy of the *rūpa*-process, makes it abundantly clear that we have not to deal with 'bodies' or 'things' as such, but that *rūpa* is a concept for dynamic flux. It is not meant to 'explain' the basis of all things, it only means that even in the world of objects which we believe to be rather static, there is an incessant flux and structurance.[3]

1. Aṭṭhasālinī IV 77-78. Although these three qualities are always together, we can distinguish them, as the author says. But then to set them up as separate categories is to revert to dogmaticism claiming a certain numerical set, rather than to raise to the level of philosophical thought.

2. Aṭṭhasālinī IV 67.

3. A similar conception in Western psychology is reached by Floyd H. Allport, Theories of Perception and the Concept of Structure, pp. 665 sqq.

However, this wide 'frame of reference' of the term *rūpa* of necessity weakens its usefulness in philosophical discussions. It is here that Buddhists split up into a conservative group who displayed a singular lack of philosophical interest and continued to use the term in all its ambiguity without ever attempting to clarify its position,[1] and another group who felt compelled to re-assess the ancient tenets and tried to give them a new ordering. It thus happens that the Theravādins list as *rūpa* certain topics which the Vaibhāṣikas and Vijñānavādins classify as *cittaviprayukta* (*saṁskāra-*) *dharma* ['topics of dynamic import not dependent on our attitude'.] In the discussion of the logical nature of those topics listed in a new way because of a strong philosophical interest, the temperament of the philosophers was of utmost importance. As a matter of fact, Buddhist philosophy remains for ever a sealed book if the psychological background of the authors is not taken into account.

The wide 'frame of reference' of the term *rūpa*, we spoke about above, is patent in the discussion of sex. The author of the Aṭṭhasālinī begins his analysis from the periphery. He points out that the shape of the hands, feet, neck, breast and other parts of the body in women is different from that of men, the pelvis in women is broader than in men, while the upper body is narrower. He then refers to the socalled secondary sex marks, such as opulence of the female breast, beardless face, and also counts such marks as the difference in hair-style. After that he points out the difference in interest, but fails to see social conditioning : girls like to play with small baskets, pestle and mortar, at dolls, and to make clothes, while boys prefer to play with carts and ploughs, to build sand-dams and dig pools.[2] Then he discusses those factors differentiating the sexes which it is difficult to consider either as physical or mental, namely, gait and movement, the difference in the way of eating, sitting, walking, lying. But all this is due to the

1. An unsatisfactory attempt has been made in Abhidhammatthasaṅgaha VI 4 sq. Not less than eleven types of *rūpa* have been established, none of them contributing to the elucidation of *rūpa* itself.

2. Aṭṭhasālinī IV 61; 63.

structuralizing and controlling power of femininity (*itthindriya*) or of masculinity (*purisindriya*), respectively.[1] Femininity and masculinity are like the seed out of which a tree grows and spreads with branches and twigs filling the whole sky. This structuralizing power, however, is not perceived by the eye, it is an interpretation of that which has been perceived, though this does not mean that femininity has been abstracted from the data of sense. It is a Gestalt through which we perceive and understand, hence sex is listed with the Theravādins as *rūpa*. As the author of the Aṭṭhasālinī in this connexion points out, the features of men and women (*liṅga-santhāna*) are perceived both by the eye and the mind (*itthiliṅgādīnī cakkhuviññeyyāni pi manoviññeyāni pi*).

Although there are many structuralizing processes in man which are common to both men and women, as for instance the structures of the sense organs of sight, hearing and so on, the structuralizing powers of femininity and masculinity form separate entities.[2] Yet this does not exclude the fact that there may be fluctuation between masculinity and femininity in the sense that women show masculine traits and men feminine traits.[3]

The Gestalt-character of femininity and masculinity respectively is apparent also from the statement that femininity and masculinity are the cause of female or masculine features and interests, but not the cause of the sex organs.[4]

1. Aṭṭhasālinī. IV 61; 63.
2. ibid.
3. ibid. IV 64. The bisexuality of human beings has found its full recognition on a purely psychological level in the Tantras. See my Yuganaddha. The Tantric View of Life.
4. Aṭṭhasālinī IV 64 : *itthi—(purisa) liṅga-nimitta-kuttākappānam kāraṇabhāva-paccupaṭṭhānam,* and IV 66 : *na tassa indriyaṁ vyañjanakāraṇam* Cp. Tikapaṭṭhānavaṇṇanā, p. 50.

The author of the Aṭṭhasālinī substantiates his statement by referring to hermaphroditism. It is, however, apparent from his exposition that he is thinking of homosexuality also. He seems to have had very strange ideas about this topic. He declares that in these sexual border cases there is only one structuralizing power, either (predominantly) male or female. He then states that when such a female border case becomes enamoured of

The Vaibhāṣikas did not separate femininity and masculinity from the general bodily structure (*kāyendriya*), as did the Theravadins. They expressly stated that the structuralizing power termed femininity or masculinity is by nature the body, because it cognizes touch.[1] It is spoken of as a power because it 'lords over the distribution of sentient beings which fall under the two categories of male and female (*sattvabheda*), and also because it 'lords over' the specific differentiations found in men and women as to shape, voice, and behavior[2] (*sattvavikalpabheda*). But however different men and women may be from each other, there is similarity among each group. This similarity which exists among the members of each group, either among women or among men, is termed *nikāyasabhāga.* The Vaibhāṣikas considered it as an eternal substance (*dravya*) having a double aspect, a universal one (*abhinna*) and a particular one (*bhinna*). The universal aspect is found in all sentient beings, the particular one varies according to the levels of existence (*dhātu*), whether this be the world of sensuality (*kāmadhātu*)

another female, her own female sex organ recedes and a male organ appears. This is independent of the structuralizing power of femininity or masculinity, because otherwise both organs had to be present all the time. The appearance of the male organ in a female as our author conceives it, is due to sensual tendencies (*rāgacitta*). While his description in this case may refer to hermaphroditism proper, his statement that such a female border case may become herself pregnant and make other females pregnant is certainly an insufficient analysis of homosexuality which does not always exclude heterosexual intercourse. See Aṭṭhasālinī IV 66.

1. Abhidharmakośa II 2 and Bhāṣya. Vyākhyā : *kāyendriyattābhāvaṁ strīpuruṣendriyaṁ spraṣṭavyavijñānajanakatvāt.*

Throughout the analysis of *rūpa* we have seen that the objective constituent of a perceptual situation is very often not distinguished from the external reference of the situation. This nondistinction gave rise to the controversy whether the deities in the *rūpāvacara*, the realm of Gestalt-experiences, had femininity or masculinity or not. The classical texts state that the beings there have all *indriyas* and that would include also *strīndriya* and *puruṣendriya.* The Vaibhāṣikas, however, contended that these *indriyas* are absent, not because, as some people believed, there was no use for them, since sexual intercourse does not obtain there, but because the desire to make use of them is absent and also because it is with the re-inforcement of the external reference that femininity and masculinity begin to operate. See Bhāṣya ad Abhidharmakośa I 30.

2. Bhāṣya ad Abhidh.-kośa II I.

or the world of Gestalten (*rūpāvacara*), according to the particular forms of existence (*gati*), such as men, gods, animals, and the like, according to the forms of birth (*yoni*) such as born from an uterus or from an egg, according to the social status (*jāti*) which determines whether one is a Brahmin or belongs to any other class of society.[1]

The conception of *nikāyasabhāgatā* by the Vaibhāṣikas has been subjected to a severe criticism by the Sautrāntikas on the ground that it is but an adoption of the Vaiśeṣika doctrine. This doctrine postulates as an eternal universal (*padārtha*) the *sāmānya* or generality of things as a unitary (*eka*) eternal (*nitya*) principle underlying and informing a multitude of individual things and beings. It further claimed that this generality was an objective entity of perception.[2] It is patent that nothing of this is true. 'Generality' as well as the other universals which the Vaiśesikas claimed to be eternal entities, are categories defined by postulates; they are best described as principles of interpretation which we apply to the data of sense-perception. The contention of the Vaibhāṣikas that they do not assume one single category as do the Vaiśeṣikas, but a number of *sabhāgatās* does not meet the criticism but only reveals the inconsistency and artificiality of the Vaibhāṣika system. Thus, for instance, they recognize the class concept 'ordinary man' (*pṛthagjanasabhāgatā*), acknowledge in addition a 'quality of being an ordinary man' (*pṛthagjanatva*) which is the non-possession of those qualities and virtues which are characteristic of a spiritually advanced and ethically educated person (*ārya*), but then they acknowledge the class concept 'man' (*manuasabhāgatā*), while failing to recognize the 'quality of being man' (*manuṣyatva*).[3] Another objection raised against their conception is that we never perceive the generality of things directly. The claim of the Vaibhāṣikas that the *sabhāgatā* exists per se (*dravya*), because in a Sūtra it is stated that if a murderer should be reborn among human beings instead of in

1. Abhidharmakośa II 41 and Bhāṣya.
2. Siddhāntamuktāvalī, 8. For a fuller discussion of this problem see Satkari Mookerjee. The Buddhist Philosophy of Universal Flux, pp. 87 sqq.
3. Bhāṣya ad Abhidh.-kośa II 41.

one of the hells provided for such crimes, he will attain the *sabhāgatā* of men (*manuṣyāṇāṁ sabhāgatām*), is a lucid example of how language creates spurious metaphysical problems.[1]

Following the Sautrāntika argument, the Vijñānavādins recognize the *sabhāgatā* only as being a mere word (*prajñapti*), having temporary validity, as just a principle of interpretation which states that "such and such sentient beings in such and such groups are similar to each other as regards their psycho-physical existence".[2]

Not only is the importance of sex found in the division of sentient beings into males and females, but of much greater importance is the role sex plays in the spiritual development of mankind. Sex forms an integral part of man; to deny it is as morbid as to exaggerate it. The argument that sex is different from other expressions of life, because man is supposed to be able to get along without sexual activity, while he cannot do so without food, not only overlooks the grave psychological damages that develop in the course of rigorous repression, but also—and this makes it a worthless argument—hopelessly muddles up ideas belonging to different strata. This argument starts with the tacit assumption that sex is *always* licentiousness and food *never* more than sustenance of life. Certainly, there is no difference, ethical or otherwise, between sexual licentiousness and gluttony, on the one hand, or between sex phantasies and visions of sumptuous meals because of sex and food starvation, on the other. Sex is a driving power that may enable man to achieve the highest and most sublime, just as it may destroy him completely. Therefore the ancient teachers (*pūrvācārya*), who in many respects had a better knowledge of human nature than many of the contemporary admirers and followers who have swallowed a considerable dose of the poison of prudery and hypocrisy, fully endorsed the importance of sex by declaring that it 'lords over' (*adhipati*) all that which makes man emotionally unstable and throws him out of his course (*saṁkleśa*) and also over all that sets him right and liberates him from the self-imposed shackles (*vyavadāna*).[3]

1. Bhāṣya ad Abhidh.-kośa II. 41.
2. Abhidharmasamuccaya, p. 11.
3. Bhāṣya ad Abhidh.-kośa II I.

Sexual border cases, such as those who are sexless or hermaphrodite (*śaṇṭha*) or those who have been castrated, who fail to achieve erection of the penis or are unable to ejaculate (*paṇḍaka*), and have not the capacity to indulge in unrestraint (*asaṁvara*),[1] because of their incapacity for having strong emotions are unlikely to commit patricide or matricide (checking the murderous instinct of human nature is important in spiritual development),[2] and are also unable to undermine or to destroy the foundation of all that is good and wholesome[3] (this being reserved for men and women with strong opinions, opinions being always supported by emotions and such emotions being very much linked with sex). On the other hand, such sexual border cases are also unable to apply active restraint (*saṁvara*),[4] to enter the path which will pacify the passionate nature of man or utilize the emotions for higher goals so that they become equilibrated,[5] or ever to attain the ultimate by turning away from all that makes up the world.[6] In this connexion it may be noted that Mahāyāna ethics included in its fold also these unfortunate cases, by declaring that, though they are handicapped to fulfil that which is necessary in the ordinary way of life, they are capable of fulfilling the Bodhisattva ideal which transcends all barriers.[7] This ethics does not know of beings being condemned forever for no fault of their own, nor of beings selected for no virtue of their own.

The ancient texts had stated more than once that all that is conditioned has three characteristics of this conditionedness. They are birth (*utpāda*, Pāli *uppāda*), death (*vyaya*, Pāli *vaya*), and modification of the existing (*sthityanyathātva*, Pāli *ṭhitassa aññathattam*).[8] This terminology has been interpreted in such a way that 'origination' (*utpāda*) was synonymous with 'birth' (*jāti*), 'end' (*vyaya*) with 'impermanence' (*anityatā*), and 'modification of the existing' (*sthityanyathātva*)

1. Abhidharmakośa IV 13.
2. ibid. IV 103.
3. ibid. IV 80.
4. ibid. IV 13.
5. ibid. VI 51.
6. ibid. IV 45.
7. See Dvags.po. lha. rje, loc. cit., foll. 46a sq.
8. Aṅguttaranikāya I 152

with 'aging' (*jarā*).[1] Apart from this interpretation it was suggested that the formula of the three characteristics of all that is conditioned, was incomplete inasmuch as it did not mention 'duration'. But by analysing the term 'modification of the existing' (*sthityanyathātva*) into two independent components, one found the desired 'duration' (*sthiti*). The result of this analysis was that the Abhidharma[2] counted four characteristics, and according to the school to which the authors belonged, interpreted them either as four topics or as three.

'Birth' (*jāti*) was defined by the Vaibhāṣikas as that entity which brings about that which is conditioned, while the Sautrāntikas and the Vijñānavādins defined it as the 'beginning of a series' which had not existed previously (*abhūtvā bhāva*).[3] The Sarvāstivādins objected against this interpretation which is purely phenomenological, on the basis of their substantial existentialism and as has happened time and time again in philosophy, fell a prey to the law of projection inherent in language. They interpreted the statement about the conditioned character of all that is conditioned'[4] in the sense that 'the conditioned character' meant one thing and 'all that is conditioned' another, which led them to assume 'birth of birth', 'duration of duration,' 'aging of aging', and impermanence of impermanence'.[5] Restricting their analysis of their entities (*dravya*) arbitrarily in this way and not allowing 'duration of birth' or 'aging of birth' or other possible combinations, they believed they had avoided the *regressus ad infinitum.*

In a similar way the Vaibhāṣikas defined 'duration' (*sthiti*) as that entity which stabilizes and makes the conditioned last. The Sautrāntikas and Vijñānavādins considered duration to be a term for the fact that the series has not yet come to an end and become inexistent. 'Aging' (*jarā*) was for the Vaibhāṣikas that factor which brings about the deterioration of the

1. Bhāṣya ad Abhidh.-kośa II 45.
2. The statement by L. de la Vallee Poussin, n. 1 on p. 223 is not correct.
3. Abhidharmasamuccaya, p. 11. Bhāṣya ad Abhidh.-kośa II 45. This formula is found in Majjhimanikāya III 25, it has high authority, but is rejected by the author of Milindapañha, p. 52.
4. Aṅguttaranikāya I 152.
5. Abhidharmakośa II 46. Aṭṭhasālinī IV 113-117 rejects this view.

conditioned, while for the Sautrāntikas and Vijñānavādins it was a term for the fact that in a given series each successive moment of this continuous flow is slightly different from the preceding one. Finally, 'impermanence' (*anityatā*) was for the Vaibhāṣikas that entity which destroys the conditioned, while for the Sautrāntikas and Vijñānavādins it was a statement about the fact that the series has come to an end.[1] The main difference was that the Vaibhāṣikas attributed the characteristics to a single entity, while the other schools attributed them to a series. This difference of conception is intimately linked with the Buddhist idea of momentariness (*kṣaṇa*). The problem is : what is the nature of a 'moment'. Is it a single indivisible unit or can it be subdivided into smaller units ? The Vaibhāsikas held the latter view. For them a 'moment' was the amount of time during which a certain characteristic achieves its full operation.[2] The other schools inclined to the indivisibility of a moment. It disappears immediately on the spot, as soon as it has appeared.[3] The argument, also advanced by the Mādhyamikas, is that, if a moment could be subdivided, it would lose its character of momentariness.

The author of the Aṭṭhasālinī attempts to keep up the original triadic conception about all that is conditioned, by taking 'origination' and 'duration' (*upacayasantati*) as referring to one conception. He understands by both terms a thoroughly dynamic process, which in modern terms we might compare with the initial and gradually increasing energy charges needed to start and keep a body moving. In this way he states that the initial charge (*ācaya*) is origination, while every successive charge (*upacaya*) is the growth of that which has received the initial charge, growth being but another term for duration. He illustrates his point by the following simile : "The initial charge, like the moment when water begins to rise in a well dug near the bank of a river, is origination; the additional charge, like the moment when the well has become full, is growth; duration, like the moment when the water overflows,

1. Bhāṣya ad Abhidh.-kośa II 45, 46. Abhidharmasamuccaya, p. 11.
2. Bhāṣya ad Abhidh.-kośa II 46.
3. Bhāṣya ad Abhidh.-kośa IV 2-3.

is continuity".[1] This simile is particularly suited to elucidating the underlying idea because in a stream of water there is continuity and homogeneity, although no instant is the same. The author then makes the significant statement that the 'initial charge' (*ācaya*) refers to the 'object charged' (*āyatana*), just as the 'object charged' refers to the 'initial charge'. In other words, although we may speak of 'the origination of a sense field' we nust not allow ourselves to be tricked by this linear arrangement of words into the assumption that 'origination' is one thing and 'the sense field' is another. This interpretation is exactly the one offered by the Sautrāntikas and through them by the Vijñānavādins.[2] In modern terms this means that *rūpa* (the above characteristics are dealt with in connexion with the conception of *rūpa*) has essentially a field character that reaches and tends to maintain a steady state. Such a field is organized by forces and being a field it is capable of flexibility and transformation.[3] It is interesting to note that these are precisely the same features that are basic to the Gestalt system in modern psychology.[4]

'Aging' (*jarā*), too, is for the author of the Aṭṭhasālinī no entity per se, but an interpretative concept used to describe certain phenomena associated with old age, as for instance the broken state of teeth, greyness of hair, and wrinkles on the face. None of these are age, for "just as the path taken by floods or conflagrations is clearly visible from the broken and scattered state and charred look of gass, trees, and other plants—the path itself, however, is not the flood or the conflagration—so also the path taken by aging is clearly visible from the broken state of teeth and similar features, it is perceived by the naked eye, but brokenness of teeth and the other features mentioned are not 'aging'.[5]

1. Aṭṭhasālinī IV 80. cpr. *uttaritaram pavattikāle* with *uttarottarakṣaṇ-anubandha* in Bhāṣya and Abhidh.-kośa II 46.

2. Aṭṭhasālinī IV 81. Bhāṣya ad Abhidh.-kośa II 46.

3. In this respect the Buddhist conception of the pliability and workability of *rūpa* is most relevant. See above, p. 163.

4. Floyd H. Allport, Theories of Perception and the Concept of Structure, pp. 113 sqq.

5. Aṭṭhasālinī IV 82.

When the author speaks of 'aging of *rūpa*' as meaning that the nature of *rūpa* (*sabhāva*) is not lost, but that its newness (*navabhāva*) has gone, this statement will be understood only from the viewpoint of momentariness. That is to say, a certain objective constituent (*rūpa*) of a particular perceptual situation does not lose the quality which it seems to have on inspection, otherwise it would not be possible to call it the objective constituent of the particular situation. But *rūpa* is not only the objective constituent of a perceptual situation, it also stands for what we believe to be a physical object. Because of the momentariness of *rūpa* as an objective constituent due to the event-character of the experience of it, the 'physical object' (*rūpa*) is essentially a homogenous series of moments. Though similar within the framework of the series, each successive moment is different from the preceding one. Thus, while each moment does not change its nature of being a moment, within the series of moments, due to their nature of immediately disappearing on the spot after having appeared, each moment loses its character of being new (from the serial point of view), and this is called 'the aging of a thing'.[1]

'Impermanence' (*anityatā*, Pāli *aniccatā*), which is intimately linked with the other concepts of birth, duration, and aging, is the end and disappearance of all that has come into existence. It is the return to non-existence (*hutvā abhāvaṭṭhena*)[2]. It is not restricted to that which is listed as *rūpa*, but encompasses the whole of existence, the mental as well as the material, to use these conventional though inappropriate terms.

Birth, aging and death are the outstanding characteristics we encounter in the world around us. It is the interpretation as to their logical nature that varies. Although the author of the Aṭṭhasālinī favors the Sautrāntika interpretation against the Vaibhāṣika doctrine, he illustrates the nature of these three enemies of mankind in such a way, that if we had no evidence to the contrary, we should be forced to include him among the adherents of the Sarvāstivādins and the Vaibhāṣikas in particular. He declares: "Three enemies of a man roam about seeking an

1. ibid. IV 84. See also Bhāṣya ad Abhidh.-kośa II 46.

2. Aṭṭhasālinī IV 85. This is precisely the position of the Sautrāntika who declared: *bhūtvā abhāvaḥ*. See Bhāṣya ad Abhidh.-kośa II 46.

opportunity to pounce upon him. Of these enemies one may be supposed to say : 'Let it be my task to take him out and to bring him into a jungle'. Another might say: 'Let it be my task to strike him to the ground, once he has been brought into the jungle.' And the third will say : 'Let it be my task to cut off his head with my sword, once he has fallen to the ground'. Such are birth and the other events in life. Birth is like an enemy who takes man out and brings him into a jungle, because the nature of birth is to bring about existence in this or that situation. Aging is like an enemy who strikes a man to the ground after he has been brought into the jungle, because it is the nature of aging to make the psycho-physical constituents of man weak and dependent, and to bring him to a state where he is lying on a bed. Death is like an enemy who cuts the man's head off after he has fallen to the ground, because it is the nature of death to bring about the end of the life of the psycho-physical constituents of man struck by old age".[1]

Not only is this simile found in the Vibhāṣā,[2] but the definition of the technical terms is in every respect identical with the Vaibhāṣika interpretation.[3] There is still another instance where the author of the Aṭṭhasālinī seems to have inclined to a view similar to that of the Vaibhāṣikas. This is where he states that the descriptive phrase 'shrinkage of the span of life, debility of sensory functions' is a metaphor, by which the effect, i.e., the shrinkage of the span of life, as referring to the passing of time, and the debility of the sensory functions, as referring to the nature of the organism, is used in the sense of the cause, i.e., aging.[4] But these instances fade into the background against the overwhelming majority of cases where he is in favor of the Sautrāntika and Vijñānavāda view. It may not be amiss to surmise that his intention was to give a

1. Aṭṭhasālinī IV 86. The translation of the Pali Text Society completely misses the import of this passage, because the translator fails to recognize the causative aspects of the definitions.

2. Bhāṣya ad Abhidh.-kośa II 45.

3. In particular, reference may be made to the definition *jarā hi kevalaṁ dharmaṁ durbalīkaroti* in Vyākhyā ad Abhidh.-kośa II 45 : "Aging exclusively weakens an entity". Cp. the term *durbalīkaroti* with dubbala......*karaṇato* in Aṭṭhasālinī IV 86.

4. Aṭṭhasālinī IV 43.

synoptic view of the Theravādins' ideas in the manner as did Vasubandhu for the Vaibhāṣikas.

As the last item in their category of *rūpa* (i.e. secondary qualities), the Theravādins list 'food' (*āhāra*).[1] It may seem strange to us on first sight that among those topics which we should describe as abstracta, all of a sudden is included something very concrete—solid food. What lies behind the inclusion of this topic in *rūpa*, is the fact that sense perceptions play an important role, not only those when food is swallowed, but in particular the sensations of the contraction of the stomach-walls, which give rise to articulations such as 'I am hungry, give me some food'. It will be remembered that hunger and thirst had been listed as objective constituents of tactual situations by the Vaibhāṣikas and Vijñānavādins, while the Theravādins were prevented from doing the same because of their conception that secondary qualities (*upādāya rūpa*) are not objective constituents of such situations.[2] The author of the Aṭṭhasālinī describes the morphology of hunger as a cycle of activity, beginning with a need or physiological tension resulting from disequilibrium set up by internal stimuli and passing through the preparatory effort of finding the situation which will satisfy the need, to the sense of satisfaction, the release of tension or state of equilibrium resulting frcm the attainment of the goal. The nature of food he describes as comprising of mass (*vatthu*) and nutritive value (*ajā*), both of them serving to remove danger from the organism and to preserve the living organism. He says :

"What is the function of mass and what of nutrition? To remove dangers and to preserve. Mass is able to remove dangers but unable to preserve; nutrition preserves but is unable to remove dangers. Both together are able to preserve and to remove dangers. What is this danger? It is physiological heat. For when inside the stomach there is no mass of boiled rice or other food, physiological heat rises and seizes the stomach-walls and makes the person cry out : 'I am hungry, give me food'. When the person has taken in food, the heat leaves the stomach

1. Dhammasaṅgani 646; Aṭṭhasālinī IV 87; Abhidhammatthasaṅgaha VI.

2. See above pp. 173 sq.

walls and seizes the food mass. Then the person becomes quieted.

It is just like a demon lurking in the shade who attacks him who enters the shade, fetters him with demoniac chains and enjoying himself in his hiding-place bites him in the head when he feels hungry. Because of being bitten this person cries out aloud. Having heard his cries, people come from all sides thinking that there is someone in distress. The demon seizes all who come, devours them and enjoys himself in his hiding-place. In this way this comparison should be understood: The physiological heat is like the demon lurking in the shade; the stomach-wall is like the person fettered with demoniac chains; the food mass is like the persons who have come from all sides; the seizing of the stomach-walls emptied from food by the digestive process of physiological heat is like the pouncing of the demon who enjoyed himself in his hiding-place until the time of feeling hungry, on the person and biting him on the head; saying 'give me food' is like the cries of the bitten man; the contentment resulting from the digestive process leaving the stomach-walls and seizing the food mass is like the time when the demon enjoys himself in his hiding-place after he has seized and eaten those who on account of the cries have come".[1]

With a discussion of the nutritive value of various kinds of food, the coarser the food the less valuable, and of arranging all sentient beings according to the gradation in the nutritive value of food they partake of, the author concludes his analysis of food.[2]

It will be readily admitted that a strictly numerical system is not only an artificial and arbitrary limitation to further investigation, but also lends itself to be interpreted in such a manner that each numerical item is an entity *per se*, which since it involves persistence through a lapse of time, commonsense would be inclined to consider as a substance. This is exactly what happened in the case of the Sarvāstivādins-Vaibhāṣikas who developed a system comprising quite a number of substances (*dravya*). Although enumeration was an integral feature of the earlier strata of Buddhism, it may be reasonably

1. Aṭṭhasālinī IV 88-89.
2. ibid. IV 90-91.

doubted whether this enumeration was ever meant in the way in which the authors of the Abhidharma literature took it, viz., to be conceived as a rigidly defined system. It is much more consistent with the spirit of Buddhism as a discipline of vital importance for the spiritual development of the individual, to consider the enumerations scattered over the vast realm of texts as an aid to memory.

The wide range of meaning of the term *rūpa*, extending from an objective constituent of a perceptual situation to an interpretative concept, made it particularly unsuited as an aid to clear thinking, and as a consequence to the communication of thought. For if the field of reference is too large, its content becomes vague and may lay us open to the charge that we do not know exactly what it is we are thinking of or speaking about. Success in thinking more clearly will be achieved when we do define the words by means of which we are attempting to express our thoughts. Therefore, throughout the history of Buddhist thought definition of terms has received the greatest attention and the quarrel between the various schools was often nothing more than a wrangling about correct definitions.[1] In clarifying the position taken up by the various schools, by definition and re-definition it happened that the term *rūpa* became restricted to mean the objective constituent of perceptual situation, and in a wider sense, the epistemological object of our perception. The realization of the character of wholeness of an experience and of the fact that the observer is part of his observation, naturally included the sensory organization by which we perceive.

But there are also other topics than perceptions. Our interests are centered on events, causal connections, activities, time, and above all on relationships, which we want to conceive and to communicate. Certainly, relationships cannot be classified as epistemological objects or as certain states of mind. This

1. Definition and classification go hand in hand, and any ordered arrangement affords a good conspectus of what is known about a certain subject matter. Classification has been the hobby of the Theravādins to an unbelievable extent. The principle of classification has been division. In such bulky works as the Yamaka, Paṭṭhāna, and to a lesser extent, Dhātukathā, hardly anything but classification on the basis of division is found.

then made it necessary to set up a new category which was designed to comprise all those topics on which interest centered and which could not be properly listed as either *rūpa* or *citta.* This new category, set up by the Sarvāstivādins-Vaibhāṣikas and taken over by the Vijñānavādins, was termed *cittavipra-yukta-saṁskāra* 'dynamic factors apart from our attitude'.[1]

When we express events in language and turn them into propositions something very curious happens. The events become transformed in such a way that the relations that exist between the members of the proposition are turned into something like objects. A person who is not aware of this fact is at once led into reading the presented facts in the obvious but wrong way.[2] This peculiarity in combination with the interest in the development of man to spiritual maturity resulted in the postulation of a particular topic called *prāpti* 'attainment, possession'[3] and its opposite *aprāpti* 'non-attainment, non-possession'.[4] That is to say, a person who has undergone a spiritual training is known to 'have attained' and to 'possess' something which others lack who have not done so. Thus '*A* possesses *B*' tells of a way in which *A* and *B* are combined. In our expressing this way we name it and in naming it a new entity, 'possessing', seems to have added itself to the complex of *A* and *B*. Similarly it may happen that '*A* does not possess *B*', which also tells about a way in which *A* and *B* are separated. Both these relations, the positive and the negative ones, the Vaibhāṣikas considered to be real entities (*dravya*), which nicely illustrates their wrong reading of 'fact'. The critique by the Sautrāntikas made it abundantly clear that the event which was turned into the proposition '*A* possesses *B*' did involve a certain succession of acts by *A* and *B*, but not in the manner which the proposition seems to exhibit—first *A*, then 'possesses', then *B*. Certainly *A* and *B* are simultaneous with each other and with possessing. This the Vaibhāṣikas themselves were forced to admit,[5] but in their eagerness to 'substantialize'

1. Abhidharmakośa II 35; Abhidharmasamuccaya, pp. 10 sq.
2. See Susanne K. Langer, Philosophy in a New Key, p. 64 (Mentor Book).
3. Abhidharmakośa II 36-4c.
4. ibid. II 39-40.
5. Bhāṣya ad Abhidh.-kośa II 36 : *sahajaprāptihetuka.*

all and everything they closed their ears to a pertinent critique and held to their conception of 'possession' being a substance, because it was prescribed by their system (*siddhānta*).[1] The Vijñānavādins took up the critique by the Sautrāntikas, included 'possession' as a 'concept' (*prajñapti*) in their system and dropped 'non-possession' completely.[2] This difference in conceiving of the logical nature of other topics is also evident in the remaining categories mentioned as 'dynamic factors apart from an attitude', as for instance, 'induced unconsciousness' (*āsaṁjñika*), 'the practice and attainment of induced unconsciousness' (*asaṁjñisamāpatti*), which ordinary and untrained people (*pṛthagjana*) mistake for emancipation from the turmoil of worldly existence, while the spiritually-minded people (*ārya*) consider it as a dangerous pitfall,[3] 'the attainment of the suspension of attitudinal and functional operations' (*nirodhasamāpatti*), 'words' (*nāmakāya*), 'sentences' (*padakāya*), and 'letters' (*vyañjanakāya*).[4]

In dealing with the world around us and also with ourselves, we believe that there are dependable regularities within the multiformity of our experiences. These regularities we ever and again try to find and the implicit belief in such orderly sequence or causation is a dominant principle in our individual minds. It is upon this belief that we base our hopes and fears, plans and techniques of action. But causation is a tricky problem and the discussions of philosophers have done little, if anything, to clarify it. It is with the advance of science that the idea of cause as exerting compulsion, as an agent impelling something to act in some way, though still being present, no longer finds serious consideration and that emphasis is placed on relationships rather than on terms.[5] Relationships have always attracted the main interest of the Buddhists of all schools, and the Vijñānavādins listed in their category of topics, apart from an attitude and an epistemological object, several terms

1. Bhāṣya ad Abhidh.-kośa II 36.
2. Abhidharmasamuccaya, p. 10.
3. Bhāṣya ad Abhidh.-kośa II 42.
4. Abhidharmakośa II 47; Abhidharmasamuccaya, p. 11. All these entities are substances (*dravya*) for the Vaibhāṣikas, while they are concepts, terms, signs (*prajñapti*) for the Vijñānavādins.
5. See L. S. Stebbing, A Modern Introduction to Logic, p. 261.

descriptive of causal relationships. They are 'regular sequence' (*pravṛtti*), 'difference between cause and effect' (*pratiniyama*), 'correspondence between cause and effect' (*yoga*), 'rapid succession between cause and effect' (*java*) 'orderly sequence' (*anukrama*), 'temporal relationship' (*kāla*), 'spatial relationship' (*deśa*), and most important of all, since it is extremely difficult, if not impossible to find, any *one* event which can be regarded as *the* cause of a given event, 'the collocation of causal factors' (*sāmagrī*).[1] This latter term clearly shows that the Buddhists never admitted the rule '*A* causes *B*' , except as a crude suggestion in non-philosophical parlance. As a matter of fact, the Buddhist conception of causation, is if we want to compare it with other theories about causation, more in line with Hume's view that in causation there is no indefinable relation, except conjunction and succession and that our tendency to accept such propositions as 'this causes that' is to be explained by the laws of habit and association. A fruitful understanding of the Buddhist conception of causation will be gained once the outstanding logicians such as Diṅnāga and Dharmakīrti are systematically studied, the latter in particular clearly formulating and making use of the law of functional dependence.

Of all schools the Vijñānavādins were the only ones who gave number (*saṁkhyā*) a status of its own in their classification of topics of interest.[2]

1. In course of time two distinct sets have become developed: *hetu* and *pratyaya*. The Theravādins recognized three *hetus* which could be counted as nine, according to their character, as wholesome, unwholesome, or undefined. They also accepted twenty-four *pratyayas*, most of them owing their existence to the profuseness of linguistic expression. According to Abhidhammattha-saṅgaha VIII 29 this large number can be reduced to four topics, but with the exception of *ālambanapratyaya* (Pāli *ārammaṇapaccaya*) none are found in the other schools of Buddhism.

The Sarvāstivādins recognized six *hetus* yielding five results, and four *pratyayas*, which are identical with those recognized by the Vijñānavādins. The Vijñānavādins recognized ten *hetus* which were essentially subdivisions of two *hetus*, and four *pratyayas*.

A good synopsis of the various *hetus* and *pratyayas* is found in Louis de la Vallée Poussin, Théorie des douze causes, pp. 51 sqq.

2. Abhidharmasamuccaya, p. 11. The Vaibhāṣikas included number of calculus in mental activity. Abhidharmakośa IV 126.

Atoms and Structure

A presentation of the ideas about our 'physical' world would be incomplete if the atomic theory of the Sarvāstivādins was not referred to. However, it must not be assumed that in this theory we have anything like the atomic theory which obtained at the beginning of modern physics, the philosophical consequence of which was that a three-term relation obtains in which the atoms in public mathematical space and time are one term, the sensed qualities in sensed space and time the third term, and the observer the mediating second term. Nor do we find in it an equivalent to the early Greek distinction between the world as immediately sensed which is not the real world, and the world as designated by the mathematically and experimentally confirmed theories of science. For the Sarvāstivādins and also for the Sautrāntikas, who held an atomic view, atoms are not discontinuous but always form a conglomeration, a structural unit. At the minimum eight atoms in the proper sense of the word as indivisible entities, form one structural unit which, however, is unable to exist alone and must be combined with and supported by at least seven similar units. The eight substances (*dravya*), in the terminology of the Sarvāstivādins, which build up one unit are the four great elementary qualities (*mahābhūta*) together with four secondary qualities (*upādāya*), viz., color-shape (*rūpa*), odor, taste, and the tangible. If these atoms, in the loose sense of the term as a cluster of atoms proper, (*saṅghātaparamāṇu*) are found in an organism they in addition comprise the tangibility of the body organization, and in the case of the particular sensory capacities, they in addition comprise the sensibility of the particular sense organization which is inseparably linked with the general body organization.[2] Although we speak of the sensory capacity of an organ it should be noted that in Buddhist conception the sensory capacity *is* the organ, the 'of' belongs only to the projectibility of language.

Between the Sarvāstivādins and Sautrāntikas a dispute had arisen as to the nature of the conglomeration of atoms : Whether the atoms touch each other or whether there are inter-

1. Abhidharmakośa II 22 and Bhāṣya.

vals between them. Or whether there are no intervals between them and yet they do *not* touch each other. The Sarvāstivādins-Vaibhāṣikas held the view that there are intervals between the atoms of the conglomeration, while the Sautrāntikas declared that there are no intervals and yet the atoms do not touch each other. The underlying idea of the atomic theory has certainly been one of structurance, as may be gleaned from the assertion that the arrangement of the clusters of atoms is different with the different organs. Thus the eye atoms are shaped like the cummin flowers, the ear atoms like a birch-tree leaf, the nose atoms like a coronet, the tongue atoms like a half-moon, the body atoms like the body itself, the atoms of the female sex organs like a drum, and those of the male sex organs like a thumb.[1]

Owing to their tendency to reduce everything to, and to deal essentially with, quantitative concepts and laws (*dravya*) as the sole and sufficient condition of structure, the Sarvāstivādins-Vaibhāṣikas overlooked the fact that quantitative laws alone, though always assignable to the patterning or structuring of events, can never describe the event and its structuring. Quantitative laws do not even account for one of the most significant aspects of structure, viz., wholeness. Wholeness itself is the outcome of structuring and structuring takes place at every level of organismic life. The critique of the atomic theory of the Sarvāstivādins by the Vijñānavādins and Mādhyamikas was therefore directed against the reduction of a living process to quantitative laws and, moreover, pointed out an inherent contradiction in terms of the atomic theory. A summary of the atomic theory and its critique is found in sGam.po. pa's Lam.rim and is given here in translation :[2]

"The Vaibhāṣikas say : The nature of atoms is such that an atom is spherical, has no parts, is single, and exists materially. The conglomeration of atoms forms objects (of perception) such as color-shape and other objects. Between the atoms in an atom conglomeration there are intervals. That these atoms

1. Abhidharmakośa I 43-44ab and Bhāṣya. Students of psychoanalysis will be reminded of the relationship between the thumb and sex.

2. Dam. chos. yid. bzhin. gyi. nor. bu. thar. pa. rin. po. chrgyan. zhes, bya. ba. theg. pa. chen. poi. lam. tim. gyi. bśad. pa. fol. 96.

appear to be in one place is like the unity of appearance of a yak's tail in the pasture. That the atoms do not fall asunder is due to the fact that they are held together by the Karman of sentient beings.

"The Sautrāntikas assert : The atoms conglomerate and though there are no intervals in between them, they do not touch each other.

"Although the adherents of an atomic theory make such a claim nothing of what they say is proved. Atoms must be single or plural. If they are single it must be questioned whether they have several sides or not. If they possess various sides, they extend into an Eastern, Western, Southern, Northern, upper and lower direction. Since in such a case they have six sides (and are divisible) the claim of their singleness collapses. If they do not possess different sides, all material things ought to be of the nature of a single atom. But this is not the case, as is plainly evident. In the Viṁśatikā is stated:[1]

> One atom joined with six others
> Must have six parts.
> If six are in one and the same place,
> The aggregate must be as one atom only.

"If you suggest that there is a multitude of atoms as aggregates, the answer is that if one atom were found to exist it would be possible to assume an aggregate of single atoms, but since a single atom is not proved, an aggregate due to a combination of single atoms is not proved."

A similar theory, though in important respects different and superior to it was evolved by the Theravādins. Apart from the fact that they do not recognize atoms as quantitative elements in structure and refer to the quantitative aspect by such terms as octad, nonad, decad and a few more, the highest number being thirteen, the quantitative aspect remains entirely subordinate to the dynamic or kinetic one. As the terms imply, the minimum of quantitative requirements for structuring are eight 'forces', viz., the four great elementary qualities (*mahā-bhūta*) of solidification (*paṭhavīdhātu*), cohesion (*āpodhātu*),

1. Viṁśatikā by Vasubandhu, verse 12.

temperature (*tejodhātu*), motion (*vāyodhātu*) and four secondary qualities (*upādāya*), viz., color (*varṇa*), odor (*gandha*), taste (*rasa*), and 'force' or 'vigor' (*ojā*), by which latter term is indicated that a firm articulation and organization of such a compound or structure obtains. These eight forces which are never found apart from each other are termed an 'inseparable organization' (*avinibbhogarūpa*) or a 'pure octad' (*suddhaṭṭhaka*)[1] This organization owes its existence to various structuralizing laws, that is to say, any such organization is the manifested form of the structuralizing law and is the empirical, factual, physical, and physiological character of nature and man. The laws that operate at different levels are above all Karman or the fact that the whole of reality is a dynamic process.[2] Then there is *citta* which as we have seen in the narrower sense of the word, is a term for our attitudes in dealing with the world and ourselves; but since an attitude involves the whole organism, the 'inseparable organization' which expresses the structuralizing law of *citta* (*cittasamuṭṭhāna*),[3] represents a behavioristic patterning, inasmuch as popularly speaking, a body not animated by a mind (*citta*), would not behave in such and such a way, and it is therefore correct to say that the particular organization as structuralized by *citta* is the particular mind or living being. Next there is the thermodynamic behavior of organismic life (*utusamuṭṭhāna*).[4] According to biology and thermodynamics any living organism is not in thermodynamic equilibrium. This obtains, because of the second law of thermodynamics, that no living being can exist unless energy comes into it from without. Such energy is supplied by food. It also represents a structuralizing force and is mentioned as the last factor in contributing to structure-formation. It may be said to be the physio-chemical nature of man (*āhārasamuṭṭhāna*).[5]

Another fact we find is that unless a body is at rest, it has kinetic energy. Kinetic energy is termed 'life' (*jīvitendriya*)

1. Abhidhammatthasaṅgaha VI 19.
2. ibid. VI 10; 18.
3. ibid. VI 10; 19.
4. ibid. VI 10; 20.
5. ibid. VI 10; 21.

which, as has been pointed out above, is considered to be a certain amount of power, by which an organism is capable of doing work, i.e., in the language of physics, to overcome resistance. In being active kinetic energy is lost or, in terms of biology, organismic life gradually loses its life. Since the number of constituents can be counted (quantitative aspect) 'life' together with the 'pure octad' forms a nonad.[1] In its further structuralization into a sensory apparatus we arrive at the sense-decads comprising of the pure octads, life (kinetic energy), and the sensory capacity which is the sense organization itself. Naming them after the dominant sensory organization we have an eye-decad, an ear-decad, a nose-decad, a tongue-decad, and a body-decad. Since the body is either male or female and since sex is as important as the other sensory functions, and found at all levels of body organization we have a sex-decad also, which is either male or female. One other decad is mentioned and that is the heart-decad.[2] It was counted as a particular decad that was essential for achieving harmony as far as the psychological processes of perception were concerned. All other senses had a basis of their own, only mind as interpretative operation had no corresponding physiological basis. As most suited the heart was selected, because all our intellectual processes are supported by emotional flux. Moreover, everybody is familiar with the fact that the emergency reactions of fear, anger, joy and the like do affect the heart. As a matter of fact, fear and sexuality, the dominant emotions in most people, increase or lower the palpitation of the heart. If we are now-a-days convinced that the higher skills of life belong to the cerebro-cortical level and not to the vegetative system of which the heart is a suitable symbol, we should not forget that the Abhidharmikas did not want to give an account of the physiological levels of organization according to postulated and deductively and experimentally verified theories.

The greatest structure or the unique event in which structurance continues to operate, is the organized human body. This body is divided into three sections : a lower one extending from the navel to the feet, a middle portion extending

1. Abhidhammatthasaṅgaha VI 18.
2. ibid.

from the navel to the wind-pipe, and an upper part from the wind-pipe to the crown of the head.[1] In all these parts we find organismic activity in a way that the organism behaves in such and such way (*cittasamuṭṭhāna*), that it follows thermodynamic laws (*utusamuṭṭhāna*), exhibits physiochemical processes (*āhārasamuṭṭhāna*), is capable of feeling pressure (*kāyadasaka*), and comprises sex (*bhāvadasaka*). The middle portion in addition has heart activity, and the upper portion sensory activities.[2]

Whatever the defects of numerical limitations may be, since they so easily induce us to believe that a static-mechanistic model and quantitative aspects will suffice to account for all organismic activity, they should not be allowed to make us forget the Buddhist conception of universal flux which definitely shows that the octads, nonads, and decads can be but events within the total structure man and that there is also an incessant structuring of events. Further, within the total structure there is constant displacement of energy and there are certain regions where such changes in the energic state occur; known as the homeostatic level of the energic balance of the structural manifold in an organism. These regions Allport aptly calls 'event-regions.'[3] Intimately connected with energy displacements,

. Aṭṭhasālinī IV 51.

2. ibid. The distribution is as follows :

Lower body :	feeling decad (*kāyadasaka*)	10
	sex decad (*bhāvadasaka*)	10
	organismic activity (*cittasamuṭṭhāna*)	8
	thermodynamics (*utusamuṭṭhāna*)	8
	physiochemistry (*āhārasamuṭṭhāna*)	8
	Total : 44 components.	
Middle body :	the same increased by heart (*vatthudasaka*)	
	Total : 54 components.	
Upper body :	the same as the lower body increased by	
	eye-decad (*cakkhudasaka*)	10
	ear-decad (*sotadasaka*)	10
	nose-decad (*ghānadasaka*)	10
	tongue-decad (*jivhādasaka*)	10
	Total : 84 components.	
	All over total 182 components.	

3. Floyd H. Allport, Theories of Perception and the Concept of Structure, p. 653.

due to stimulation raising the energic state of a particular event region above the homeostatic or autonomous level, and then communicating it throughout the whole structure, are sets or dynamic patterns which tend to determine what is to be perceived. Such 'sets' are known as expectancy and intention. In the first case an individual 'expects' a certain stimulus to appear and gets ready for it, while in the second case the individual responds. As Allport points out 'expectancy' and 'intention' within the 'set' go together and the emphasis upon the one or the other does not imply two different aspects but only two phases of the same total process.[1] Both topics, energy displacement (*ussada*) and set (*ābhujita*), the author of the Aṭṭhasālinī has admirably elaborated. He says :

"In the case of expectancy-intention (*ābhujitavasena*), when a bowl filled with food is brought, he who takes a morsel of it and examines it as to whether it is hard or soft, is 'set' for the primary quality of solidity (*paṭhavīdhātum eva pana ābhujati*), although in this morsel there is also temperature and mobility. If he puts his hand into hot water for examination, he is 'set' for temperature (*tejodhātum*), although there is also solidity and mobility. If in the hot season he opens a window and lets the window strike his body, while the wind gently strikes his body, he is 'set' for mobility (*vāyodhātum*), although there is also solidity and temperature. In this way the 'set' determines the object of perception (*evam ābhujanavasena ārammaṇam karoti nāma.*)[2]

"He who stumbles or dashes his head against a tree or while eating bites upon a stone, takes solidity as the objective constituent of his perception due to its preponderance (*ussadavasena*), although there is also temperature and mobility. He who treads on fire, takes temperature as the objective constituent of perception because of its preponderance, although there is also solidity and mobility. When a strong wind blows so as to make us deaf as it were, he takes mobility as the objective constituent of perception because of its preponderance, although there is also solidity and temperature.

1. Floyd H. Allport, Theories of Perception and the Concept of Structure, p. 216

2. lit. : 'thus because of the set the perceiving individual determines the objective constituent of his perception'.

"Tactile cognition does not rise all at once in him who makes any one of the primary qualities the objective constituent of perceptions. Stimulation (and sensation) are immediately (*ekappah ārena kāye*) sensed by him who is pricked by a bunch of needles. (Otherwise), wherever the pressure sense organization (*kāyappasādo*) attains a higher energetic state (*ussanno*), there rises tactile cognition. And it arises first wherever stimulation is strongest. Also when a wound is cleaned with a feather, the filaments stimulate the pressure sense organization (*kāyappāsadaṁ ghaṭṭeti*), and wherever the organization has a higher energic level there tactile cognition arises. In this way, due to energy displacements the objective constituents of tactile perceptions are determined".[1]

As the author of the Aṭṭhasālinī plainly states : sets and stimuli are responsible for our passing from object to object.[2] Thus a dynamic view holds throughout for man and the world around him, even when a distinction is made to the effect that the world around us is said to be unorganized (*anupādinna*) and only our own existence is organized (*upādinna*). This does not mean a distinction between unorganic matter and live matter but only points out the greater importance of ourselves as perceiving subjects, although 'greater' here implies no value judgment.

Considering all that has been said about the structurance going on in man, we cannot be but surprised at the comprehensive conception of man the Buddhists had from earliest times. In spite of their predominant interest in spiritual development and growth they never made the mistake of reducing man to a mental substance (Locke) or to an association of sensed data (Hume) or to inspected wants (Mill, Bentham). If the idea of spiritual growth and development has any *raison d'etre*—and the Buddhists affirm it—then it must take into account the whole man and not a fragment. Buddhist discipline starting with the actual man always insisted on wholeness.

1. Aṭṭhasālinī IV 96-97.
2. ibid. IV 98 : *ajjhāsayato vā visayādhimattato vā.*

Conclusion

Knowledge of the world around us and of ourselves begins with perception. Perceptual phenomena are experienced as certain qualities which in vision we call hue or color. Other examples are the sound we hear, the odors we smell, taste, and an experience of prèssure, warmth, and cold. But there is another class which is mainly concerned with the formal properties of things, we perceive, such as shape, outline, size, volume and in a wider aspect, grouping. It is most significant that we do not experience these qualities, dimensions, as such and in isolation but as things and events presenting a 'whole character'. Experience comes in Gestalten which moreover may be organized into strong and firmly articulated forms or into weak and poorly articulated ones. The Gestalten we are experiencing are termed *rūpa.* In using the term Gestalten and speaking of the holistic character of our experiences we must make one important distinction. The Buddhists did not assume or believe that the 'whole' was something more than, or at least different from the parts, possessing laws of its own according to which it selects and organizes the parts. The unique 'whole-character' is by no means denied, it is even firmly insisted upon, but an 'independent' whole is rejected. This distinguishes the Buddhist conception of *rūpa* as Gestalt from the Gestalt of the gestalt psychologists.[1] Taking into account the dynamic conception so characteristic of Buddhism, *rūpa* can be said to be a generic term for structured events.

While for presentational purposes it is perfectly correct to speak of *rūpa* as the objective constituent of perceptual situations, and in extension of the term due to the external reference of the situation, as the epistemological object, the total something

1. See Sthiramati's Vṛtti on Vasubandhu's Triṁśikā, p. 16. "The whole is not something different from its parts in their operation together, because we do not perceive a whole after having abstracted in parts" (*na ca saṁcitam avayavasaṁhitamātrād anyad vidyate tadavayavān apohya saṁcitākāravijñānābhāvāt*).

The same critique is found in Floyd H. Allport, Theories of Perception and the Concept of Structure, pp. 141 sqq.

It is a remarkable fact that Sthiramati's important work like many others, has not yet found an English translation .

of our perception, the question remains whether the some*thing* can actually be separated from the some*how*. The Sarvāstivādins-Vaibhāṣikas assumed that it was possible and forthwith developed a system of substances (*dravya*) as the some*thing* forming the basis of the some*how* of our perceptions. The Vijñānavādins contented that the some *thing* is but a transformation, a projection, as it were, of the some*how*. The Theravādins avoided committing themselves in either way. And the Mādhyamikas pointed out that in direct immediate experience, the problem of the some*thing* and the some*how* does not obtain at all, substantialism (*dravya*) and mentalism (*vijñāna*) are modes of interpretation,—nothing more.

THE PATH

(*mārga*)

The way out

The analysis of that which we are accustomed to call mind and its states or, from a dynamic angle, our attitudes and the function-events that operate in them and build them up (*citta-caitta*), as well as the investigation of perceptual situations in which we claim to be in cognitive contact with 'things' believed to make up our 'physical' world (*rūpa*),—all of which is our world, Saṁsāra,—is a necessary means to enable us to evolve the Path by which we may attain not only peace of mind amid transitory, death-doomed, determinate objects in nature and equally transitory inspected selves, but also spiritual contentment and a joyous acceptance of facts, which as a lasting possession will free us from bondage. The Path, therefore, occupies a very important and prominent place within Buddhist thought.[1] The nature of any path is such that it leads from one place to another. In Buddhism, The Path leads from Saṁsāra to Nirvāṇa. To walk a path naturally involves the problem of the nature of Saṁsāra and Nirvāṇa as the starting-

1. The 'Path' has been the subject-matter of a particular class of literature in Tibet. Two sections can be distinguished, known as *lam, rim* and *lam zab* respectively. The former is based on the Sūtras and to a lesser extent, on the Tantras. The latter is based on the Tantras and deals with meditative process exclusively. It is usually transmitted from teacher to disciple because certain exercises cannot be practised without the guidance of a teacher who himself has gone through the particular discipline. Therefore distinction also is made between an ordinary (*thun.moṅ*) and extraordinary (*thun. moṅ. ma.yin.pa*) part. Even today texts dealing with the extraordinary aspect are handled very carefully and only initiated persons get access to them. Pad ma-dkar, po. giving an outline of this aspect in his Bla. bsgrub, thun. mon. ma. yin. pai. khrid. rim. gñis.gdan.rdzogs, does not fail to say at the end of his work: "While the ordinary means for attaining ultimate reality is open to everybody, this teaching of the extraordinary means has formerly been kept very secret. May the Guru (i.e. The Buddha's and the host o D ākas (i.e., spiritual powers) pardon me for having divulged this teaching out of a loving disposition to mankind" (fol. 14b).

point, on the one hand, and the goal, on the other, the Path itself being the link between the two.

The reality of Saṁsāra has never been doubted and Buddhists never made the fatal mistake of judging it as an illusion (*māyā*). It is true, Saṁsāra may lose its patent reality character and its hold over us when through certain spiritual exercises[1] we arrive at a point from which we experience our world in a different way and in a new light. But this new manner and new light is and remains an experience and however vivid the experience may be it does not justify an ontological predication to the effect that our world is an illusion.

In contrast with Saṁsāra which is 'conditioned' (*saṁskṛta*), Nirvāṇa is said to be 'unconditioned' (*asaṁskṛta*), 'peaceful' (*śānta*), 'unborn' (*ajāta*), 'unoriginated' (*anutpāda*); it is 'the cessation (*nirodha*) and non-existence (*abhāva*) of misery and of emotionally unbalancing motivations'. These are only some of the attributes and many more such descriptive terms and phrases can easily be culled from the vast mass of texts belonging to the various schools of Buddhism. As so often happened and in this particular case also, linguistic expression has given rise to 'metaphysical' problems which actually were no problems at all and, posited as problems, only tended to confuse clear thinking. The descriptive phrase, 'There exists something unborn',[2] contains both an affirmative and a negative element. The Sarvāstivādins-Vaibhāṣikas selected the existentially affirmative part and interpreted Nirvāṇa in such a way that it was meant to denote an entity in which there is absence of motivation and which like a dam stops the continuation of emotional instability, activeness, and origination.[3]

The Sautrāntikas considered Nirvāṇa as 'non-existence' (*abhāvamātra*) of misery and emotional instability and 'non-appearance' (*aprādurbhāva*) of new misery.[4] They compared Nirvāṇa with the disappearance of a flame, which is a process

1. There is a meditation practice called *māyopamasamādhi* (Tib. *sevu ma. lta.bui.tiṅ.ṅe.'dzin*). Emphasis lies on the *upamā* 'like', 'a concentration in which we see our world as if it were an illusion'.

2. Udāna VIII 3 and 2.

3. Madhyamakavṛtti, p. 525.

4. Abhidharmakośa II 55d-56b and Bhāṣya. See also Vyākhyā.

and not an entity in itself. It will be observed that the Sautrāntikas in no way denied Nirvāṇa, but gave it rather a dynamic interpretation which was taken up by the followers of Mahāyāna Buddhism, referring to this dynamic aspect by the term *apratiṣṭhitanirvāṇa*.[1] The critique by the Sautrāntikas, directed against the thing and substance conception of the Sarvāstivādins, clearly points out that properties (such as 'being peaceful, being the end of misery', and so on) are not individual things; and as a critique, that which the Sautrāntikas have to say is absolutely correct. But if a critique loses its character of just being a critique and becomes something like an isolated system then Nirvāṇa in this critical interpretation turns into 'non-existence' pure and simple, being on the same level as 'existence'. The only difference is that the two constructs 'existence' and 'non-existence' are existentially affirmative and existentially negative respectively. The tendency to establish rigid systems has been at work since earliest times, and all schools without exception, who took up a certain position, became spiritually stagnant. Through systematization it happened that the way out of Saṁsāra became a path leading from one form of existence to another form of existence or from existence to non-existence. To insist on either conception as the sole truth certainly militates against the Buddhist idea of a Middle Path that avoids the extremes of existence and non-existence.

The Theravādins did nothing to solve this dilemma. Some of them accepted the Sarvāstivāda view, as did for instance Buddhaghosa,[2] others took over the Sautrāntika view, as did the author of the Aṭṭhasālinī.[3]

It is the indisputable merit of the Mādhyamikas and Tantriks—the Mādhyamikas in a more intellectually understandable way and the Tantriks in a more psychological man-

1. *apratiṣṭhita* means not to fall into the activism of Saṁsāra and not to fall into the quietism of (*static*) Nirvāṇa. See for instance Lam. *zab. kyi, rnam. par. bśad.* pa. *zab. lam.gyi. sñe. ma.fol.* 11b.

2. Visuddhimagga VIII 247 : *na rāgābhāvamattam* is a critique of the Sautrāntikas, and XVI 67 sqq. is an acceptance of the existence-theory of the Sarvāstivādins.

3. In III 468 the author uses the term *apātubhāva* in the same sense as the Sautrāntikas. Other instances where the author follows the Sautrāntika view have been pointed out within the text.

ner—to have pointed out the fallacies of these one-sided interpretations and to have solved the problem by recapturing the living spirit of Buddhism in immediate experience where such predications as 'existence' and 'non-existence' are wholly out of place[1] and where the claim of an ontological object corresponding to the experience is a sign of bad reasoning. Since philosophers, as a rule, are convinced of their own intellectual acumen and the validity of their thesis, but doubt the intelligence of their opponents and try to disprove their thesis in no uncertain terms, the Mādhyamikas who hold no thesis of their own[2] and accomplish the *reductio ad absurdum* on principles and procedure fully acceptable to the holder of a thesis, can with a hearty laugh return the compliments by saying :

"those who assume existence I call similar to cattle,
But those who believe in non-existence are still more stupid than these".[3]

Saṁsāra and Nirvāṇa are not two entities, but essentially terms for describing an experience and owe their existence as separate entities to a rather objectionable analysis and the habitual tendency of ours to take our abstractions and constructs as the whole truth about the whole of reality. Saṁsāra is in no way inferior to Nirvāṇa, nor is Nirvāṇa in any way superior to Saṁsāra. Value judgments only detract us from reality. From the standpoint of experienced reality and not from speculation, Nirvāṇa and Saṁsāra are one and the same, as Nāgārjuna has so aptly expressed it :

"There is not the slightest difference of Saṁsāra from Nirvāṇa,
Nor is there the slightest difference of Nirvāṇa from Saṁsāra.

1. Madhyamakavṛtti, p. 524 : *bhāvābhāvaparāmarśakṣayo nirvāṇam ucyate.*

2. "A position (*pakṣa*) breeds a counter-position (*pratipakṣa*), and neither of them is real", Madhyamakavṛtti, p. 359.

3. Dohākośa-upadeśa-gīti by Saraha (mi.zad. pai. gter. mdzod. man. ṅag. gi. glu). bs Tan. 'gyur, Derge edition, rgyud. vol.zhi. fol. 2ca. Quoted twice by sGam. po. pa in his Dam. chos. yid. bzhin. gyi, nor . bu. thar.pa. rin. po. chei. rgyan. zhes, bya. ba. theg. pa. chen. poi. lam. rim. gyi. bśad. pa. fol. 98b.

That which is the limit of Nirvāṇa is also the limit of Saṁsāra,
In between them not the slightest shade of difference is found".[1]

This has important consequences concerning The Path itself, for it means that the starting-point is the same as the goal. Hence The Path cannot be something different either. "The difference between the starting point (*gzhi*), The Path (*lam*), and the goal (*'bras.bu*) exists only on the part of him who discourses on it, in reality (*don.la*), there is no reason to differentiate between them and it is permissible to say that starting point and goal are indivisible or that path and goal are indivisible (*dbyer.med*)".[2] This realization demands that we accept reality as it is and do not introduce a division which will only create difficulties. Although this conception of The Path falls outside the scope of the Abhidharma, it has to be mentioned because it is the logical outcome of that which has been foreshadowed in the various works of the Abhidharma literature. As far as this literature is concerned, Nirvāṇa alone is unconditioned and The Path as being evolved by us in our striving for Nirvāṇa is something conditioned.

The Theravāda Conception of the Path

Although The Path is basically one it may be viewed from various angles. Of these[3] only two are of primary importance, inasmuch as they denote the essence of The Path : "seeing" (*dassana*) and "paying closest attention to that which has been observed" (*bhāvanā*).[4] Owing to their importance they have been developed into a *darśanamārga* "a path of seeing" and *bhāvanāmārga* "a path of attention" in the *Mahāyāna* schools of Buddhism. Since a path leads from one place to another and since it may do so by various halting places, such halting places corresponding to certain individual types of man, to

1. Mūlamadhyamakakārikā XXV 19, 20.
2. Lam. zab. kyi. rnam.par. bśad.pa. zab. lam.gyi. sñe. ma. fol.8b.
3. See for instance Visuddhimagga XVI 95.
4. On the meaning of *bhāvanā* see Aṭṭhasālinī III 327; Abhidharmakośa VI 1; VII 27; cp. Abhidharmasamuccaya, p. 70.

speak figuratively, the one path leading from Saṁsāra to Nirvāṇa has been split up into four sections counted as four paths.[1] It is only the First Path leading to a stage termed 'entering the stream' (*srota-āpatti*, Pāli *sotāpatti*), i.e., the stream which finally carries an individual along its current to distant Nirvāṇa, that is connected with "seeing". The three other paths, leading to a stage of 'once-returning' (*sakṛdāgāmin*, Pāli *sakadāgāmi*), never returning' (*anāgāmin*, Pāli *anāgāmi*) and 'Arhantship' (*arhant*, Pāli *arahā*) are connected with "paying closest attention to that which has been observed on the first path". It is obvious that because of the gradation of the Four Paths "seeing" on the First Path is more like catching a glimpse of reality and by attending to its characteristics and by making them a vivid experience must be developed into proper seeing and understanding. Thus the author of the Aṭṭhasālinī states :[2] "The term 'seeing' is used in reference to the Path of Entering the Stream. It is called 'seeing', (*dassana*) because it catches sight of Nirvāṇa for the first time. Although the cognitive moment (*gotrabhū*)[3] gets a glimpse of Nirvāṇa for the first time, it may be likened to a person who has come to a king on a certain errand and who has seen the king from afar riding on an elephant's back by a certain road, and who on being asked whether he had seen the king, were to reply that he had not seen the king because the purpose of his errand had not been accomplished. So also this cognitive moment, though it has seen Nirvāṇa, is not seeing in the proper sense of the word because the necessary work, the getting rid of emotional instability, has not been achieved. This cognition only performs the function of adverting in The Path". At another place the author says that this cognitive moment is like adverting though itself it is not adverting.[4] This means that the realization of Nirvāṇa, the seeing of reality, is something like a perceptive process, but since Nirvāṇa is not a thing in itself and therefore cannot be spoken of in terms of ordinary sense perception where

1. Visuddhimagga XXII 2 : Aṭṭhasālinī III 466-539.
2. Aṭṭhasālinī II 24.
3. See also Aṭṭhasālinī III 508: *gotrabhūñāṇaṃ nibbānam ārammaṇam kurnmānam*. See also Visuddhimagga IV 74; XVII 81; XXII 5-13. XXIII 7.
4. Aṭṭhasālinī III 511.

a perceiving subject and a perceived object are postulated, 'seeing' and 'adverting' are but inadequate terms for that which may be called a 'depth-experience'.

As to the three remaining Paths the author of the Aṭṭhasālinī states :[1] " 'Concentrated attention' (*bhāvanā*) is spoken of with reference to the three remaining paths. The triad of these remaining paths arises by virtue of paying the closest attention to that which has been perceived on the First Path. This triad does not see anything new that has not been seen previously, hence it is called 'paying closest attention to that which has been perceived' ".

None of the paths can be followed without meditation or at least in connection with meditation The Path is easy.[2] Meditation, however, has a double aspect. It may help us in finding the wholeness-character of our experiences and thereby release us from our fragmentary dealing with the world in terms of mere utilitarian considerations. Or it may lead us to a realization of the meaning of our experiences. The former, born out of healthy attitudes, leads back to a still more healthy attitude in dealing with the particulars of this world, the latter leads over and beyond this world, though not in a spatial sense. Because of the direction the meditative processes may take, a distinction is made between a 'worldly' (*lokiya*) and a 'superworldly' (*lokuttara*) meditation, the 'superworldly' meditation being different from the 'worldly' one only by its association with the Paths.[3]

The author of the Aṭṭhasālinī begins his explanation of the First Path with an investigation of the meaning of the term 'superworldly' (*lokuttara*). He says that this type of meditation is termed 'superworldly', because it crosses the world, crosses over the world, and stands overpowering the three worlds after having passed beyond them.[4] It furthermore leads man out of the vicious circle of birth and death (*niyyānika*), because through this type of meditation man comes to understand misery, to stop the new origination of misery, to realize the

1. Aṭṭhasālinī II 24. Cp. Abhidharmakośa VI 28 cd.
2. Abhidharmakośa VI 66.
3. Aṭṭhasālinī III 466.
4. ibid.

end of misery, and to practise the way guaranteeing the cessation of misery.[1] It is the cognition and incorporation into our individual life of that which is termed the Four Truths that distinguishes this meditation from all other meditational practices. "While healthy attitudes and meditative practices ranging over the three worlds (of sensuality, Gestaltung, and non-configurativeness) build up and make grow birth and death in a never-ending circle and hence are called building-up practices, it is not so with this meditation. Just as if a man were to erect a wall eighteen cubits high, while another man were to take a hammer and to break down and to demolish any part as it gets erected, so also this meditation sets about to break down and to demolish death and re-birth that have been built up by healthy attitudes and meditative practices ranging over the three worlds, by bringing about a deficiency in those conditions which tend to produce birth and death, and therefore this meditation is also called 'the tearing down one, *apacayagāmī*'.[2]

That which is broken down is whatever views a person may hold about himself (*sakkāyadiṭṭhi*), scepticism (*vicikicchā*), and the clinging to rites and rituals (*sīlabbataparāmāsa*), on the intellectual side, and the unwholesome forces of cupidity (*rāga*), antipathy (*dosa*), and bewilderment (*moha*) on the emotional side.[3] The destruction of these forces enables man to set his foot on the first spiritual level (*bhūmi*). In particular it enables him to gain the state of a person who has entered the stream. This state is one of the 'results of Śrāmaṇya' (*sāmaññaphala*).[4]

1. Aṭṭhasālinī III. 466. Cp. Abhidharmasamuccaya, p. 65.
2. Ibid.
3. Aṭṭhasālinī III 467. According to Abhidharmakośa VI 53 cd this belongs to the path of once-returning.
4. Aṭṭhasālinī III 468. According to Abhidharmakośa VI 51, *Śrāmaṇya* is the 'immaculate way' and according to VI 54 it is *Brāhmaṇya*, the *brahmacakra*. This terminology is already found in the ancient Sūtras, but here it has special implications. The Buddha is Brahmahood (*brahmabhūta*, Dīghanikāya III 84), so Brahmahood cannot be separated from Brahma expressiveness (*brahmavihāra*) which comprises benevolence (*maitrī*), compassion (*karuṇā*), joy in the good and wholesome performed by others (*muditā*), and equanimity (*upekṣā*). As will be seen later on, the Theravādins excluded the positive qualities of compassion and joy from their ideal of Buddhahood. In this respect they stand alone, none of the other schools accepted such a negative

In realizing this state the same difficulties obtain as in the case of ordinary worldly meditations, which gives rise to various types of persons, such as those who proceed with difficulties or those who remove obstacles easily.

The interest in how man appears to himself and which are the functions that operate at various levels and in various attitudes, has always been paramount. So also the attainment of certain 'superworldly' stages does not mean that 'superworldly' is some transcendental hocus-pocus breaking into our lives from somewhere and in some manner which we can never understand. The author of the Aṭṭhasālinī leaves no doubt that the 'superworldly' is an attitude, similar to a healthy attitude in ordinary life, but with the difference, that it is controlled by 'the conviction that I shall come to know that which hitherto has been unknown' (*anājñātamājñāsyāmītīndriya*, Pali *anaññātaññassāmītindriya*).[1] Again, the 'unknown' is not something unknowable, but is a result of the fact that through a change of attitude from a mere worldly utilitarian attitude to a 'superworldly' understanding attitude, our eyes become opened to that which was always present but which we did not observe because we were occupied otherwise, and which we did not care to observe and to be aware of because of our preoccupations. "As a man having come to a vihāra where he has never been before, and being seated in the midst of it might say with reference to his not having gone there before, 'I have come to a place where I have never been before', and being decorated with garlands he has never been decorated with before, being dressed

view. The positive conception of Buddhahood is best expressed in Lam. zab. kyi, rnam. par. bśad. pa. zab. lam. gyi. sñe. ma. fol. 29a :

"The boundless forces (*tshad. med-apramāṇa-maitrī, karuṇā, muditā, upekṣā*) are the sole cause of attaining the basic meditation stages (i.e. four *rūpāvacara* and four *arūpāvacara*)· Because due to this they extend to the worlds, they are termed *brahmavihāra* (*tshaṅs.pai.gnas.pa*). In the ultimate sense *brahma* (*tshaṅs.pa*) is unveiled Buddhahood".

1. Aṭṭhasālinī III 471 : "In the cycle of Saṁsāra which knows no beginning I shall come to know the unknown, the place of immortality of the nature of the Four Truths". According to Abhidharma-kośa 119 the stage of one who has entered the stream also contains the *ājñāendriya* 'knowledge of attainment', while according to Aṭṭhasālinī III 657 this belongs to the three higher levels.

in a garment he has never worn before, and having eaten a meal he has never tasted before, might say with reference to these experiences, 'I have eaten a meal never tasted before', so also it is with reference to the terms of the description : 'unseen' (*adiṭṭha*), because not seen before by the eye of discrimination (*paññācakkhu*); 'unattained' (*appatta*), because not reached before; 'unknown' (*avidita*), because not made clear by knowledge of experience (*ñāṇa*); and 'unrealized' (*asacchikata*), because not seen directly (*apaccakkha*)".[1]

An attitude always expresses itself in man's behavior. So also a 'superworldly' attitude will find its expression in the behavior of him who has grown up to it. As very characteristic of such an attitude is the fact that in distinction from a worldly healthy attitude, here kind words (*sammāvācā*), action beyond reproach (*sammākammanta*), and proper living (*sammājīva*) are present. While a healthy attitude had five 'path-functions',[2] the incorporation of these three forms of expressiveness emphasizes the importance of the Path in 'superworldly' attitudes. The main distinction between a worldly and a superworldly attitude lies in the fact that these three forms of expressiveness belong as an integral part of a superworldly attitude, while the same three forms may be occasionally present in healthy attitudes,[3] but never at the same time.[4]

It is here again that the artificiality of a numerical system becomes patent. The ancient texts had spoken of an Eightfold Path. As long as it was meant as a suggestion, no objections could be raised against such a numerical presentation, but when the import of the various 'members of the path' (*aṅga*) were analyzed it became apparent that the number eight could not be kept up, although this number had been hallowed by its association with The Buddha's words. The author of the Aṭṭhasālinī—and he does not stand alone—points out that livelihood (*ājīva*) is never an entity per se, but

1. Aṭṭhasālinī III 475. The last term. *paccakkha*, Skt. *pratyakṣa* is important in the Buddhist theory of cognition. It is pure perception devoid of any judgments.

2. See above pp. 74 sq.

3. Aṭṭhasālinī III 472 : 252.

4. ibid. III 481.

only a generic term for our expressions in words and deeds. Livelihood as such only owes its existence to the fact that we depend in our lives on so many things which we procure by words and deeds. Thus livelihood has no function of its own and naturally fails to establish the validity of the eightfoldness of the Eightfold Path. But since The Path demands the number eight, some meaning must be found for 'livelihood' so that it may be included in The Path as 'proper livelihood' (*sammā-jīva*).[1]

The author of the Aṭṭhasālinī begins his attempt to solve this difficult problem by pointing out the muddleheaded conceptions about ethical behavior which we have in ordinary life where we condone a certain action in one case, and frankly disapprove of it in another case, although the action is one and the same. He says : "Transgression at the level of overt behavior is done for reasons of one's livelihood and also without these reasons. The same holds good for transgressions at the communicative level. In this latter case, when kings and government officials who are addicted to sports set out for hunting, for highway robbery, and for adultery just in order to show off, their behavior receives the name of unwholesome action at the level of overt behavior. Refraining therefrom is called proper overt behavior. Whatever misdemeanor people show in the fourfold ways of speech, if it is done for no reasons of gaining one's livelihood, is termed unwholesome action at the level of communication. To refrain from it is termed proper speech. When hunters, fishermen, and other professionals kill, steal, and misbehave themselves in sexual matters, this is known as wrong livelihood. Abstaining therefrom is termed proper livelihood. When people, after having taken a bribe, tell lies, utter calumnies, harsh words, engage in fruitless talk, this is known as wrong livelihood. Abstaining from this is proper livelihood".[2]

The very fact that in a superworldly attitude there is nothing of that which we disapprove of as an evil action, be it

1. Aṭṭhasālinī III 479. For the Vaibhāṣikas 'wrong livelihood' is a category of its own. Abhidharmakośa IV 86.

2. Aṭṭhasālinī III 480. In 481 the author cites a view which is also found in Abhidharmakośa IV 86; 77.

by body or by speech, and also nothing of that which we condone as a bad way of living, shows the depth of understanding of ethical problems and the height of Buddhist ethics. To put it into modern terms: an act in itself is absolutely neutral and it receives its evaluation as either good or evil according to the particular discipline that is taken up. Within the frame-work of a discipline, an act is then either good or bad and in this relatively isolated system it is absolutely good or bad. Thus, in taking upon ourselves a discipline that is necessary for attaining a so-called superworldly attitude, killing is evil and it remains evil whether it is a wanton act of killing as in hunting for sport or a professional act as in slaughter houses. But this evaluation is valid only for the discipline of The Path and does not extend to other disciplines. There are other disciplines in which killing and the training for indiscriminate killing is a virtue, as is exemplified by military service, where disobeyance of the articles of war at once entails a court-martial.[1]

While in this way The Path is related to our outward behavior it also has a psychological counterpart in the so-called 'members of enlightenment' (*bodhyaṅga*, Pāli *bojjhaṅga*) of which there are seven: inspection (*smṛti*, Pāli *sati*), discrimination of entities as to their intrinsic value in pursuing the path to enlightenment (*dharmapravicaya*, Pāli *dhammavicaya*), assiduous striving (*vīrya*, Pāli *viriya*), tension release (*praśrabdhi*, Pāli *passaddhi*), concentrated absorption (*samādhi*) and equanimity (*upekṣā*, Pāli *upekkhā*).[2] These act as antidotes against mental inertia, frivolity, fixation, struggle, indulgence in sensual pleasures and self-mortification, and addiction to wild speculations, such as eternalism and nihilism. For enlightenment means to awaken from the sleep of emotional instability, to penetrate to the meaning of the Four Truths, and to realize Nirvāṇa.[3]

Although the attainment of enlightenment, the progress toward superworldly attitudes, is stated to be a positive ideal, the statement by the author of the Aṭṭhasālinī and by Anuruddha that in a superworldly attitude there is no compassion and no

1. Worse than this, modern states tend to adopt an absolutive ethics of killing by making military service compulsory for everybody.
2. Aṭṭhasālinī III 475. Abhidharmakośa VI 66-71 and Bhāṣya.
3. Aṭṭhasālinī III 473-474.

joy at the good and wholesome performed by others,[1] is all the more surprising. The argument that compassion extends to sentient beings, while the functions in a superworldly attitude are directed toward Nirvāṇa,[2] is a hopeless argument and only falls in with the negative character of Nirvāṇa as mere 'non-existence' even if the non-existence of emotions is some kind of existence. To exclude compassion from the ideal of enlightenment laid the Theravādins open to the charge of a complete lack of altruistic feeling. Actually, in this respect they stand alone. No other school of Buddhism accepted this conception. The Vaibhāṣikas introduced a distinction between compassion plain and simple and Great Compassion (*mahākaruṇā*). It is true, compassion extends to sentient beings, it may be a sentimentality, some kind of philanthropy which because of its lack of discrimination, often does more harm than good, but Great Compassion does not know of any distinction between sentient beings, it is the expression of the highest meditative concentration, it is realized when one actually succeeds in rising above the world.[3] Moreover, considering the habitual indolence of mankind and the ingrained aversion to attend to anything that does not follow an accustomed pattern—to teach such people and to make teaching a life-time job as was done by The Buddha—needs Great Compassion (capital letters !).[4]

The early texts of Buddhism had spoken of three 'deliverances' (*vimokṣa*, Pāli *vimokkha*)[5] which, on the one hand, represented certain types of concentrated absorption (*samādhi*)[6] and according to the division into a 'worldly' and a 'superworldly' aspect were termed 'pure' (*śuddha*)[7] or 'immaculate' (*anāsrava*).

1. Aṭṭhasālinī III 472. Abhidhammatthasaṅgaha II 21.
2. Aṭṭhasālinī III 472 : *karuṇāmuditā pana sattārammaṇā, imā dhammā nibbānārammaṇā ti tā p'ettha na gahitā.*
3. See the long discussion about the difference between ordinary compassion and Great Compassion in Bhāṣya ad Abhidharmakośa VII 33.
4. When in Abhidhammatthasaṅgaha II 15 it is stated that certain people believe that in those attitudes in which equanimity (*upekṣhā*) prevails, there is neither compassion nor joy, it seems that they mistook indifference (I couldn't care less) for equanimity, which certainly does not exclude compassion.
5. Paṭisambhidāmagga II 35.
6. Abhidharmakośa VII 23 cd. (*Bhāṣya*) ; 24.
7. ibid. VII 25.

In their latter aspect as 'immaculate' the deliverances were termed 'gateways to liberation' (*vimokṣamukha*[1] and represented superworldly Path proper.

Essentially these three types of concentration are related to certain aspects of the contemplated object. To understand these aspects leads to enlightenment. The names of the three deliverances are *śūnyatā* (Pāli *suññatā*), *apraṇihita* (Pāli *appaṇihita*), and *ānimitta* (Pāli *animitta*). By *śūnya* the fact is realized that everything conditioned, be it natural objects or postulated selves, has no individuality of its own persisting over and beyond the conditions that brought those entities about. By *apraṇihita* the fact is realized that everything conditioned is unable to yield lasting happiness and hence is misery, and by *ānimitta* is understood that everything is transitory. The relationship between the deliverances and the aspects of the whole of reality is as follows :

śūnyatāvimokṣa	*anātman*
apraṇihitavimokṣa	*duḥkha*
ānimittavimokṣa	*anitya*

However, as far as The Path is concerned only two of the three deliverances are able to give their name to The Path. This is because of the different approach in the Abhidharma. In the Sūtras the deliverances had been termed so by virtue of the quality (*saguṇato*), of the objective reference (*ārammanato*), and of the approach (*āgamanato*) to reality and it was the nature of reality which reflected on The Path. Thus by virtue of the goal to be approached which is *śūnyatā* The Path itself is termed *śūnyatā*.[2] However, this term has for the Theravādins no philosophical implications. It is a mere attribute describing the absence of something, viz. the absence of the emotions of cupidity, aversion, and bewilderment, which is Nirvāṇa. Similarly taking this absence and non-existence of emotions as the objective reference, The Path may be designated by it. The Abhidharma conception is concerned only with the 'approach

1. Abhidharmakośa VII. 25.
2. Aṭṭhasālinī III 484.

to Nirvāṇa' which may be viewed from two angles: insight (*vipassanāgamana*) and path (*maggāgamana*) so that with respect to the path insight is of primary importance, while with respect to the goal to be achieved the path being walked is of primary importance.[1]

The same explanation is given with reference to the 'unbiased', *apraṇihita*, which as a term for the goal extends its name to The Path. It also is related to insight. By virtue of its quality The Path is termed so, because there do not exist any leanings toward cupidity, aversion, and bewilderment, hence 'being without any leaning' 'unbiased', (*appaṇihita*). Because of the absence of such leanings Nirvāṇa is also called 'without any leanings' and The Path having Nirvāṇa as its objective reference is then termed in the same way.[2]

The reason that the 'imageless', *ānimitta,* does not give its name to The Path is that though the insight into it stands where the goal is to be found, in its application it deals with the destruction of such ideologies as eternalism (*niccānimitta*), theory of persistence (*dhuvanimitta*), hedonism (*sukhanimitta*), and Pure Ego theories (*attanimitta*), so that it is without ideological images (*ānimitta*) only where the goal is found, otherwise it is busy with ideological images (*sanimitta*).[3]

Another reason for the fact that there is no *animittamagga* (imageless path) is the nature of the path as accepted as having eight definite members or definite functions. The imageless deliverance is seeing the whole of reality as impermanent (*aniccānupassanīya hi vasena animittavimokkho kathito*). Through this deliverance confidence gains a controlling position within our mental life. Confidence (*saddhā*, *saddhindriya*), as has been explained above,[4] is that element in our attitudes which gives us assurance and certitude about further progress, because it purifies and brings lucidity into our conceptions about that with which we are dealing, unlike mere belief which obfuscates our minds. Such confidence effectively destroys the unwarranted assumption, so often met with in our ordinary dealings with

1. Aṭṭhasālinī III. 484.
2. ibid. III 486.
3. ibid. III 487.
4. See above p. 63.

the world, that whatever we cherish for the moment will persist unchanged, whether this be the object of our perception or of our own individualities. But confidence is not a member of The Path in its eightfold aspect, nor is it a member of those elements which lead to enlightenment. Hence that which is not a member of The Path cannot give its name to The Path itself. On the other hand, the *śūnyatāvimokṣa* which realizes that there does not exist any individuality apart from the conditions which for a certain time produce it or, to put it in a more philosophical language, that there is no Pure Ego (*anātman*) either as a substratum of our mental life or as a transcendental entity, is equal to a highly developed sense of discrimination, of analytical appreciative understanding (*paññindriya*). Similarly the *apraṇihitavimokṣa*, through which we can pursue our way toward Nirvāṇa without ever side-tracking into the manifold forms of emotional instability, which is the realization of the misery of all conditioned existence, and which through this realization liberates us from addiction to conditioned existence, is a highly developed state of concentrative absorption (*samādhindriya*). Both analytical appreciative understanding and concentrative absorption are 'members' of The Path and can extend their names to The Path itself.[1]

There is one other reason given for the fact that in the Abhidharma we do not speak of an *animittamagga*. The Path, so we are told, receives its name by essence and opposition (*sarasato ca paccanīkato*), that is to say, by its intrinsic nature (*sabhāvato*) and by its function of opposing and abolishing certain obstacles (*paṭipakkhato*).[2] Since The Path as *śūnyatā* and as *apraṇihita* refers to the fact that like Nirvāṇa it is the absence of emotional instability (*rāgādīhi suñña*) and the nonleaning toward any form of emotional instability (*rāgappaṇidhiādīhi*) and thus reveals its essence (*sarasato*), the one reason for its receiving this name has been fulfilled. The other reason is that *śūnyatā* opposes and destroys the addictedness to any form of Self (*attābhinivesassa paṭipakkho*), just as *apraṇihita* opposes and destroys any leaning (*paṇidhissa*). Thus its function as opposition is pointed out as the second reason for naming The

1. Aṭṭhasālinī III 488.
2. ibid. III 489.

Path. But although in essence The Path is 'imageless' (*animitta*), since there is absence and non-existence of such concepts as emotional instability or such ideological concepts as eternalism, and thus might receive its name from this essence of The Path, yet the *animitta* does not oppose anything. It does not oppose the view of transitoriness which has as its objective constituent the elements of our existence (*saṁkhāranimittārammaṇāya aniccānupassanāya*) and sees them as transitory. Because of its being in harmony with (*anulomabhāve*) the real nature of things, and therefore not serving as an opposition, the *animitta* cannot extend its name to The Path.[1]

The author of the Aṭṭhasālinī, representing the Theravāda view, unwittingly raises a problem, which if it had been pursued to its logical consequences, would have led to the acceptance of the Mādhyamika view that The Path and the goal can by rights not be separated. [For when Nirvāṇa is *śūnyatā* and *apraṇihita* as is The Path, no logical reason exists to make a distinction between path and goal.] And also the fact that *śūnyatā* serves to destroy the idea of a persisting individual nature (*anātman*) corresponds to the Mādhyamika view which states that *śūnyatā* is no end in itself, but is only meant to crush the belief in concrete existence. Indeed, those who hold the view of Śūnyatā as a goal are incurably stupid. As has been expressed by Nāgārjuna :

> "Those who hold a view of Śūnyatā
> Are said to be incurable".[2]

The three properties of being impermanent (*anitya*), being not worth-while to cling to (*duḥkha*), and being not such that the assumption of a Self or Pure Ego would be justified (*anātman*), are so intimately related that any one of the three entails the other two, so that it seems as if all three are presented to the perceiving and observing individual in one and the same moment of advertence, though actually the three are not together at the same time as far as The Path is concerned.[3] Thus to

1. Aṭṭhasālinī III 489.
2. Mūlamadhyamakārikā XXIV 11.
3. Aṭṭhasālinī III 490.

see things as impermanent enables us also to see them as not worth-while to cling to and as not representing some individual nature above and beyond their conditioned existence. In this way, the penetrating insight into the nature of things and selves, which as a perceptual act perceives certain properties, leads to knowledge by experience (*ñāṇa*) of the futility of 'things. For him who perceives the three properties of impermanence, non-worth-while-ness, and no-Self-or-Pure-Ego-ness, the five psycho-physical constituents of his existence are like a corpse tied to a person's neck. Knowledge by experience which has as its objective constituent the elements of existence, rises with reference to these elements. It is just as if a Bhikṣu who wanted to buy a bowl, were to see one brought by a bowl-vendor and, thinking highly pleased, 'I will take this one', were to find three holes in the bowl on examination; he would not become disinterested in the holes, but in the bowl. So also perceiving the above mentioned three properties, one becomes disinterested and unattached to the elements of existence".[1]

While the essential feature of the First Path is the seeing of reality (*dassana*, *vipassanā*), in particular the seeing of the First Truth which states the fact that in the whole of reality there is nothing to which it is worth-while to become addicted, because everything is impermanent, unable to yield lasting happiness, and has no character of its own. This truth enables us also to see the other Truths. The Second, Third, and Fourth Paths are the embodiment of truths perceived in our lives by continuous and closest attention to that which has been perceived (*bhāvanā*). The deeper the realization grows that everything is impermanent and that the desire for its immortality is a source of suffering, because by virtue of its transitoriness it breaks in our hands as soon as we attempt to lay hands on it, the feebler becomes our addiction to the sensuously and sensually stimulating objects that surround us and of which we partake as determinate personalities. But not only does this addiction grow less, ill-will also decreases, because addictedness and ill-will are related to each other in such a way that the one enhances the other. If I am addicted to a particular thing I want to possess it alone and I shall try to hinder anybody else

1. Aṭṭhasālinī III 491.

from sharing that which I covet and I shall not refrain from scheming even against his life. The aggrandisement of the sense of self which has its root in possessiveness, is coupled with ill-will towards others. It is an inseparable union. Therefore possessiveness and ill-will are mentioned as growing feebler together on the Second Path.[1]

It cannot be expected that we will get rid of these enemies to a humane way of life without constant vigilance and a continual awareness of the impermanence of our cherished selves. But the effectiveness of paying the closest attention to the Truths perceived, is evident from the fact that covetousness and ill-will make themselves felt only occasionally (*adhiccuppattiyā*) and that they rise slowly (*pariyuṭṭhānamandatāya*). "In a Sakṛdāgāmin (Once-returner) emotional instability does not come about as often as in the case of the majority of people who follow the cycle of births; it comes about only occasionally, and if it comes about it does so, sporadically like shoots in a sparsely sown field. Moreover, if it arises, it does not do so as is the case with the majority of people following the cycle of births, in a crushing, spreading, covering manner and producing darkness. It arises very feebly because its power has been exhausted by the Two Paths. It arises in a thin form, like a film of cloud or like fly's wing".[2]

The weakening of emotional outbursts and the rarer occasions of such manifestations is by no means incompatible with our everyday life in which we work, eat and drink, and have children. However, there have been people who claimed to have advanced to this stage or second level of spiritual development and who asserted that the emotions in them are just as violent as with ordinary people who do not attempt to grow spiritually. The only difference is that such emotional outbursts occurred with greater intervals. Such a view is not well grounded. Certainly, it cannot be expected that from the very beginning of our striving our emotional nature will become automatically gentle, for emotions are very deep-rooted and it is no easy task even to weaken them. But this does not mean that they remain as they were before. Every attempt

1. Aṭṭhasālinī III 525.
2. ibid. III 525.

at discipline has its effects, however slight they may be. The argument for the violent nature of emotions on this level, namely, that such people have sons and daughters, is a hopelessly bad argument and it only reflects the attitude of a moralist who does not see and is unable to understand that emotionality is not merely sex and that sex is not only violence. Spirituality is assuredly not sterility, mentally or physically. The author of the Aṭṭhasālinī, rejecting this view of violent emotions because of the fact that there are sons and daughters, simply states: "Sons and daughters also come by the rubbing together of limbs".[1]

There is one other feature characteristic of the Second Path and also of the remaining paths. This is the fact that there is nothing more to be learned. A person who has advanced to this stage and is walking The Path is a knower (*ājña*). But in order to succeed in weakening and in finally getting rid of all possibilities of ever falling again into emotional unbalance, he over and again re-cognizes the Truths perceived on the First Path. The continuous re-cognition which is a dominating feature in his outlook and mental make-up is technically known as *ājñendriya* (Pāli *aññindriya*).[2]

The Third Path which leads to a stage of Anāgāmin (Never-returner) is practised in order to get completely rid of those fetters which on the Second Path have already become weak and loose.[3] There are five fetters known as 'fetters which tie man down' (*avarabhāgīya*, Pāli *orambhāgiya*). Of these 'sensuality and the desire for sensuous and sensual relation' (*kāmacchanda*) as well as 'ill-will' (*vyāpāda*) are such that they stop man from getting out of the clutches of this ordinary world of sensuality (Kāmadhātu), while the 'view that our physical existence is the whole truth' (*satkāyadṛṣṭi*), 'scepticism' (*vicikitsā*), and the 'observance of rites and rituals' (*śīlavrataparāmarśa*)

1. Aṭṭhasālinī III 526.
2. ibid. III 526. Bhāṣya ad Abhidh.-kośa II 9ab. It comprises ine function-events: *manas, sukha, sanmanasya, upekṣā, śraddhā, bala, smṛti, samādhi, prajñā.*
3. Aṭṭhasālinī III 527 : *sakalāgāmimaggena tanubhūtānaṁ saṁyojanānaṁ nissesapajahanatthāya.*

make man return to this world of sensuality.[1] Actually, the three latter fetters are shaken off on the First Path, the path of seeing the Truths. It is the fetters of sensuality and ill-will, those which enhance the sense of ego and possessiveness together with grudging others what they have, that are shaken off on the Second and Third Path, which are paths of practising the Truths. This distinction is of utmost importance. It shows that it is a fairly simple task to get rid of intellectual fetters. It is easy to accept the findings of science, to use modern examples, to discard the 'ghost-in-a-machine' theory of the relation between body and soul, to attend to a problem seriously instead of talking hazily about it and in order to conceal one's ignorance about it, resorting to sophistry and misapplied scepticism, to discard mere ritualism because in all honesty in most cases it has turned into a meaningless formalism;[2] but it is a gigantic task to tame or to sublimate our deep-rooted emotions. I may believe anything about myself, whether it makes sense or not, but anything that attempts to encroach upon my precious ego will meet with undisguised hostility. Emotions are not sublimated by recognizing the validity of a proposition or by seeing things by ourselves, but only by paying the closest attention to that which is the nature of any living process, by working hard on ourselves. Hence the emotions are refined by a path of practice (*bhāvanāmārga*). When, therefore, the texts speak of three paths that have to be walked to the end, viz., the Second, Third, and Fourth Path, they imply the difficulty of refining our emotional nature.

The Fourth Path leading to the state of Arhantship is practised in order to shake off the remaining fetters, 'the fetters belonging to the higher levels of human life' (*ūrdhvabhāgīya*, Pāli *uddhambhāgiya*), since without having got rid of them completely man cannot achieve his goal and find his own dignity.[3]

1. Dīghanikāya III 246; Visuddhimagga IV 155; Aṭṭhasālinī III 348; Abhidharmakośa V 43 bc, and Bhāṣya.

2. A distinction must be made between 'ritual' as a symbolic transformation of experiences and 'formalism'. The former is something very much alive, the latter is dead stuff. If it is kept up, formalism becomes an euphemism for hypocrisy.

3. Aṭṭhasālinī III 528; Abhidharmakośa V. 45 and Bhāṣya.

There are also five such fetters : attachment to the world of Gestalten (*rūparāga*), attachment to non-Gestaltung (*arūparāga*), conceit (*māna*), frivolity (*auddhatya*, Pāli *uddhacca*), and ignorance (*avidyā*, Pāli *avijjā*) not in the sense of not knowing something but in the sense of not having a clear understanding of reality.[1]

Since the division of the paths is such that on The Path of Seeing (*darśanamārga*) the various views we hold about ourselves are shown to have no foundation whatsoever and consequently are expelled, while on the paths of attentive practice (*bhāvanāmārga*) the deep-rooted emotions of our nature are sublimated, the question has been raised whether to include the first topic of the Eightfold Path, viz., correct view (*samyagdṛṣṭi*, Pāli *sammādiṭṭhi*) is not contrary to the nature of the paths of attentive practice. One argument offered was that we speak of an anti-poisonous drug regardless of the fact whether there is poison present or not, and so also we might speak about correct view whether there is still wrong view or not. This would make correct view a mere name and depriving it of any function.[2] At the bottom of this view lies the conception of the interplay between thesis (*pakṣa*) and antithesis (*pratipakṣa*), which does not lead to a synthesis as is assumed and postulated in the Absolutism of Fichte and Hegel, but to a mutual cancelling.[3] For when wrong view (*mithyādṛṣṭi*) has been expelled by its antithesis right view (*samyagdṛṣṭi*), right view itself becomes meaningless because it has meaning only so long as it can bear on wrong view. However, even if one allows a nominal existence of right view in order to keep up the validity of the numerical character of the Path, the argument for its existence in this form fails to take into account the factual, as the author of the Aṭṭhasālinī points out. Whenever man attempts to grow beyond the

1. Aṭṭhasālinī III 528.
2. ibid. III 529.
3. T.R.V. Murti, The Central Philosophy of Buddhism, makes the unhappy attempt to interpret the Madhyamaka and Vijñānavāda philosophies as absolutistic systems and to compare them with Kantian and Hegelian systems. Unfortunately the author is unaware of the fact that only subjects standing on a same level can be compared and not those which have a different view-point. The result is that he does not do justice to any topic.

standard of the mass-man value, whenever he begins to question instead of blindly accepting, he becomes automatically separated from the mass. At this moment there is the grave danger that just because of his becoming separate and different from the amorphous mass, he develops a feeling of superiority, puffs himself up by an overweeningly favorable opinion of his powers and accomplishments; in short, he becomes conceited. Conceit (*māna*) is the worst and deadliest enemy to true spirituality. It is a view, though hollow and stupid, which we hold about ourselves, the view (*dṛṣṭi*) that we belong to an 'inner circle' or to the 'elect' whatever they may be. It is only 'right view', viz., the view that an Ego, pure, impure, transcendental or what not, is a myth, that can cope effectively with conceit. "It is right view that expels this conceit".[1] Conceit which is at the basis of all unhealthy attitudes lingers on until the goal has been attained and it has to be 'killed' (*vajjha*) over and over again on each path we travel. He who is 'in the stream' (*srota-āpanna*) still harbors a kind of conceit which can only be killed by the path of Once-returning, and he who has attained the stage of a Once-returner harbors a type of conceit which only the path of non-returning can kill, and he who has attained the stage of a Never-returner still harbors a type of conceit which only the path of Arhantship can effectively destroy. In this way each 'member' of the Eightfold Path serves a definite purpose and does not have a merely nominal existence.[2]

The Path in its four stages is essentially meant to overcome unhealthy attitudes and to produce a certain type of man in whom unhealthy attitudes can no longer operate. Twelve unhealthy attitudes were enumerated, of which eight had their basis in cupidity (*lobha*) and either represented a joyful or indifferent mood together with certain views or without them and had come about either by a natural disposition of the individual or by following the example of those who suffered from unhealthy attitudes. Two further unhealthy attitudes were rooted in antipathy (*dosa*) and a sullen mood, also brought about by the natural disposition of the individual or by following bad examples. The last two unhealthy attitudes had their roots

1. Aṭṭhasālinī III 530: *sā tam mānam pajahatī ti sammādiṭṭhi.*
2. ibid. III 530.

in delusion-bewilderment (*moha*) and since delusion-bewilderment need not necessarily be in the wake of either cupidity or antipathy but can operate of its own, these unhealthy attitudes were marked by an emotionally indifferent mood and distinguished only by scepticism, the inability to grasp the real nature of things, and by frivolity, attending to all and everything without ever attempting to understand what is being attended to. Since the Path of Seeing or the path of entering the stream toward Nirvāṇa destroys wrong views, because the Truths have been caught sight of, the result is that a person who has attained the state of being in the stream (*srota-āpanna*), though still possessing unhealthy attitudes, has got rid of at least those five unhealthy attitudes which comprise wrong views, i.e., one rooted in cupidity which either has a happy or indifferent mood, one which is due to the natural disposition of the individual or to his following a certain example, one unhealthy attitude rooted in delusion-bewilderment, as well as an indifferent mood, and scepticism. While it is comparatively easy to shun the more intellectual unhealthy attitudes, to sublimate or to make ineffective the deeper-lying emotions, the path of once-returning which is a path of practice, serves to weaken the two remaining unhealthy attitudes rooted in cupidity and of a joyous mood. It is the path of non-returning which alone is able to make these two unhealthy attitudes ineffective. The path of Arhantship, the last stage of the path of practice, makes the remaining five types of unhealthy attitudes ineffective[1]. This gradation shows the difficulty in overcoming our deep-rooted emotions : it is easier to overcome cupidity than to conquer aversion and all that it entails. And aversion can be overcome only when the slightest trace of cupidity no longer obtains, because only then have aversion and antipathy become meaningless. Therefore, its conquest comes last after cupidity has been overpowered by two paths, the one being able only to weaken cupidity and the other to do away with a weakened enemy.

The various types that result from traversing the paths are by no means uniform but vary according to the degree of attainment in overcoming the deeper layers of emotional instability. With only minor divergences the description of them

1. Aṭṭhasālinī. III 537; cp. III 530.

tallies with the one given by the Sarvāstivādins-Vaibhāṣikas. It will suffice to refer to these types in the discussion of the Vaibhāṣika conception of the Path.[1]

The Vaibhāṣika Conception of the Path

The Vaibhāṣikas recognize a variety of aspects of The Path, whether it is a worldly or a superworldly path (*laukika-mārga, lokottaramārga*), whether it is seeing the truths (*darśana-mārga*) or practising in one's life that which has been perceived (*bhāvanāmārga*) which is also a path of getting rid of the impediments to the attainment of Nirvāṇa (*prahāṇamārga*), or whether it is a path on which nothing more is to be learned, everything having been accomplished before (*aśaikṣamārga*). All these aspects, which may be spoken of as distinct paths, are subsumed under four headings, each referring to the salient features of the paths : path of preparation (*prayogamārga*), the successful traversing of which gives rise to the path without obstacles (*ānantarya-mārga*), after which comes the path of deliverance (*vimukti-mārga*), and the special path (*viśeṣamārga*) different from all preceding paths.[2]

In order to be able to set out on the path to win the goal, it is necessary to prepare ourselves for this gigantic task. Preparation is of two types, a remote preparation and a proximate one. The proximate preparation forms part of the path of preparation itself. The remote preparation, which certainly cannot be dispensed with, implies that above all, for that which is necessary for the task ahead of us, more than one existence is needed. Indeed, the shortest period in which we may hope to succeed in winning the goal, comprises of three existences as human beings.[3] The first existence will be needed just to lay

1. The Theravāda description of these types of individuals is given by Buddhaghosa in his Visuddhimagga XXIII 55 sqq.

2. Abhidharmakośa VI 65 and Bhāṣya.

3. This does not mean that there is transmigration of a permanent soul. As a matter of fact, Buddhism does not recognize transmigration, but only incarnation. The stream of existence flows on like a river which may appear to preserve its course, though this often changes, and in which the water rushes on never remaining the same. In other words, the elements and events in a structure change ceaselessly, and though the structure seems to persist even this is gradually changed by the changing structuralizing events.

the foundation of all that is good and wholesome (*kuśalamūla*) out of which, as a ripe fruit, spiritual maturity may come about in the course of our subsequent existences. This foundation of the good and wholesome is qualified as 'conducive to and forming part of the process of liberation' (*mokṣabhāgīya*) and comprises of listening to (*śruta*) and pondering over (*cintā*) the message of The Buddha and of making the resolution (*praṇidhi*) to follow the Buddhist doctrine and discipline, this resolution overshadowing all our behavior in words and deeds[1].

After the foundation has been laid, which is no simple task because of its demanding the most difficult from us, viz., to be aware of all our activities and of their results on our environment whether animate or inanimate, and actually can be said to be a life-time striving, we have a guarantee that not only the stream of our existence will continue in a human form, as for us as human beings this is the best possible state and means of exerting ourselves, but we also shall have acquired the power to produce those qualities which form part of and lead to an understanding of reality as never understood before (*nirvedhabhāgīya*).[2]

Together with producing the qualities conducive to an understanding of reality the desire to see the Truths with our own eyes and to experience them in our lives grows and we begin to study, to ponder over that which we have studied, and to meditate on that which we have pondered over for a long time[3]. As a matter of fact, the qualities which lead to an under-

1. Abhidharmakośa VI 24-25. This step forms part of the *bodhicittotpāda* in Mahāyāna works. See for instance Bodhicaryāvatāra I 15.

"This attitude directed toward enlightenment is, in brief, of two types: An attitude of resolution to win enlightenment and an attitude engaged in winning enlightenment".

2. Abhidharmakośa VI 20. *nirvedha* is interpreted as *niścita vedha* 'decidedly true penetration of the aim'. It is the Path which pierces and destroys doubt. See Bhāṣya ad VI 20.

3. Abhidharmakośa VI 5. The Vaibhāṣikas contended that discrimination born from hearing (*śrutamayī prajñā*) deals with the name, discrimination born from pondering (*cintāmayī prajñā*) deals with the name and the subject matter, sometimes selecting the name, sometimes selecting the subject-matter, and discrimination born from meditation (*bhāvanāmayī prajñā*) deals with the subject-matter. This view is criticized by Vasubandhu, because it makes the *prajñā cintāmayī* superfluous. His explanation is that *śrutamayī*

standing of reality result from meditation, and not from a mere hearing of certain topics and the pondering over them and in particular they are connected with the meditative stages discussed (*dhyāna*) elsewhere[1].

However, to acquire the qualities conducive to understanding is not an easy task and in order to be successful it is necessary to overcome those passions which result in cupidity and sensual attachment (*rāga*) and also to develop the capacity to concentrate by learning not to attend to all and everything without doing anything properly. For those who by nature are liable to get involved in sensual attachment (*rāgacarita*) the contemplation of the 'impure' (*aśubha*), i.e., the gradual decomposition of a corpse, is recommended, while those who are unable to attend to one topic, are told to practise breath control, which has a definitely quieting effect.[2] When through these practices the necessary calm and detachment has been achieved, we can set out to try to learn more about the nature of the object of our contemplation. This is done by 'applying inspection' (*smṛtyupasthāna*).[3] 'Inspection' is understood here in a wider sense than merely professing to describe the apparent characteristics of the objective constituent of the inspective

prajñā is a certitude which derives from that which is termed an instrument of valid knowledge (*pramāṇa*) as applied by a reliable and qualified person (*āptavacana*). *prajñā cintāmayī* is certitude arrived at by rational investigation. *prajñā bhāvanāmayī* is certitude brought about by meditative absorption.

These three types of discrimination are also mentioned by Buddhaghosa in Visuddhimagga XIV 8 as *cintā-suta-bhāvanāmayā* and explained in XIV 14 in the following way which, with the exception that the order is different, agrees closely with Vasubandhu's interpretation : "Discrimination which does not stem from having heard from others but evolves from one's own pondering over the matter is *cintāmayā* ; discrimination which stems from having heard from others and evolved by virtue of that which has been heard, is *sutamayā*, and discrimination which has evolved by having become meditatively absorbed in any kind of subject-matter, is *bhāvanāmayā*".

1. See above, pp. 119 sq. According to Abhidharmakośa VI 20 these qualities are gained in the stages of *dhyāna* of the Gestalt-world in the first preliminary stage of *dhyāna* (*anāgāmya*) and in that stage which does not comprise *vitarka* (*dhyānāntara*) See also Abihdharmakośa VIII 22.

2. Abhidharmakośa VI 9-12. A more exhaustive treatment as found in Visuddhimagga III 121. See also above, pp. 101 sqq.

3. Abhidharmakośa VI 14.

situation[1] inasmuch as 'inspection in the Buddhist sense of the word comprises both of the cognition of that which makes a thing that which it is (*svalakṣaṇa, svabhāva*) and of the cognition of the general characteristics of the thing itself (*sāmānyalakṣaṇa*). Thus, for instance, that which makes our body what it is, is its organization of the four great elementary qualities (*mahābhūta*) and of those qualities derived from them (*bhūta*) which are termed *rūpa* comprising color and shape, while the general characteristic of this organization is the fact that as something conditioned it is impermanent, (*anitya*), unable to yield lasting contentment because of its being an incomplete cycle of activity in which temporary feeling of happiness is marred by a residuum of unhappy feeling due to the fact that the cycle has not been completed successfully and hence is, generally speaking, unsatisfactory (*duḥkha*), does not have a reality of its own (*śūnya*), and does not have an individuality of its own over and above the conditions that bring these characteristics about (*anātma*). The difference between these two sets of characteristics is essentially the distinction we make between a thing and its states, or, in philosophical terms, between non-primary characteristics belonging to the thing and primary characteristics belonging to its states. This distinction between non-primary and primary characteristics (*svalakṣaṇa—svabhāva* and *sāmānyalakṣaṇa*) not only shows that the thing is an abstraction of a certain kind, it may even mislead us into thinking that the thing is something apart from the situation in which it finds itself. To have pointed out this circumstance is the merit of the Mādhyamikas who declared that the *svabhāva* is no *svabhāva* at all (*niḥsvabhāva*). It will, however, be observed that what the Buddhists call *svabhāva* in certain respects corresponds to our primary characteristics. We cannot here discuss the nature of this distinction and abstraction; it is sufficient to point out the two types of characteristics. The distinction made as regards our body is valid also for the other constituents of inspective situations: feeling, (*vedanā*) mental processes (*citta*) and those elements (*dharma*) that constitute our world.[2] As a cognitive act 'inspection' is by nature analytical understanding (*prajñā*). The

dynamic, transformational view of Reality

1. Abhidharmakośa and Bhāṣya.
2. ibid. 15.

relation between 'inspection' and 'analytical understanding' has been explained by the Vaibhāṣikas in the following way. 'Discrimination', 'analytical understanding' (*prajñā*) bears on its object due to the predominant role of 'inspection' (*smṛti*) which keeping the particular perceptual situation constant, presents the objective constituent of the situation for discrimination. Vasubandhu criticizes this view and offers instead the following interpretation. 'Discrimination' applies 'inspection' and according to the manner in which the object is seen by 'discrimination' it is taken hold of, 'addressed' (*abhilapyate*) by 'inspection'.[1] In applying 'inspection' there is a gradation of learning, proceeding from the grosser to the subtler, as is expressed also by the order of the objective constituents of inspective situations. At the same time it removes certain misconceptions and superstitions. The inspection of the constituents of our body destroys attachment to it, because the veil of aestheticism is torn. A warning must be expressed here against a possible misunderstanding. The tearing down of all that we believe to be beautiful is no aim in itself but only a means to sever attachment and addiction and this can only be achieved by temporarily depreciating that which we held in high esteem. If it becomes an aim in itself no further progress on the path is possible. Professional iconoclasts have never contributed to human development in a positive way. Inspection of our feelings reveals the unsatisfactoriness of even pleasurable feelings, because the underlying unpleasurable feeling-tone releases a new cycle of activity with all its harrassing aspects of finding a solution to the problem. Inspection of our attitudes shows that there is nothing static and nothing permanent about them; and inspection of the elements that constitute our world, internally as well as externally, makes it abundantly clear that nowhere is a Self to be found.[2] It is with the attainment of inspection of the subtle, when we see all constituting elements as impermanent, unsatisfactory, unreal and non-individual that

1. Bhāṣya ad Abhidharmakośa VI 15. The explanation of *smṛtyupasthāna* which according to this interpretation is *smṛter upasthānam*, is not found elsewhere. According to Buddhaghosa, Vism XXII 34 it is *sati yeva upaṭṭhānam* 'inspection' is presence, hence presence, application of inspection.

2. Abhidharmakośa VI 15. Visuddhimagga XXII 34.

the qualities 'conducive to an understanding of reality in its reality' (*nirvedhabhāgīya*) are produced in us.

Inspection properly conducted is a process of deep concentration and absorption that affects the whole of our existence which we have arbitrarily split up into a physical and a mental aspect, a division that has made us forget that the mental and physical occur within a unity and should not therefore be thought of as modifications of, or changes in, two things—a mind and a body. Thus as the first indication of success there arises heat (*ūṣmagata*), which is not only felt bodily but is also a distinct mental event and force that burns away emotional instability. This heat may last for quite a long time—actually it lasts as long as the concentrative state of absorption continues—and will gradually increase until it reaches its maximum value or 'top' (*mūrdhan*).[1] Both the initial heat and the top heat bear on the Four Truths, each Truth revealing four aspects, so that a total of sixteen aspects obtains. This number sixteen is a common feature of Abhidharma works, although the interpretation of these sixteen topics may vary.[2]

Both 'heat' and its 'maximum value' are pathways on which we can proceed as well as fall back. Their main function is to lead us to a more vivid realization and a deeper understanding of the nature of the constituents of our reality.[3] After the 'maximum value' has passed through three degrees of intensity it is on the highest degree of intensity that there comes about an event of highest importance and of momentary duration. It is the acceptance (*kṣānti*)[4] of the validity of the Truths which have been directly experienced and which also has three degrees of intensity. Out of the last there results an experience which is termed 'highest worldly realization' (*laukikāgradharma*)[5] which like the preceding event is of momentary duration. Acceptance and highest worldly realization are the culminating points of modifiable processes. Heat and its maximum value may be directed to an understanding of the Truths in such a

1. Abhidharmakośa VI 17.
2. See accompanying table.
3. Abhidharmakośa VI 17-18 and Bhāṣya.
4. ibid. VI 18c.
5. ibid. VI 19c.

way that the ultimate and highest level of knowledge may be achieved. However, due to the fact that through those experiences of heat and its maximum value we come to understand certain aspects of reality which we had not observed or taken the time to attend to, we may at any moment come to an acceptance of that which we perceive even if it would be possible to proceed to a deeper understanding. In other words, we may stop before we have exhausted all possibilities. Once this happens we are stuck. It is, therefore, necessary to postpone acceptance as long as possible. The point at which acceptance sets in is not only the final limit to the preceding process, it also separates one class of individuals from the other ones. It is out of the levels of spiritual penetration, i.e., from the demarcation line of the setting in of acceptance, that the spiritual classes of individuals (*gotra*) such as the Śrāvaka lineage, the Pratyekabuddha lineage, and the Buddha lineage, come about.[1]

To develop these four experiences of heat, maximum value, acceptance, and highest worldly experience, is the direct path of preparation, everything that went before was the remote preparation for enlightenment.

Immediately after the highest worldly experience has been attained there arises an immaculate *dharmajñānakṣānti* which bears on the unsatisfactoriness of the world of sensuality.[2] As the name implies, it is an acceptance of reality as it is and in this acceptance we find that particular knowledge by experience (*jñāna*) which in dealing with the constituents of reality (*dharma*) sets us free. This acceptance, though not knowledge itself, expels all doubts, because by nature it is an impassionate investigation into the nature of reality.[3] Therefore, this particular acceptance, too, which comes about after long practice of concentration and meditation and is not trammeled by emotionally toned considerations, is the path without obstacles (*ānantarya-mārga*.[4] Absence of doubts alone can give us knowledge about the nature of reality (*dharmajñāna*) which like its maternal soil, acceptance, is immaculate. With gaining 'acceptance' the

1. Bhāṣya ad Abhidh.-kośa VI 23 cd.
2. Abhidharmakośa VI 25cd 26a.
3. Abhidharmakośa VII 1 and Bhāṣya.
4. ibid. VI 28.

person striving to win enlightenment, becomes a spiritual aristocrat (*ārya*) and may win the first fruit of his striving, the status of a person who has entered the stream toward enlightenment, Nirvāṇa (*srota-āpanna*). With gaining 'knowledge' the same person gains possession (*prāpti*) of a certain extinction of certain instabilities (*nirodha*).[1] Since through knowledge alone he becomes liberated, knowledge is the path of deliverance (*vimuktimārga*).[2]

Out of this knowledge of the unsatisfactoriness of the world of sensuality (Kāmadhātu) which, as has always to be remembered, is not propositional knowledge, comes an acceptance of the unsatisfactoriness of the higher meditative worlds, Rūpadhātu and Ārūpyadhātu. This acceptance, in turn, brings about knowledge. Being subsequent to the former events these two types of acceptance and knowledge are termed *anvayajñānakṣānti* and *anvayajñāna* respectively.[3]

Similarly, four such events arise with each of the remaining three Truths of Origination of Unsatisfactoriness (*samudaya*), Cessation of Unsatisfactoriness (*nirodha*), and Way to Cessation of Unsatisfactoriness (*mārga*). In total, there are eight aspects of 'acceptance' (*kṣānti*) and eight aspects of 'knowledge' (*dharmajñāna*). Thus we have

Unsatisfactoriness of Kāmadhātu	*duḥkhe dharmajñānakṣānti*
	—,,—*dharmajñāna*
of Rūpa and Ārūpyadhātu	—,,—*anvayajñānakṣānti*
	—,,—*anvayajñāna*
Origination of Unsatisfactoriness of Kāmadhātu	*samudaye dharmajñānakṣānti*
	—,,—*dharmajñāna*
of Rūpa and Ārūpyadhātu	—,,—*anvayajñānakṣānti*
	—,,—*anvayajñāna*
Cessation of Unsatisfactoriness of Kāmadhātu	*nirodhe dharmajñānakṣānti*
	—,,—*dharmajñāna*
of Rūpa and Ārūpyadhātu	—,,—*anvayajñānakṣānti*
	—,,—*anvayajñāna*

1. In particular this is the *pratisaṁkhyānirodha*, one of the three unconditioned elements. See Abhidharmakośa II 36cd, 55d and Bhāṣya.
2. Abhidharmakośa VI 28.
3. ibid. VI 26d.

Way to Cessation of Unsatisfactoriness of Kāmadhātu	*mārge dharmajñānakṣānti*
	—,,—*dharmajñāna*
of Rūpa and Ārūpyadhātu	—,,—*anvayajñānakṣānti*
	—,,—*anvayajñāna*

Of these sixteen events, the first fifteen are the Path of Seeing the Truths (*darśanamārga*), the sixteenth event already partakes of the Path of Practising that which has been seen (*bhāvanāmārga*).[1] While the first fifteen events are more like isolated events, though co-operating in such a way that one event follows the other and that each is different from the preceding one, the sixteenth event can only repeat itself and therefore forms a continuity.

Comprehension (*abhisamaya*) of the Truths is for the Vaibhāṣikas a gradual process, proceeding from one topic to another in the order indicated above. To this conception of a gradual comprehension of the Truths, the Vaibhāṣikas were forced by their peculiar method of analysis of propositions, which we could observe in connexion with their definition of 'possession' (*prāpti*). This they had analyzed to the effect that the proposition '*A* possesses *B*' was meant to assert first *A*, then possession, and lastly *B*.[2] The same procedure obtains also here. The Four Truths had been converted into the proposition that unsatisfactoriness is recognized, the origin or cause of unsatisfactoriness is abolished, the abolition of unsatisfactoriness is realized, and the path toward the abolition of unsatisfactoriness is practised.[3] Certainly there is a succession of events in the complex of the Four Truths, but this succession is not as the linguistic expression seems to have it, that first we have unsatisfactoriness, then we have its origination, then its abolition and thereafter the way to its abolition. Thus the Vaibhāṣikas, together with a few other little known schools, stand alone in their conception of a gradual comprehension of the Truths. Both Vasubandhu[4] and Buddhaghosa recognize that there is some

1. Abhidharmakośa VI 28 and Bhāṣya.
2. See above, p. 178.
3. Cp. Aṭṭhasālinī III 466. Abhidharmasamuccaya, p. 65. Visuddhimagga XXII 95 sq.
4. Bhāṣya ad Abhidh.-kośa VI 27b.

kind of succession, but this succession is such that the Four Truths are simultaneous with each other and with that which happens in their realization, hence a 'unique' comprehension (*ekakṣaṇa*). Buddhaghosa almost uses the same words as Vasubandhu when he comments on the canonical passage that "he who sees unsatisfactoriness also sees its origin"[1] by declaring that one truth is made the subject of discourse in this quotation, because this very one truth functions also with reference to the other truths.[2] The simultaneousness of the Four Truths he illustrates by a number of similes of which one may be adduced here. "Just as the rising sun the moment it appears performs four operations: illumining those things which are visible objects, dispelling darkness, spreading light, and diminishing cold, so also this knowledge by experience of the path, in one instant understands and comprehends the Four Truths: comprehends unsatisfactoriness, abolishes its origination, practises the path toward its abolishment, and realizes its cessation".[3]

Of the fifteen events which form the Path of Seeing the Truths, the eight types of 'acceptance', (*kṣānti*) enable us to do away with that instability in our life which is the view we hold about ourselves together with those emotional responses which are connected with the views we hold, but not the other emotions as they can be overcome only by constant closest attention to the Truths. The views we hold about ourselves have quite an ancestry. Man is fettered to a world of sensuous and sensual stimulation and reaction by his delusion-bewilderment (*moha*) about what is true. In this bewilderment he does not recognize the basic unsatisfactoriness of all that he encounters and resorts to an ill conceived scepticism (*vicikitsā*) out of which is born wrong view (*mithyādṛṣṭi*). This wrong and distorted view about that which he finds in and around himself leads him to believe in his particular existence as the sole truth (*satkāyadṛṣṭi*) which, in turn, gives rise to 'metaphysical' problems, the extreme views of eternal existence or eternal annihilation (*antagrāha*). According to the superstitions, man develops certain observances

1. Saṁyutta-nikāya V 437; Visuddhimagga XXII 98.
2. Visuddhimagga XXII 98; *ekaṁ saccam ārammaṇaṁ katvā sesesu kiccani-pphattivasena.*
3. Visuddhimagga XXII 95.

which he believes to be able to bring about the realization of his dreams (*śīlavrataparāmarśa*). This formalism makes him attach special importance to the view he holds about himself (*rāga*) and this addictedness has in its wake conceit (*māna*) and contempt (*pratigha*).[1] Out of this vast realm of formidable power the 'acceptances' effectively deal with the powers of the Self by undermining the ground on which they operate through an impassionate investigation into their nature.

The sixteenth event (*mārge 'nvayajñāna*) which is the first moment of the Path of Practising the Truths (*bhāvanāmārga*), is also the realization of the first result which the immaculate way of practice offers.[2]

There are two possible ways of attaining the Path of Seeing the Truths which must be traversed before the Path of Practising the Truths can be traversed. The one possibility—and this is the easier way—is to practise the worldly path of closest attention (*laukika bhāvanāmārga*) as laid down in the meditative processes leading to the realization of a world of Gestalten and a world of non-configuration, by which we also become free from the fetters which tie us down to a world of sensuous and sensual stimulation and response.[3] However, this practice, though of high value and importance because of its effect on our emotional nature, cannot lead us beyond that which we call our world. It can only lead us to the highest point of worldly experience by making us dissatisfied with the lower levels of our existence. Through this practice we may pass through all the stages of meditation (*dhyāna*) up to the last stage (*bhavāgra*) but if we do not succeed in developing a vision of the Truths, we remain what we are, ordinary beings, and the best that can be said about us is that we have a healthy attitude toward the world. Since meditation tends to conquer our emotional nature, because in order to enter the various stages it is imperative that we become detached, the moment we enter into the preliminary stage of actual meditation and then onward into the following stages, we have the possibility of developing the 'qualities conducive to a deeper understanding of reality' (*nirvedha-*

1. Abhidharmakośa V 33.
2. ibid. VI 31.
3. See above chapter on Meditation.

bhāgīya) out of which the immaculate Path of Seeing the Truths is born.[1] The advantage of meditation (*dhyāna*) in connection with the Paths is that the final goal is attained earlier, because a person who combines both aspects, the worldly and the superworldly, is 'in possession' (*prāpti*) of the abolition of those unsettling elements which belong to the world of sensuality, the worldly 'possession' being of a temporary nature only, if alone, and the superworldly of a permanent nature.[2]

However, if a person has not practised meditation, this does not exclude him from entering on the Path of Seeing the Truths and subsequently from entering on the Path of Practising the Truths, both in their immaculate aspects of being free from all passionate considerations. The only difference is that such a person's progress toward the final goal will take a longer time since he has to work harder to overcome all that which may lead him out of his way.

Provided that a person who has not practised meditation (*dhyāna*) whereby certain fetters would have been thrown off, and therefore is still 'fettered by all fetters' (*sakalabandhana*),[3] comes upon the Path of Seeing the Truths, he is likely to win the first fruit of this Path, because the impulse that has been given cannot but have its effect. But his approach to this status is slow, because all those emotional fetters that tie him have to be cut loose and these fetters have various degrees of heaviness and intensity. Nine degrees are distinguished which result from a subdivision of three main degrees. The order in which they are overpowered is as follows:

I	II	III
1. strong-strong	4. medium-strong	7. weak-strong
2. strong-medium	5. medium-medium	8. weak-medium
3. strong-weak	6. medium-weak	9. weak-weak.

The Path itself also has nine degrees of intensity and its operation in overcoming the intensities of our emotions is such that the Path as being weak-weak yet overpowers the emotions which are strong-strong. This means that, on the one hand, whatever we do is sure to have its effect, however little effort we put into

1. Abhidharmakośa VI 20 cd.
2. ibid. VI 29 c; 55.
3. Bhāṣya ad Abhidh.-kośa VI 63 d; 29 cd; II 16 cd; 36 cd.

our work, and, on the other, it is easier to overcome the coarser emotions than the subtler ones which more than often escape our notice.[1]

Although the emotions proper are overcome by the Path of Practising the Truths, the Path of Seeing the Truths destroys the views we hold about ourselves together with the emotions that attach to these views. In order to attain the status of a person who is in the stream toward Nirvāṇa (*srota-āpanna*), the first fruit of our striving, it is necessary to overcome at least the first four or five degrees of intensity of our emotional responses in relation to our sensus and sensual world.[2] If these intensity degrees should have been overcome already by a worldly meditation practice, the person on the Path will skip the first status and approach the second status or Sakṛdāgāmin (Once returner) which is marked by the fact that the intensity degrees including the eighth degree have been overcome. Such a person is known as 'one who has become detached to a high degree' (*bhūyovītarāga*).[3] If the ninth degree, too, has been overcome by having become completely detached from the sensual world (*virakta, kāmavītarāga*), and moreover when no attachment of any intensity degree to any of the meditative stages including the 'no-thing-ness sphere' (*ākiñcanyāyatana*) obtains, such a person approaches the status of an Anāgāmin (*Non-returner*).[4] The approach to any of these statuses comprises the fifteen events representing the Path of Seeing the Truths, the sixteenth event denotes the fact that a person has attained the status he was capable of attaining. Hence he is a person 'staying in a certain status' (*phalastha*).[5]

The overcoming of each intensity degree of the unsettling elements ranging from our ordinary world of sensual responses to the highest realms of Gestalten and of non-configuration, is literally an expulsion of this particular element (*prahāṇa*). This expulsion does not meet with any obstacles (*ānantaryamārga*). It also is an event of being freed from its disturbing influence (*vimuktimārga*). Both events, expulsion and freedom, are know-

1. Abhidharmakośa VI 33 and Bhāṣya.
2. ibid. VI 29 cd -30a and Bhāṣya.
3. ibid.
4. ibid.
5. ibid. VI 31 ab.

ledge events (*jñāna*), because emotions can be overcome only by knowledge and never by acquiescence to them.[1] This distinguishes the Path of Practising the Truths (*bhāvanāmārga*) from the Path of Seeing the Truths (*darśanamārga*), which involves a moment or event of acceptance and an event of knowledge.

After a person has succeeded in expelling the eighth intensity degree (weak medium) of the highest worldly state (*bhavāgra*), a meditative state of absorption takes place in which it is not possible to speak of either perception-ideation or non-perception non-ideation (*naivasaṁjñānāsaṁjñāyatana*),[2] he may then aspire to become an Arhant by expelling the last intensity degree (weak-weak) of the last trace of instability still left over. The first event in this process, the expulsion of the unsettling element through knowledge by experience (*jñāna, ānantarya-mārga, prahāṇa*), has been termed Vajropamasamādhi 'concentrative absorption which is like a diamond', because it effectively destroys the last remnant of emotional instability, the diamond being a favourite simile of hardness and indestructibility.[3] Since this absorption can be developed with reference to any type of knowledge of the Four Truths and in the various stages of the meditation process there is a variety of such diamond-like absorptions.[4] However, these Vajropamasamādhis which lead to the status of an Arhant, can only be developed after the status of an Anāgāmin has been attained, because in the latter case the necessary foundation for becoming an Arhant has been laid due to the almost complete absence of emotional instability.[5] Together with the expulsion and destruction of the last intensity degree, of the last trace of instability, the knowledge of exhaustion (*kṣayajñāna*) is born,[6] which is both a path of unhampered expulsion and a path of freedom. Once there is this knowledge that all emotional instability has lost its power, the person is an Arhant, a person for whom there does not exist anything for which he has to strive any more or which he must make the

1. Abhidharmakośa V 65d.
2. See above pp. 131 sq.
3. Abhidharmakośa VI 44d.
4. ibid. Bhāṣya.
5. Bhāṣya ad Abhidh.-kośa VI 31ab.
6. Abhidharmakośa VI 44d-45a and Bhāṣya.

object of study (*aśaikṣa*).[1] In particular cases, after the knowledge of exhaustion (*kṣayajñāna*) there arises another knowledge, the knowledge that emotional instability will never be brought about again (*anutpādajñāna*).[2] These two types of knowledge together are Enlightenment (*bodhi*).[3]

According to Buddhism the goal of man's life is enlightenment which in more familiar terms may be called spiritual maturity. In the achievement of this goal one factor is of supreme importance—the concept which the individual has of himself. Upon this self-concept depends the development of character, the achievement of adjustment and integration. The development of ethical and social values also depends on this factor, because what a person thinks of himself cannot fail to have an influence on the levels of his aspiration at every state. I am fully aware of the fact that the use of the term self-concept in connection with Buddhist discipline will rouse a storm of protest from certain modern followers of Buddhism who believe that a self-concept is incompatible with spiritual development along the Buddhist Path. What they do not see is that the term self-concept is a purely operational term and not a theory about a Self. It is nothing concrete and existent. It is a potential particular that needs something added to it before any fully concrete thing exists. This happens as soon as we stop with acceptance which is the keystone of a certain level or status.[4] This status means, in Buddhist terms, that any of us who has stopped with acceptance, *is* in the stream (*srota-āpanna*), *is* a Sakṛdāgāmin, *is* an Anāgāmin, or *is* an Arhant. Once we have attained any such status we have admitted that we are stuck. But life is never something static. To be and to remain alive we must not allow ourselves to be carried into some shallow back-water. This is only possible if we do not acquiesce in anything anywhere, if we continue striving, indefinitely. Striving is assuredly not a smooth affair and hence it is disliked by most people who are quite happy to stay where they happen to be. It needs a special effort, a 'special path' (*viśeṣamārga*),

1. Abhidharmakośa VI 45b.
2. ibid. VI 50 and Bhāṣya.
3. Abhidharmakośa VI 67 ab.
4. See above, p. 220.

to overcome this inertia, as the Vaibhāṣikas were fully aware.[1] And Vasubandhu shows his deep knowledge of human nature when he declares : "Since the attainment of a certain status does not imply that the path to a higher status has also been attained, a person staying in a particular status does not *eo ipso* approach a higher status without exerting himself for it".[2] The very fact that any status and any fixed type of self-concept is basically an admission of our having become static, was the reason that in Māhāyana Buddhism even the Arhant ideal became disreputable, not because the Arhant was a disreputable person, but because as the expression of a status this ideal militated against the thoroughly dynamic character of Buddhism.

So far the Path in its various aspects has been discussed with reference to the emotional nature of man, being the most difficult side of him to sublimate and to control. The emotional nature is present everywhere in man and its particular form decides the selection of the meditation object to begin with on setting out to win enlightenment.[3] But of no less importance is a person's intellectual acumen, his capacity to concentrate and to think clearly. Two types are distinguished: One, who starts by having confidence (*śraddhā*) in that which others tell him, because they are deemed to be dependable persons by virtue of having practised for themselves certain aspects this man is termed *śraddhānusārin* 'following by virtue of having confidence'; the other is he who is an independent thinker and makes his own studies of what the texts have to say and is termed *dharmānusārin* 'following the doctrine'. Of these two types, the latter is of superior intellectual acumen, in him the function of appreciative analytical understanding (*prajñā*) is particularly keen.[4] The difference between these two types becomes marked when they have attained a certain status by having traversed stages on The Path. Then the former is known as *śraddhādhimukta*, his interest centering on the religious experience involving confidence and trust, and may be said, in our terms, to represent the religious type of man, while the latter due to his analytical

1. Abhidharmakośa VI 65b d.
2. ibid. VI 32.
3. See above pp. 216 sq.
4. Abhidharmakośa VI 29ab.

method has gained a certain view of reality and is known as *dṛṣṭiprāpta* and may be said to be the intellectual type.[1] This difference is a distinguishing factor between the various types of Arhants. Those who have evolved out of a religious temperament have only a temporary liberation and may any time fall from their exalted status,[2] while only he who is the intellectual type attains non-temporary liberation and if he falls he cannot fall from that which he actually possesses[3] He is known as an 'Unshakable One' (*akopya*).[4]

While many schools of Buddhism did not recognize the fall of an Arhant, such as among others the Theravādins, the Vaibhāṣika view recaptured something of the dynamic character, but being still bound to the older tradition, failed clearly to evolve a more positive ideal.

The typological classification has been very much elaborated. Only the more important varieties may be mentioned here. There are seven types of spiritual aristocrats (*ārya*), apart from the two types of Buddhas, the Buddha himself and the Pratyekabuddha, who are special forms of the 'unshakable' Arhant type. These seven types are :

1. Śraddhānusārin
2. Dharmānusārin

by way of temperament in their initial state of ordinary human beings, who on having entered The Path more distinctly reveal their intellectual acumen and become

1. Abhidharmakośa VI 31 cd.

2. ibid. VI 56. He is termed a *samayavimukta*. To this distinction corresponds the classical differentiation between *cetovimukti* and *prajñāvimukti*. The former is liberation from passions, the latter from ignorance. See VI 761.

3. ibid. VI 59 and Bhāṣya. According to the Vaibhāṣikas a Buddha, too, may fall, but only from the enjoyment of the spiritual good he has achieved, not from his Buddhahood. The 'unshakable' Arhant may fall from the enjoyment of that which he has achieved, not from its possession, and he may also fall from (i.e. fall short of) that which he has not yet acquired. Any other Arhant may even fall from that which he has already obtained.

4. ibid. VI 50; 56. He alone has the *anutpādajñāna*. On this see above p. 229.

3. Śraddhādhimukta
4. Dṛṣṭiprāpta — by way of predominance of confidence and analytical understanding respectively.
5. Kāyasākṣin — by way of concentrative absorption in which the temporary suspension of mental functions is realized (*nirodhasamāpatti*).
6. Prajñāvimukta — by way of having become liberated from emotional instability through discrimination, and
7. Ubhayatobhāgavimukta — by way of having become emancipated through concentrative absorption as well as discrimination.[1]

The very fact that the names of these types are class-names tells us a good deal about their nature. A large number of persons must have been met with who combined a number of properties which justified this terminology, because otherwise we would have hesitated to call them so. But it is an unprofitable attempt to try to find out how many varieties of classes there may be, to justify their inclusion in any of these types.[2]

1. Abhidharmakośa VI 63 and Bhāṣya. An identical list is found in Visuddhimagga XXI 74-76. Here a person who attends to impermanence and is convinced of it is a *saddhānusārī* on passing through the path to the first result of being in the stream. When this aim has been achieved he is termed a *saddhāvimutta*. He who attends to unsatisfactoriness and through tension release attains concentrative absorption is a *kāyasakkhī*. He who enters the world of non-configuration and attains the highest status therein, is an *ubhatobhāgavimutta*. He who attends to the fact that nothing has any individuality of its own and has keen discrimination is on his path to the first goal termed a *dhammānusārī*, when he has attained this goal a *diṭṭhippatta*, and when he attains the highest status a *paññāvimutta*.

2. Thus 147, 825 varieties of Śraddhānusārins have been calculated, and 29, 565 kinds of Dharmānusārins. This means that for certain scholastics the spirit of Buddhism had become less important than enumeration.

Classification by way of absence of intensity degrees of emotional instability has been extended since earliest times to the Srota-āpanna (*saptakṛtparama, kulaṁkula,* Pāli *sattakkhattuparama, kolaṅkola*), Sakṛdāgāmin (*ekavīcika* Pāli *ekabījin*), and Anāgāmin (*antarāparinirvāyin, upapadyaparinirvāyin, sābhisaṁskāraparinirvāyin, anabhisaṁskāraparinirvāyin, ūrdhvasrotas,* Pāli *antarā-*

The Vijñānavāda Conception of the Path

The Vijñānavādins continue the line of thought expounded in the Abhidharma works of the Sarvāstivādins-Vaibhāṣikas but with a marked difference in interpretation due to a changed outlook, which is not merely the traditional antithesis of 'pluralism' and 'monism'. As has been shown above, the Sarvāstivādins believed in a plurality of kinds of substance[1] and consequently accepted a still greater plurality of substances than kinds.[2] The Vijñānavādins, on the other hand, believed that there was only one substance, mind. They were, in C.D. Broad's terms,[3] 'differentiating attribute monists' and 'substantival monists'; some of them, however, accepted a 'specific property pluralism' (dualism), while others held to a 'specific property monism'. The former are known in Tibetan works as *gzhan. stoṅ. pa.* They declare that our empirical world as a world of purely conditioned existence has no reality of its own (*raṅ-stoṅ*), while only the underlying Ultimate, Tathāgatagarbha, is real in itself but free from and devoid of the former (*gzhan, stoṅ*).[4] Those who held to a 'specific property monism' were more closely related to the Mādhyamikas who did not commit themselves by a thesis of their own.

parinibbāyī, upahaccaparinibbāyī, asaṅkhāraparinibbāyī, sasaṅkhāraparinibbāyī, uddhaṁsoto). Abhidharmakośa VI 34-39. Visuddhimagga XXIII 55-57. In the definition of these types, Buddhaghosa inclines to the Sautrāntika formulation as far as the *sābhisaṁskāraparinirvāyin* and *anabhisaṁskāraparinirvāyin* are concerned. In the case of the *upapadyapārinirvāyin* he gives definition which is not the Sautrāntika view, but is nevertheless rejected by the Vaibhāṣikas. As to the *ūrdhvasrotas* Buddhaghosa only knows him as going to the Akaniṣṭha heaven to find Nirvāṇa there. The Vaibhāṣikas distinguish another type who goes to the *bhavāgra*.

1. They accepted *rūpa* which roughty corresponds to our 'material substance', *citta-caitta* 'mental substance', *rūpa-citta-viprayukta*, 'substance which is neither material nor mental' and *asaṁskṛta* 'substance which is different from all other substances'.

2. Their total was 11 *rūpa*, 1 *citta*, 46 *caitta*, 14 *rūpa-citta-viprayukta*, 3 *asaṁskṛta*—75 substances.

3. C. D. Broad, The Mind and its Place in Nature, pp. 26 sq.

4. See for instance Phyag. rgya. chen. poi. man. ṅag. gi. bśad thyar. rghyal. bai. gan. madzod, fol. 60a sq.

Usually in works dealing with Indian and Buddhist philosophy the Vijñānavādins are considered to be the 'idealists' among Buddhist schools, but so are all Mahāyāna Buddhist schools, because—again to follow the valuable distinction made by CD. Broad[1] —they understand the nature of the universe to be such that the most sublime and most valuable, Buddhahood, becomes manifested in ever greater intensity and to an ever wider extent. But what actually distinguishes the Vijñānavādins from all other schools of Buddhism, is their mentalism, though not of a Leibnizian or Berkeleian type, but more in line with the view of Bradley who thinks that the Absolute is wholly mental stuff or 'experience', as he terms it.

This monistic conception[2] has important consequences. Since there is nothing but mind (*cittamātra*) as ultimate reality (*dharmatācitta*),[3] the question of rejecting and expelling something no longer has any literal meaning. The Path is not a way to get rid of something by dumping it somewhere and then to proceed lighter and lighter (often misunderstood as emptier and hollower than before), but is a means of understanding and comprehending how all that which in the old terminology had been declared that it ought to be given up and expelled, has come about. Thus Asaṅga who is a specific poperty monist (beside being a differentiating attribute monist and substantival monist) states:

> "Since there exists no entity apart from ultimate reality,
> The passions have been declared by the Buddha to be the way out (of the passions)"[4]

In his commentary on this aphorism he says that since there is no entity whatsoever apart from ultimate reality, because no entity can exist over and beyond ultimate reality, the ultimate nature of passions which appears as a distinct passion is also the way out of it.

1. C. D. Broad, The Mind and its Place in Nature, p. 654.
2. Monism does not militate against a plurality of kinds of mind, because the apparently different kinds may differ only in arrangement and terminology. Thus the Vijñānavādins had 8 *citto*, 51 *caitta*, 11 *rūpa*, 24 *viprayukta*, and 6 *asaṁskṛta*-100 varieties, all of them being 'transformations' (*pariṇāma*) of the one substance mind.
3. Mahāyānasūtrālaṁkāra, comm. ad XIII 19.
4. Mahāyānasūtrālaṅkāra XIII 11.

Similarly, ignorance (*avidyā*) and enlightenment (*bodhi*) are one and the same though not as a mathematical equation.[1]

Only a correct approach (*yoniśaḥ pratipad*) to our emotional, as well as our intellectual nature, can ensure liberation from unbalancing effects[2], but whatever savours of repression and rejection cannot be a correct approach. Bodhisattvas by virtue of their ceaseless striving have acquired the capacity to make a correct approach and therefore they do not lack in positive emotional values. Instead of being emotionally and intellectually starved and dried up, a Bodhisattva has infinite love for all sentient beings. As Asaṅga expresses it:

"A Bodhisattva's great love for sentient beings has deeply
penetrated into his very existence,
Therefore he is ceaselessly engaged in the good of beings
as if they were his only child"[3]

Not only is there a correct approach to our emotional nature which, figuratively speaking, tears the veil of self-centered passionateness, there is also a correct approach to our intellectual side which, speaking equally figuratively, rends the veil of ignorance about all that can be known and there is no limitation to knowledge. The Ultimate, in Buddhism, is something knowable, though not known by theory or discursive method, but by direct experience.

In order to achieve liberation from emotional instability and from ignorance, or in other words, to gain emotional sustenance and knowledge, various stages and levels have to be traversed. There are five main paths:

Sambhāramārga
Prayogamārga
Darśanamārga
Bhāvanāmārga
Niṣṭhāmārga[4]

In discussing these five paths and their various aspects I follow the exposition of sGam.po.pa (Dvags.po.lha.rje) who,

1. Mahāyānasūtrālaṁkāra comm. ad XIII 12; *avidyā ca bodhiś caikam iti.*
2. ibid. comm. ad XIII 13; *tān eva rāgādīn yoniśaḥ pratipadyamānas tebhyo vimucyate.*
3. ibid. XIII 20.
4. Abhidharmasamuccaya, pp. 65 sqq.

though being a Mādhyamika, accepts the arrangement of the stages of and on The Path as laid down by the Vijñānavādins, and gives such a clear account of the inter-relation of events, as can be done only by one who has travelled The Path to its very end; and that of Asaṅga who in his Abhidharmasamuccaya is mainly concerned with the correct definition of terms.[1]

The First Path or Sambhāramārga is the period in which we equip ourselves with all that is necessary to set out on the toilsome path towards winning enlightenment in order to be all the more able to work selflessly for the welfare of all sentient beings. For this purpose only excellence (*puṇya*) and knowledge which is never separated from experience (*jñāna*) will do. As Asaṅga says :

> "The equipment of Bodhisattvas is unsurpassable excellences and knowledge;
> The former serve to make him rise in Saṁsāra, the latter to pass through it without being emotionally and intellectually unbalanced.[2]

The Sarvāstivādins had already insisted that the winning of enlightenment is not achieved in one existence; one existence was necessary to lay the foundation for this task. For the Vijñānavādins time as such has disappeared, as may be gleaned from Asaṅga's definition of this Path of Equipment :

> "Continuously (*saṁtatyā*) paying closest attention (*bhāvanā*) to positive values in an ever increasing manner,
> The sustenance (*āhāra*) derived from it, is the all accomplishing equipment of him who has a steadfast mind.[3]

For ordinary human beings who are just beginning to grow up to be human beings and to behave humanely, this equipment means to observe ethics and manners in every walk of life, to keep restraint on the senses so that sensual attachment may not grow, to be moderate in eating and drinking, to be wakeful during the first and last hours of the night which should

1. sGam. po. pa's analysis is in his Dam. chos. yid. bzhin. gyi. nor. bu. thar. pa. rin. po. chei. rgyan. shes. bya. ba. theg. pa. chen. poi. lam. rim, gyi. bśad. pa., foll. 105b sqq.
2. Mahāyānasūtrālaṅkāra XVIII 38.
3. ibid. XVIII 4.

be devoted to contemplation and meditation on the positive qualities. The Buddha developed by traversing The Path, to strive energetically and to attend to whatever work there may be, to develop tranquillity and insight, and to be fully aware of all actions and their effects on our environment. In particular it means to develop discrimination (*prajñā*) by either hearing the positive doctrine of Buddhism or by pondering over it, or by attempting according to the capacity of each of us to make it a living experience.[1] In addition to this, a Bodhisattva has to bring everything to highest perfection. Asaṅga, therefore, declares that liberality (*dāna*) and ethics (*śīla*), two of the perfections a Bodhisattva has to acquire and to practise, constitute that which is known as excellence (*puṇya*), while discrimination (*prajñā*), another perfection of a Bodhisattva, leads to the highest form of knowledge or knowledge by immediate experience (*jñāna*). Liberality and ethics as well as discrimination are inseparably linked with three other perfections for becoming effective, viz., patience (*kṣānti*, often this term means acceptance, and since no perfection is separate from knowledge, the understanding of human nature is also patient acceptance, a tolerant view of others' shortcomings), strenuousness (*vīrya*), and concentration (*dhyāna*). And all of them are necessary in order to ascend to higher and higher levels of spirituality (*bhūmi*).[2] At this stage, whether still a simple beginner or already a more advanced Bodhisattva, a person practises inspection (*smṛtyupasthāna*) in order to learn more about the nature of that which immediately concerns us; our body, our feelings, our attitudes, and the constituents of this our immediate reality. He further strives to bring it about that (i) the unhealthy and unwholesome which has already arisen in his life disappears and (ii) that the unwholesome in human nature which has not yet arisen will not arise; (iii) that the good and wholesome which is the counteracting force to the unhealthy and unwholesome, if it has not yet made its way into our life, arises and (iv) that it spreads if it has already come into our life.[3] Finally he practises

1. Abhidharmasamuccaya, p. 65.
2. Mahāyānasūtrālaṅkāra XVIII 41 and a commentary.
3. The technical term is *samyakprahāṇa*, Tib. *yaṅ.dag.par. spoṅ.ba*, 'correct rejection', but in meaning it corresponds to Pali *sammappadhāna*.

certain forms of concentrative absorption (*ṛddhipada*) in which the desire to attain full concentration (*chandas*), strenuousness (*vīrya*), a natural disposition (*citta*), and meticulous investigation (*mīmāṁsā*) are the keynote. These three practices are distributed in such a way that each of them forms a lower, a medium, and a superior Path of Equipment.[1]

The Path of Equipment is also the Path of Preparation, although the Path of Preparation is not just the Path of Equipment,[2] because in addition to being equipped for further travel we prepare ourselves for seeing reality. During this period the four qualities leading to a deeper understanding of reality (*nirvedhabhāgīva*) are developed. The first quality ('heat' *ūṣmagata*) is the realization that the objective constituents of our perceptual situations are not literally external, physical objects, but are 'mental addresses' (*manojalpa*) in the sense that what had been called the intrinsic character or the nature of a thing (*svalakṣaṇa*) and its general characteristic (*sāmānyalakṣaṇa*) are 'discourses' within a purely perceptual 'world'. This stage is also termed 'clarity' (*āloka*) and is synonymous with an acceptance of that which has been found by a thorough investigation into the nature of things (*dharmanidhyānakṣānti*).[3] Every effort has to be made to intensify this clarity until it reaches its maximum value (*mūrdhan*). Through the increase of clarity the realization that there is only mind (*cittamātra*) becomes settled and one sees that the percepts of all things we encounter are inside mind and that there is nothing else but mind. In other words, that which we are accustomed to call an external physical object and which we claim to know by our senses is none other than the percept which is known by the mind. Whatever we perceive is perceived in relation to our body and this in turn in relation to other things in space, but perception is the activity of our experiencing mind. In this way the external

1. sGam. po. pa, loc. cit. fo..106a. See also Abhidharmasamuccaya, pp. 71-73. Cp. Abhidharmakośa VI 68d-69bl.

2. Abhidharmasamuccaya, p. 65 : *yaḥ sambhāramārgaḥ sa prayogamārgaḥ. yas tu prayogamārgaḥ sa na sambhāramārgaḥ.*

3. Commentary ad Mahāyānasūtrālaṅkāra XIV 23-24. See also sGam. po. pa, loc. cit., fol. 80a.

physical object that is seen or touched can be said to be as internal to the mind as it is external to the body and the body (as the percept) is just as internal to the mind as it is external to other objects in space. Since it is impossible to assign any special location to mind, it is utterly impossible to perceive objects outside mind and even inside mind. Outside and inside owe their existence to the symbolific activity of mind which in this activity not only distinguishes objects by their qualities of color and shape and the spatial relations that exist between them, but also gives us at the same time symbolic information about our own body and its relation to the physical world. This symbolific activity of mind is absolutely private to the observer and confusion arises when we have to discriminate between our private perceptual 'world' and the public physical 'world', which in ordinary life we need not do, as a rule. Percepts, however, are never anywhere else but where they are perceived to be; externality belongs as much to the perceptual world as do the other relations between perceptual symbols. But what we call our physical 'world' is essentially a set of conceptual symbols and what we call our perceptual 'world' is also a set of symbols, and both sets of symbols are the forms in which mind expresses itself. Hence there is only one world and no mysterious displacement or projection from a perceptual world into a physical world (*grāhyavikṣepaḥ prahīno bhavati*).[1] There is only the one private world of the symbolific activity of mind (*grāhakavikṣepaḥ kevalo 'vaśiṣyate*).[2] Once this has been recognized and accepted the stage of acceptance (*kṣānti*) has been reached and it is not difficult to come, on the basis of this, to what is called the highest worldly experience (*laukikāgradharma*).

Certainly, to accept the view that there is only mind (*cittamātra*), evinces a far deeper analysis of and penetration into the nature of reality than the rather naive realistic conception of the Sarvāstivādins, bordering on metaphysical materialism, which does not discriminate between the various levels and their symbolic sets. In other words, acceptance has been considerably postponed by the Vijñānavādins. But to postpone acceptance needs constant labor and our disposition must be dominated

1. Commentary ad Mahāyānasūtrālaṅkāra XIV. 25.
2. ibid. XIV. 26.

by several powers with which will enable us to postpone acceptance as long as possible, because acceptance, though giving us a point from which to look out onto reality, at the same time has a fossilizing effect. As sGam.po.pa points out, during the first two stages leading up to acceptance, the dominant functions (*dbaṅ.po*, Skt. *indriya*) in our mental make-up or disposition are confidence (*dad.pa*, Skt. *śraddhā*), strenuousness (*brtson. 'grus*, Skt. *vīrya*), inspection (*dran.pa*, Skt. *smṛti*), absorption through concentration (*tiṅ. ṅe. 'dzin*, Skt. samādhi), and discrimination (*śes.rab*, Skt. *prajñā*). As soon as the stage of acceptance and the resulting highest worldly experience have come these same functions continue operating not as aiding dominances, but as unshakable powers and convictions (*stobs*, Skt. *bala*).[1]

However, it may be asked whether the point where acceptance sets in, has been postponed long enough and whether the realization that our immediate experience is mental tells us anything about the nature of reality. The answer, I am afraid, must be No. Mentalism does not tell us that the reality of which we are aware is itself mental, though it does not exclude this possibility, and as to mind it merely says that its activity is symbolific. Hence, as the Mādhyamikas were quick to point out, acceptance of mentalism is premature. A further analysis, as was done by the Tantriks who were Mādhyamikas, would have led to a certain form of mentalistic neutralism.[2]

With the attainment of the highest worldly experience (*laukikāgradharma*) the Path of Preparation has come to its end and the Path of Seeing (*darśanamārga*) begins immediately after the conception of the private character of the symbolific activity of mind (*grāhakavikṣepa*) has subsided, when the 'private world' and the 'public world' are no longer indurating constructs of mind and pure experience obtains.[3] Apart from the sixteen knowledge events found already in the Sarvāstivādins' Path of

1. sGam. po. pa. loc. cit., fol. 106b. On *indriya* and *bala* see also Abhidharmasamuccaya, p. 74.

2. I owe this term to C. D. Broad. It would be a fruitful task to make a methodological study of Buddhist philosophy instead of hunting for chance analogies in Western philosophies. Buddhist philosophy remains still to be written.

3. Mahāyānasūtrālaṅkāra X IV 28-41 and commentary.

Seeing, during this stage the seven 'members of enlightenment' are present and, what is more, highly effective. These are : inspection (*dran.pa*, Skt. *smṛti*), appreciative analytical understanding of the constituents of reality (*chos.rnam.par. 'byed.pa*, Skt. *dharmapravicaya*), strenuousness (*brtson. 'grus*, Skt. *vīrya*), enthusiasm (*dga.ba*, Skt. *prīti*), tension relaxation (*śin.tu.sbyaṅs. pa*, Skt. *praśrabdhi*), concentrative absorption (*tiṅ.ṅe. 'dzin*, Skt. *samādhi*), and equanimity (*btan.sñoms*, Skt. *upekṣā*). Because of their deeper penetration to reality the content of these functions is naturally different from that of the previous levels where they were present but not so effective[1].

While traversing this Path of Seeing, petty self-centeredness with all its likes and dislikes has given way to a new self-concept which is in harmony with reality. It is due to the realization that it is only with respect to the relation between the postulated introspected self known by common-sense and philosophical theory and the postulated external object known in the same manner (—this object may be another person as contrasted with my own person—) that a relation of other-ness between the perceiving subject and the perceived object exists. But before reality, which is one experience, is split up into subject and object, there is one-ness with reality and same-ness (*samatā*) of self and object. It is this one-ness of reality in Buddhism which is the root of infinite compassion toward suffering mankind. As Asaṅga expresses it :

> "Ever and again penetrating to the sameness of ultimate reality (in all that exists)
> He always adopts an attitude toward sentient beings which brings out their sameness with himself".[2]

This realization moulds a man's life, in the following way :

> "Having come to understand that the world is but creative forces, is without any individuality of its own, only an increase of unsatisfactoriness,

1. sGam. po.pa, loc. cit, fol. 106b. Here, to give one example, inspection does not merely see that the characteristics of things are mind-dependent, but that these characteristics are no characteristics in themselves. See Phyag.rgya. chen. poi. man. ṅag. gi. bśad. sbyar. rgyal. bai. gan. mdzod, fol. 88b.

2. Mahāyānasūtrālaṅkāra XIV 30.

He abandons a useless self-concept and relies on a lofty self-concept of supreme usefulness.
Without a self-concept yet having a self-concept, exempt from suffering yet feeling unsatisfied,
He works for the benefit of all without expecting any payment as does a person who is only bent on his own welfare.
With a mind freed by supreme emancipation yet fettered by strong ties.
Not seeing an end of suffering he exerts himself and works.
The world is unable to bear its own suffering, how much less the suffering of all others put together.
Inconsiderately the world looks only for one existence, a Bodhisattva does otherwise.
The benevolence and tenderness, the exertion and indefatigableness of the Buddha-Sons with respect to sentient beings
Is the greatest miracle in all worlds, and yet it is no miracle because all beings are the same with and to him".[1]

The Path of Seeing is, in one sense, preliminary to the most important stage in spiritual development, the Path of Practising that which has been seen (*darśanamārga*), in another sense, it is already present and co-existent with the Path of Seeing, since we cannot help acting on what we have seen unless we are moving corpses. The Path on which we pay the closest attention to that which we have perceived is of two types : a worldly path of practice and a superworldly path. The former comprises the eight stages in meditation (four *rūpāvacara* and four *ārūpyāvacara*). Meditation is necessary for three reasons, as sGam. po.pa points out. Meditation is a concentrative effort in which an ordinary diffused mind is brought into focus whereby all instability, particularly emotional instability which goes hand in hand with a disorderly mind, and which can only be remedied by concentrated attention to the working of our mind, is given up. The absence of emotional instability has as its positive expression the four boundless qualities of benevolence, compassion, participating joy, and impartiality. The positive

1. Mahāyānasūtrālaṅkāra XIV 37-41.

values that are developed through meditation form then a solid basis for the superworldly practice of always being aware of that which the Four Truths imply for our behavior in life.[1]

The superworldly path is traversed for gaining two types of knowledge; the one is without indurating constructs of mind (*nirvikalpa*) and serves to bring our own Buddha qualities to utmost purity,[2] the other is a type of knowledge in which the findings of the previous type of knowledge have a definite position (*yathāvyavasthāna*) and which serves to bring sentient beings to spiritual maturity. As it addresses itself to sentient beings who have not yet attained Buddha-hood, it is a kind of worldly knowledge which may be said to be inspired by ultimate reality inasmuch as it obtains after the superworldly knowledge (*loko-ttara-pṛṣṭhalabdhaṁ laukikam*).[3]

It is on this Path of closely attending to that which has been perceived, (viz. the eight types of acceptance of that which has been perceived, as constituting the Path of Seeing, and the eight types of knowledge resulting from the aforesaid acceptances that were there or the Path of Seeing which ultimately forms the Path of Practice,[4] that the Eightfold Path so well known has its ultimate *raison d'etre*.[5] Certainly, it takes much time and still much more labor on our side to set foot on the various steps: Correct View of Reality (*samyagdṛṣṭi*), Correct Conception of Reality (*samyaksaṁkalpa*), Correct Exertion as supported by Reality (*samyagvyāyāma*), Correct Observation of Reality (*samyaksmṛti*), Correct Speech (*samyagvāc*), Correct Action (*samyak-karmānta*), Correct Mode of Life (*samyagājīva*), and Correct Concentratedness (*saṁyaksamādhi*).

It is on this Path also that the various aspects, listed as separate paths by the Sarvāstivādins-Vaibhāṣikas, come into

1. sGam.po.pa, loc. cit., fol. 107a.

2. There are eighteen Buddha qualities (*buddhadharma*) : ten powers (*bala*), four absences of fear (*vaiśāradya*), three observations (*smṛtyupasthāna*), and one Great Compassion (*mahākaruṇā*). The powers again are types of knowledge. Most schools accepted these eighteen Buddha qualities, but the interpretation varied. A full account of these Buddha qualities is given in Abhidharmakośa VII 28-33. Abhidharmasamuccaya, p. 98-99.

3. Mahāyānasūtrālaṅkāra XIV 43 and commentary.

4. sGam. po. pa, loc. cit., fol. 107a.

5. ibid., fol. 107b.

operation. Thus The Path comprises the nine intensity-degrees we found with emotional instability and the relationship between The Path and the corresponding emotion that is overcome by it is such that the most subtle remnant of emotional instability can be overcome only by the Path when it has attained its highest power, and vice versa. Here we make the preparation for overcoming our instability (*prayogamārga*), here we succeed in overcoming this instability (*ānantaryamārga*), here we realize that we have got rid of our instability (*vimuktimārga*), and here by special efforts we rise to higher and higher levels of spirituality (*viśeṣamārga*).[1]

The Path of Seeing Reality (*darśanamārga*) and the Path of Practising Reality (*bhāvanāmārga*) by which spiritual progress is made, comprises ten levels (*bhūmi*). The first level is termed 'The Joyful One' (*pramuditā*), because representing the Path of Seeing this level makes us see that enlightenment is not too far away and in this seeing we realize that reality is found everywhere (*sarvatragatathatā*) and not in some mysterious and for ever unattainable realm.[2] The remaining nine levels make up the Path of Practising Reality. On each level wider and more comprehensive realization of reality is attained.

The second level is termed 'The Stainless one' (*vimalā*) because ethics and manners which are indispensable for spiritual development cannot any more be broken and as a consequence a person on this level will not debase himself by acts that show nothing of humane qualities. Reality is experienced as possessing the most sublime qualities and displaying infinite richness (*paramatathatā*).

"The Illumining One' (*prabhākarī*) is the name of the third level. It is so called, because through concentrated absorption clear light is brought about, and reality is found to inform everything by its sublime values (*paramaniṣyandatathatā*).

The fourth level is "The Flaming One" (*arciṣmatī*), because the spiritual attainment of this level like a flame burns away the

1. Abhidharmasamuccaya, p. 70.

2. Mahāyānasūtrālaṅkāra XX-XXI 32. In discussing the various levels and the deeper realization of reality, I follow sGam. po. pa, loc. cit., fol. 108. sg.

veils of emotional and intellectual instability. Since no petty ego obtains reality is seen to be such that it cannot be made someone's personal property (*aparigrahatathatā*).

On the fifth level, termed "The One Difficult to Conquer" (*sudurjaya*) because it is a difficult task and still more difficult to succeed in bringing sentient beings to spiritual maturity and to prevent them from falling, reality is realized as not being different according to the status a person may have attained (*abhinna-jātīyatathatā*).

"The One Which Is Present" (*abhimukhī*) is the name of the sixth level. Here Saṁsāra and Nirvāṇa are presented to our view as having the same value, neither of them being such, that the one may be preferred to the other. Reality is seen to be neither pure nor impure (*asaṁkliṣṭāvyavadātatathatā*).

The seventh level bears the name "The One Who Goes Far" (*dūraṁgamā*), because on this level we find the unique path that can be walked to its very end. Here the realization comes that reality is one and indivisible, regardless of the manner in which it may be presented to other beings who are of different intellectual capacity (*abhinnatathatā*).

The eighth level is termed "The Unshakable One" (*acalā*) because it cannot be upset by such considerations as whether there are images or no images. Reality remains what it is, it is not made better by that which we call good nor is it made worse by that which we term evil (*anupacayāpacayatathatā*).

The ninth level or "The One Which Has Good Discrimination" (*sādhumatī*) is characterized by four types of understanding,[1] viz., understanding of the name, of the thing, of the voice, and of the presentation of the experience.

The tenth level, "Cloud of Dharma" (*dharmamegha*), contains innumerable Dhāraṇimukhas and Samādhimukhas, and being knowledge, encompasses all that can be known, just as a cloud fills the sky. And just as rain quenches the thirsting earth, so this 'cloud' pours down the rain of the Dharma and extinguishes the raging fire of all kinds of instability.

When through countless ages the Path of Practising Reality has reached its highest perfection it passes into the Path of Finalization (*niṣṭhāmārga*) by which the Buddha level (*budha-*

1. *pratisaṁvid.* See Abhidharmakośa VII 37-40.

bhūmi) is attained.[1] This Path begins with the Vajropamasamādhi, the concentrative absorption which is as indestructible as a diamond, which cannot be upset by worldly conditions, which cannot be obscured by any darkening powers, which cannot be shaken by the indurating constructions of a worldly mind, which has the same flavor as Reality, and which views the common reality in all that can be known. The Vajropamasamādhi obtains when at the end of the Path of Practice all fetters have been shaken off, it comprises of a path of preparation (*prayogamārga*) and a path of unobstructedness (*ānantaryamārga*). The result of this concentrative absorption is the deeply moving knowledge that all instability, whether emotional or intellectual, has exhausted its power (*kṣayajñāna*) and that no instability of any type can ever appear again (*anutpādajñāna*). At this time the eight operational forces of the Eightfold Path together with Full Liberation (*samyagvimokṣa*), and Full Knowledge of Liberation (*samyagjñāna*) have become an inalienable possession for which it is no longer necessary to strive (*aśaikṣa*).[2] It is Reality in its entirety.

Conclusion

The Path is inseparably connected with the idea of progress. In this respect it is important to note that Buddhist philosophers never doubted the possibility of *perpetual* progress but never held the view of *uniform* progress which implies that every later state of *s* is better than every earlier state of *s*.[3] However, they differed from each other as to the problem where the value of a thing lies. Some of them did as we usually do. For when we speak about progress we talk as if the whole value of a thing lay in its successive states and we even go so far as to talk as if the whole value of a thing resided in its final state. This is of course a mistake, as the Vijñānavādins and Mādhyamikas clearly saw. It is true, the value of a thing does depend in some way on the values of its successive states, but it does not

1. sGam. po. pa. loc. cit., fol. 117a.
2. ibid., fol. 108a. Abhidharmasamuccaya, pp. 76 sq.
3. This would mean that Saṁsāra gradually becomes Nirvāṇa and all that we would have to do would be just to sit idle and wait. For the rejection of such a view, see sGam. po. pa. loc. cit., fol. 2a.

depend on these alone. The value of a thing is a quality which inheres in its entire history, from its beginning to its end, if it has an end. When the Vijñānavādins declare that to walk the Path of Practice takes already two Asaṁkhyeyas,[1] to say nothing of the time that is needed for arriving at this particular stage of the The Path, and when they insist that a Bodhisattva has to and does work without ever looking for an end of his striving, because Reality is everywhere, without beginning or end, they make use of the strongest arguement that can be found to assert that continuous striving is the essence and value of The Path and of Buddhism as a path through life. To lose oneself in a static ideal, to center the whole value in the final state of a thing, is to deny reality and an attempt to escape from it, which forever will remain unsuccessful, because Reality is more than the segment we believe to be reality. We may be too stupid to see Reality as a whole because apart from the abstractions we have made, we tend to forget that we have abstracted one aspect or the other from the rest of Reality, but that does not speak against Reality. In realizing that when we play off Saṁsāra and Nirvāṇa against each other we are dealing with abstractions and not with Reality, the Vijñānavādins and Mādhyamikas by asserting that Reality is a mixture of unity and relative isolation prevented the ideal of Buddhism, living Reality, from becoming self-stultifying. Where there is Reality there is The Path, retaining its full meaning and value of perpetual progress, as unlimited as the ideal itself.

1. Mahāyānasūtrālaṅkāra XIV 44. One Asaṁkhyeya is the lapse of as many years as we would express by a 1 followed by 140 zeroes.

INDEX

(All words, including the Sanskrit, Pali, and Tibetan terms, follow the English alphabet. T.=Tibetan.)

TABLES

The following tables do not pretend to exhaust the topics in the Abhidharma. They are only meant as a guide. As far as possible I have tried to preserve the dynamic character of the Buddhist conceptions.[1]

1. For the tabulation of mental events see particularly Anagarika B Govinda, The Psychological Attitude of Early Buddhist Philosophy and its systematic representation according to Abhidhamma tradition, Patna University 1937, pp. 205 sq.

TABLE A.

The Structure of Mind according to the Aṭṭhasālinī :

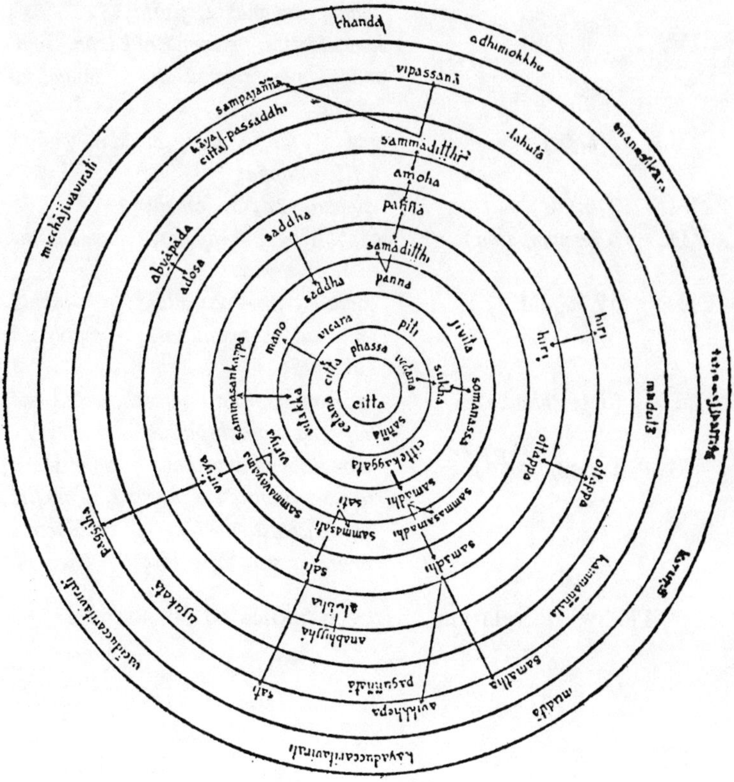

Mind (*citta*), in centre, radiates into its states and function-events as

I.	(5 *phassapañcaka*) :	*phassa, vedanā, saññā, cetana, citta*;
II.	(5 *dhyāna*) :	*vitakka, vicāra, pīti, sukha, cittekaggatā*;
III.	(8 *indriya*) :	*saddhā, viriya, sati, samādhi, paññā, mano, samanassa, jīvita*;
IV.	(5 *magga*) :	*sammādiṭṭhi, sammāsaṅkappa, sammāvāyāma, sammāsati, sammāsamādhi*;
V.	(7 *bala*) :	*saddhā, viriya, sati, samādhi, paññā, hiri, ottappa*;
VI.	(3 *mūla*) :	*alobha, adosa, amoha*;
VII.	(5 *kammapatha*):	*anabhijjhā, abyāpāda, sammādiṭṭhi, hirī, ottappa*;
VIII.	(12 *yugalaka*) :	*kāya—citta—passaddhi, -lahutā, -mudutā, -kammaññatā, -paguññatā, -ujukatā*;
IX.	(6 *piṭṭhiduka*) :	*sati-sampajañña, samatha-vipassanā, paggāha avikkhepa*;
X.	(9 *yevāpanaka*) :	*chanda, adhimokkho, manasikāra, tatramajjhattatā, karuṇā, muditā, kāyaduccaritavirati, vācīduccaritavirati, micchājīvavirati*

Their interrelation has been indicated by arrows.

TABLE B.

The Structure of Mind according to the Abhidhammatthasaṅgaha :

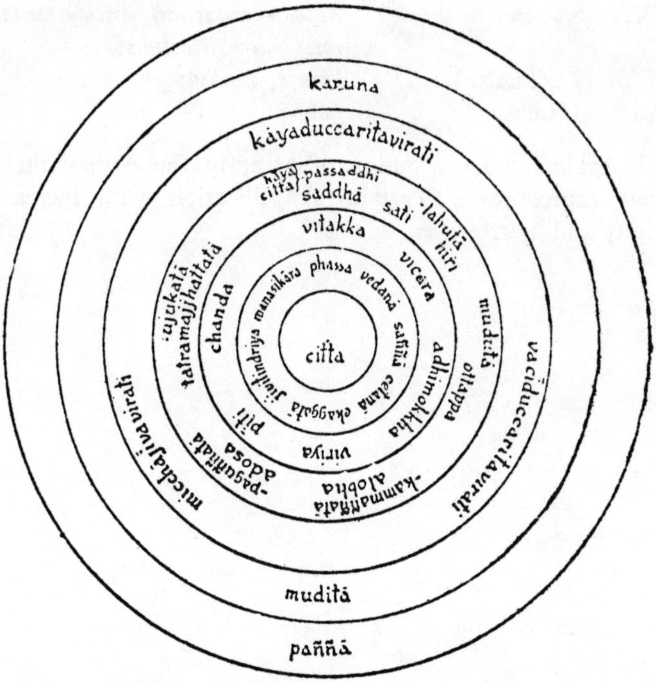

Mind (*citta*), in centre, radiates into its states as

I. (7 *sādhāraṇa*) : *phassa, vedanā, saññā, cetanā, ekaggatā, jīvitindriya, manasikāra*;

II. (6 *pakiṇṇaka*) : *vitakka, vicāra, adhimokkha, viriya, pīti, chanda*;

III.	(13 *sobhana*) :	*saddhā, sati, hiri, ottappa, alobha, adosa, tatramajjhattatā, Kāya-citta-passaddhi, -lahutā, -mudutā, -kammaññatā, -paguññatā, -ujukatā;*
IV.	(3 *virati*) :	*kāyaduccaritavirati, vācīduccaritavirati, micchājīvavirati;*
V.	(2 *appamāṇa*) :	*karuṇā, muditā;*
VI.	(1 *paññā*) :	*paññā*

Against the conception of Mind in the Aṭṭhasālinī the above represents a certain simplification with increasing rigidity and narrowness.

TABLE C.

The Structure of Mind according to the Abhidharmakośa :

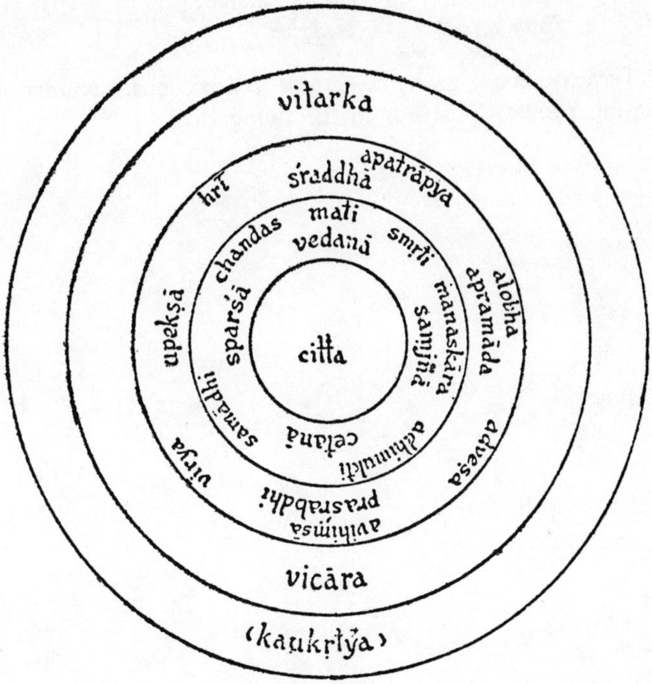

Mind (*citta*), in centre, radiates into its states as

I. (10 *mahābhūmika*) : *vedanā, saṁjñā, cetanā, sparśa, chandas, mati, smṛti, manaskāra, adhimukti, saṃādhi*;

II.	(10 *kuśalamahā-bhūmika*) :	*śraddhā, apramāda, praśrabdhi, upekṣā, hrī, apatrāpya, alobha, adveṣa, avihiṁsā, -vīrya*;
III.	(2 *aniyata*) :	*vicāra, vitarka*;
IV.	(*adhikaṁ kvacit*) :	*kaukṛtya*

Poverty and rigidity are most conspicuous. Numerical limitation proves disastrous to the living spirit.

Table D.

The Sixteen Aspects of the Four Truths :

It will be observed that the names and their general interpretation are the same with the Vaibhāṣikas (Bhāṣya ad Abhidharmakośa VII 13) and Vijñānavādins (Abhidharma-samuccaya, pp. 38, 61, 65, 77). Except for two terms the conception of the Theravādins (Visuddhimagga XXII 97) is entirely different.

Vaibhāṣika-Vijñānavādins			Theravādins
I. Duḥkha (Truth of Unsatisfactoriness) :			
anitya	impermanence	*pīlana*	strain
duḥkha	Unsatisfactoriness	*saṅkhāta*	conditioned state of affairs
śūnya	emptiness	*santāpa*	torment
anātmaka	non-individuality (unreality)	*vipariṇāma*	change
II. Samudaya (Truth of the Origination of Unsatisfactoriness):			
hetu	motive-power	*āyūhana*	instigation
samudaya	origination	*nidāna*	relation
prabhava	powerfulness	*saṁyoga*	connexion
pratyaya	conditioning force	*palibodha*	impediment
III. Nirodha (Truth of the Annihilation of Unsatisfactoriness):			
nirodha	disappearance	*nissaraṇa*	escape
śānta	peace	*viveka*	detachment
praṇīta	exaltedness	*asaṅkhāta*	unconditioned state of affairs
niḥsaraṇa	escape	*amata*	immortality

IV. Mārga (Truth of the Path toward the Annihilation of Unsatisfactoriness):

mārga	quest	*niyyāna*	liberation
nyāya	reasonableness	*hetu*	motive-power
pratipad	attainment	*dassana*	clear view
nairyānika	liberation	*adhipateyya*	spiritual rule

Table E.

The Relationships between the Path, the spiritual levels (*bhūmi*), the perfections (*pāramitā*), and Reality according to sGam. po. pa (Dvags. po. lha, rje):

Path	Spiritual Level	Perfection	Reality
Sambhāramārga	*ādikarmikabhūmi* (beginner's level)		
Prayogamārga	*adhimukticaryābhūmi* (level of interested behavior)		
Darśanamārga	1. *pramuditā*	*dāna* (liberality)	*sarvatragatathatā*
Bhāvanāmārga	2. *vimala*	*śīla* (ethics and manners)	*paramatathatā*
	3. *prabhakārī*	*kṣānti* (patience)	*paramanisyandatathatā*
	4. *arciṣmatī*	*vīrya* (strenuousness)	*aparigrahatathatā*
	5. *sudurjayā*	*dhyāna* (meditation)	*abhinnajātīyatathatā*
	6. *abhīmukhī*	*prajñā* (analytical appreciative understanding)	*asaṁkliṣṭavyavadātatathatā*
	7. *dūraṅgamā*	*upāya* (expediency)	*abhinnatathatā*
	8. *acalā*	*praṇidhi* (resolution)	*anupacayāpacayatathatā*
	9. *sādhumatī*	*bala* (power, valour)	
	10. *dharmamegha*	*jñāna* (transcending knowledge)	
Niṣṭhāmārga	*Buddhabhūmi* (Buddha level)		

TABLE F.

The Relationships between 'Totalities' (*kṛtsnāyatana*), 'Meditation stages' (*dhyāna*), 'Deliverances' (*vimokṣa*), and 'Masteries' (*abhibhvāyatana*) :

	Kṛtsnāyatana	Dhyāna	(samāpatti)		Vimokṣa	Abhibhvāyatana
1.	*pṛthivī* (earth)		*sāmantaka*		1st *vimokṣa* ←→	1sr *abhibhvāyatana*
		1st	*dhyāna*			2nd
2.	*āpas* (water)		*dhyānāntara*	←→	(*aśubha*)	
3.	*tejas* (fire)		*sāmantaka*		2nd *vimokṣa* ←→	3rd *abhibhvāyatana*
4.	*vāyu* (wind)	IInd	*dhyāna*			4th
5.	*nīla* (*blue*)		*sāmantaka*			
6.	*pīta* (yellow)	IIIrd	*dhyāna*			5th
7.	*lohita* (red)					6th
			sāmantaka			7th *abhibhvāyatana*
8.	*avadāta* (white) →	IVth	*dhāyna*	→	3rd *vimokṣa* ←→	8th
					(*śubha*)	
9.	*ākāśa* (space)					
	(*āloka*) (*light*)					
			sāmantaka			
10.	*vijñāna* (conscious ness)	Ist	*Ārūpya*			
			sāmantaka			
		IInd	*Ārūpa*		4th	
				←→	5th *vimokṣa*	
			sāmantaka		6th	
		IIIrd	*Ārūpya*		7th	
			Sāmantaka			
		IVth	*Ārūpya*			
					8th *vimokṣa* (*nirodhasamāpatti*)	

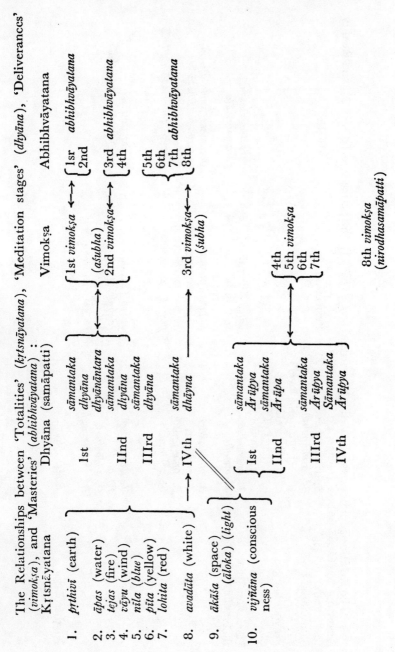